Women in Power

Women in Power

World Leaders since 1960

GUNHILD HOOGENSEN AND
BRUCE O. SOLHEIM

Foreword by Kim Campbell

Westport, Connecticut
London

Library of Congress Cataloging-in-Publication Data

Hoogensen, Gunhild, 1966–
   Women in power : world leaders since 1960 / Gunhild Hoogensen and
Bruce O. Solheim; foreword by Kim Campbell.
     p. cm.
   Includes bibliographical references and index.
   ISBN 0–275–98190–8 (alk. paper)
   1. Women in politics–History–20th century. 2. Women in
politics–History–21st century. 3. Women presidents–Biography.
4. Women prime ministers–Biography. 5. Leadership in women–Case studies.
6. Political leadership–Case studies. I. Solheim, Bruce Olav. II. Title.
HQ1236.H66   2006
305.43′3209045–dc22   2006015398

British Library Cataloguing in Publication Data is available.

Library of Congress Catalog Card Number: 2006015398
ISBN: 0–275–98190–8

First published in 2006

Praeger Publishers, 88 Post Road West, Westport, CT 06881
An imprint of Greenwood Publishing Group, Inc.
www.praeger.com

Printed in the United States of America

The paper used in this book complies with the
Permanent Paper Standard issued by the National
Information Standards Organization (Z39.48–1984).

10 9 8 7 6 5 4 3 2 1

Contents

Tables

Foreword

Throughout my life, I have found myself in positions where I was the first female – starting with my election in the spring of 1963 as student council president of my high school. In the course of my political career, I had many perplexing experiences that I suspected were related to my sex but which I didn't know how to analyze. After an election thrust me into "political retirement," I had the opportunity to delve into the study of gender leadership, as well as teach the subject at the Kennedy School of Government at Harvard University. Many of my students there were up and coming leaders themselves, and their curiosity and commitment to good governance was inspiring. Today, I speak to organizations all over the world on the subject and I am as convinced as ever that there is a desperate need for the type of thoughtful analysis that Gunhild Hoogensen and Bruce Solheim offer in this book.

In virtually all societies, leadership is gendered masculine. This is not because women do not lead, but because the positions that define leadership have been dominated by men. When women occupy these positions, they are not seen to "belong" there in the same way that men are seen naturally to do. Rather than revise their predispositions about women and leadership, people are more likely to find ways around the contradiction, by seeing the woman leader as an anomaly. This translates to the phenomenon that most women leaders do not enjoy the same level of visibility, apart from notice of their sex, and are quickly forgotten after they leave that role.

In 1996, I joined an organization called the Council of Women World Leaders, whose membership is comprised of women who have held the top office in their country. The main reason for forming the organization was to help counterbalance this trend of seeing leadership as masculine by making visible the women who have held the office of President or Prime Minister. Sometimes, when I am addressing an audience about the Council, I challenge the audience by promising to pay $100 to anyone who can name all its members. I have issued this challenge to some of the most powerful and open-minded people in the world and so far, I have never had to pay the $100. Visit www.womenworldleaders.org to see how you would have fared against this challenge.

Therefore, I am especially pleased that Hoogensen and Solheim have chosen to examine not only trends and theories of gender politics, but also highlighted twenty-two women who have occupied the top office in their countries. Their stories are as diverse as the women themselves, and I am honored to be in their company. Their leadership skills offer inspiration and instruction on overcoming challenges and finding the best in yourself as well as those around you.

But their individual stories are also threads of the tapestry which includes so many women who lead in so many ways. Analyzing the reality of women in political leadership will help each of us examine the leadership schemas which we have personally formed. Recognizing that we all have preconceptions about who can lead helps us to broaden our own views and ensure that the landscape that determines how people see the world of leadership includes women.

Kim Campbell
Former Prime Minister of Canada

Preface

Why do we generally accept the use of the term "women leaders?" We do not say "men leaders." This is common practice largely because having a leader (president or prime minister) who is a woman is still considered a "novelty" in most parts of the world. Only fifty-eight women have ever served as an elected president or prime minister. When we tell people that we are writing a book about women who have become presidents and prime ministers they lament, "why should we care whether a leader is a woman or a man as long as they are competent?" If this was a gender-blind world, their lament would make sense. But we are not there yet. A book that examines the experiences of women in top leadership positions assumes not only something unique about the experiences, but also assumes that there is something valuable to be learned through these experiences. It also assumes that there is something laudable about women fulfilling roles as world leaders.

Of course, the views we have of women, the ways in which we group such diverse individuals together as a group on the basis of the biological characteristics, and their political standing in the world, are often contested. It is not just "other" or non-Western cultures that challenge views on genders (particularly if one uses Western, dominant feminist views as the standard for gender over the past few decades), but also Western cultures themselves.

A recent example of contested gender, particularly pertaining to the roles, rights, and freedoms allotted to women in the United States is a book that rails against the harm that feminists, particularly radical feminists, have caused in American society. The Washington Editor of

National Review (a conservative-oriented magazine) Kate O'Beirne takes a
view that might contradict that which we present here, in that while we
examine and implicitly applaud the leadership of the women we high-
light, O'Beirne, in her book, *Women Who Make the World Worse and How
Their Radical Feminist Assault Is Ruining Our Schools, Families, Military, and
Sports*, wishes to demonstrate how women (at least radical feminist
women) have obtained possibly too much power in leadership roles,
changing their societies for the worse. As our book hopes to demonstrate,
feminism (or more appropriately feminisms) has many shades, which
express a need to recognize the value of women in a wide variety of
roles in society, but reflect varying and sometimes contradictory
assumptions about women, their needs, their roles, and their potential
contributions to society.

What is interesting about the possible popularity of a book such as
Women Who Make the World Worse is that it attempts to tap into narrow
stereotypes about gender research, and in particular Western (U.S.) style
feminism, and argue that most American women feel no sense of attach-
ment or sympathy for these stereotypical views. The value in such a work
could be in demonstrating the varying viewpoints that exist within feminist political theory, particularly that feminist theories have developed
considerably since the 1960s and 1970s radical feminist movement. However, this book instead chooses to ignore the debates that have occurred
over the past thirty to forty years since the height of radical feminism, and
instead rails against women who have apparently managed to exert some
influence on the development of gender equality in the United States.

Does gender research, and in particular feminism(s) have to be interpreted as only "man-hating" (one of the dominant stereotypes this particular book hangs upon) and destructive of the male and masculine
psyche? Can gender research and feminism(s) more particularly not be
a benefit to both men and women, exploring gender roles, constructed
and/or "natural?"

Confusion, contradiction, and challenge are not unknown features of
this area of research. Gender is a fundamental identity quality, it speaks
directly to who we are, who we want to be, and how we perceive others.
Identifying contradictions within the body of feminist literature is not as
challenging, however, as identifying the contradictions within our own
perceptions of gender and gender roles. A book such as *Women Who Make
the World Worse* may have some entertainment quality by largely hanging
on to extreme interpretations of gender theory, but it would benefit from
examining its own contradictions as well.

This exercise would be well taken by most who are interested, in one
way or another, in gender issues. We need to "come clean" regarding our
assumptions about gender. We, as the authors of this book, should be
clear that we value the presence of women as world leaders, even if we

may not exactly know where an increasing number of female leaders might take us. We may very well be "ideologues" in this sense, that we take a political position on the role of women and are willing to argue in favor of women entering all roles of life as they so choose. Kate O'Beirne, author of the provocative *Women Who Make the World Worse*, should likewise acknowledge her own position. Although there may be some valuable insights in this book, and an elucidation of some trails that might have been better off not followed, the author's own lack of ideological acknowledgment makes the work equally as "shrill" as those works she wishes to condemn.

Some typical assaults against a radical (see Chapter 2) feminist view that *generally* speaking argues in favor of androgyny, among other things, are the arguments that women want to be stay-at-home mothers, men are naturally aggressive and competitive, and that men should proudly exhibit their masculinity. In fronting this view of the genders, O'Beirne's methods are no different than those of her "adversaries," in that O'Beirne presents her views as a truth. That many of us do not have fixed or ready-made ideas of gender is explained fairly well in this book, but it falls on simplistic logic and opens itself up to the contradictions that we argue arise in many, particularly narrow, gender analyses. For example, O'Beirne vociferously fights for the importance of fathers in families, demonstrating their necessary roles in children's upbringing (suggesting, therefore, that the "radical feminist" agenda is in favor of eliminating fathers from the picture). Soon after, however, she contradicts the importance of this role by excusing men's higher pay due to the fact that they work much longer hours than do women (women need to be home by 5 pm to get the kids, however men apparently do not need to concern themselves with this). She also contradicts the importance of men in families when examining male versus female combat deaths. O'Beirne expresses shock and disdain over the unnecessary deaths of mothers who have entered the U.S. Armed Forces, but accepts the deaths of the many fathers who fall in conflict. Men and women dying in conflict is abhorrent, and perhaps in this case O'Beirne might better focus less on the gender issues in the military regarding women dying, and more on the American political culture that so readily sends its citizens to war.

There are so many variants of feminisms, some of which do contradict each other (which is what scholarship is about), that it is no longer possible to reify feminism as an agenda for androgyny or victimization. The dominance of the white, middle class, American 1960s feminism has long been challenged by feminists themselves around the world. This does not make them antifeminist, but scholars who argue for different views. It is this multiplicity of views that is important when learning about the experiences of women world leaders.

Were more women to become presidents or prime ministers and were more women worldwide to enter into positions of political power (matching their percentage of the world population), then we suspect that the vast array of values (albeit not identical values) that women would bring with them into office would do a better job of promoting social justice and peace in the world (even opening doors for like-minded male leaders who have been denied power) and, reduce, if not eliminate, the tendency to speak of "women leaders." This book explains how and why certain women came to power as president or prime minister in twenty-two different countries representing almost every major region of the world. *Women in Power* presents twenty-two women world leaders who since 1960 have held top positions of power. Biographies of these leaders are embedded within regional analyses that reveal not only the personal circumstances that each woman faced, but also the political milieu from which she emerged. We learn about the obstacles as well as the advantages these women faced, and derive insights about the structures that exist in our own societies regarding the power relations between men and women. *Women in Power* also devotes a chapter to differing theories of feminism in which we discover that feminism is not the same around the world. Finally, in an effort to understand how the United States can appear to be the bastion of women's liberation around the world and yet have only 15 percent representation of women in power and no woman president to date, we turn our attention to the upcoming 2008 U.S. presidential election and the possible candidates.

We wish to thank our families who supported us in the madness that is book writing (much less coauthoring across the pond), and to our editor Hilary Claggett. This book is dedicated to all the present and future leaders out there, both men and women, who are dedicated to promoting equal rights, social justice, and peace.

1

Introduction

> In every age and country, the wiser, or at least the stronger, of the two
> sexes has usurped the powers of the State, and confined the other to
> the cares and pleasures of domestic life. In hereditary monarchies,
> however, and especially in those of modern Europe, the gallant spirit
> of chivalry, and the law of succession, have accustomed us to allow a
> singular exception; and a woman is often acknowledged the absolute
> sovereign of a great kingdom, in which she would be deemed incap-
> able of exercising the smallest employment, civil or military.[1]

On May 13, 2004 the Italian-born Sonia Gandhi led her Congress
Parliamentary Party to victory in the Indian general elections. Over a
three-week period almost 380 million people voted amongst a total
population of over one billion, unexpectedly handing the Congress Party
and the Gandhi-Nehru dynasty the reigns of power once again in the
largest democracy in the world. Less than one week later Gandhi declined
the post of prime minister, despite considerable party and public pressure
to assume the post. In her speech to the Congress Parliamentary Party
Gandhi claimed that power and position were not her aim, and that she
would remain as president and chairman of Congress and therefore
active within the party despite rejecting a top post in government.
She would have been the first foreigner and first Roman Catholic
to assume the post, but not the first woman. That honor went to her
mother-in-law, Indira Gandhi (see Chapter 4).

The Nehru/Gandhi dynasty has dominated the Indian National
Congress (otherwise known as the Congress Party) in India for generations. The Congress Party has ruled India for a total of forty-four years

since India gained independence in 1947. Sonia Gandhi married into the powerful Gandhi family in 1968, after having met her husband Rajiv Gandhi, son of the assassinated former Prime Minister Indira Gandhi and grandson of the first prime minister of an independent India, Jawaharlal Nehru, at Cambridge University, England. Rajiv Gandhi assumed the office of prime minister of India directly after the assassination of his mother, Indira Gandhi, on 31 October 1984, and was elected to the post two months later in a landslide victory. Rajiv Gandhi left office in 1989 following the Congress Party's failure to win the elections, largely due to scandal. However, he continued to be politically active, and in 1991 was assassinated by alleged Tamil militants. His wife, Sonia, was immediately sought after by members of the Congress Party to continue the Gandhi leadership. Sonia Gandhi declined at that time, however, the appeals continued, and she reconsidered seven years later, becoming Congress Party president in 1998 and getting elected to parliament in the 1999 elections. Her hurdles at this time were her foreign origin, her long-standing hesitancy to enter politics after her husband's death, her slow adoption of the Indian nationality (she lived in India for 15 years before becoming Indian herself in 1984), and her poor command of the Hindi language. Her opponents tried to profit from xenophobic sentiments within the Indian population by playing up the fact that she was Italian by birth. However this argument was very weak—Sonia Gandhi is the eighth person of foreign origin to hold the post of party president, and the third foreign woman to hold the post, after Annie Beasant and Nelli Sengupta.

What is interesting in Sonia Gandhi's case is that her gender was not an impediment to winning power. Her trump card was her family name, in that the Nehru/Gandhi family appears to be the family "born" to rule (whether the family members are actually born into or married into the family). More interesting is her decision not to assume the post of prime minister, the very role her family name "dictates" that she assumes. However Sonia Gandhi made the unusual choice to decline. Unusual because she knew all along that as a two-term party president that if the Congress party won, she as president of the party would be the natural choice for the position of prime minister. Sonia Gandhi instead steps back, choosing to "clean house" within her party rather than become the government leader of India on the basis of her conscience—she could not assume the position due to her principles and her lack of interest in power. The popular Gandhi family has nevertheless had a poor survival rate in the position of prime minister, as evidenced by the murders of her husband and mother-in-law. It could be not only conscience but survival also that has influenced the latest leader of the Congress Party. Sonia Gandhi remains as president of the

Congress Party as well as the leader of the majority. This has effectively provided her with continued political control over the party, while her choice of prime minister, Manmohan Singh, is left to manage the country.

Sonia Gandhi is one of the most powerful political persons in India despite her not taking the post of prime minister. She is listed by *Forbes* magazine as being the third amongst the world's 100 most powerful women. Her experience and choices are unique and particular, and she claimed, and still does, that she listened to her inner voice—a rather benign, "soft" reason for not assuming the highest office in the land. At the same time she has been accused of being a dictator to the Congress Party—decisions are the ones that reflect the interests of Gandhi, not of the party itself. Does the fact that she is a woman have any bearing upon these choices? Is her experience similar to other women around the world who have attained such high political positions? Women face a complex combination of factors, not only as prospective leaders but also as women, that influence their abilities and chances to become world leaders. Structural conditions such as patriarchy (which manifests itself in different ways around the world—patriarchy in Canada is not the same as patriarchy in India) may work against them, however, human agency—what these women decide to do and accomplish despite structural hurdles—is equally important. It takes a good deal of external support to create a world leader (not least finances, but also acceptance), however, it also depends on the strengths of the potential leader herself, and from a deep desire to do better for her nation to a blind grab for power. This book hopes to provide a glimpse into the dynamic complexities that surround the abilities of a few remarkable women, who, whether you are politically in agreement with them or not, have been able to reach beyond the many barriers that face women throughout the world and become leaders of nations.

BARRIERS? WHAT BARRIERS?

In the vast majority of societies around the world, women have been relegated to the "private sphere." Not to be equated with the "private sector," a term encapsulating the competitive world of private enterprise, the "private sphere" here refers to the opposite—a nonengagement with society, the realm "behind closed doors," the private, the domestic, the home. Woman's clearly intimate connection with the continuation of the human race, her reproductive role in carrying, birthing, and breastfeeding the newest citizens of the world, has largely relegated her to a "caring" role, of children, husband, and home, which is separated from the "public sphere." Activities in the public sphere, be it wage labor (as her labor in the home is not paid labor), public service and/or political roles, would interfere with a woman's ability to properly care for children and the home. As well, the demands of caring for children would interfere with the demands of public life. That women have been, generally speaking, barred from public life has been in part exemplified by the fact that up until the past century, most women had been denied the right to vote.

The right to vote has been a relatively recent phenomenon for women. As women were not considered citizens in Ancient Greece and Rome (regardless of their social status or wealth through their familial relationships), they did not participate politically, nor voted. As democracies began to emerge in Europe the situation was no different for women. Arguments for women's enfranchisement have been around since the 1600s, but clearly took time to take effect on the sympathies of the male public. Women were considered to not have the right temperament to vote—the right to vote could only be accorded to independently minded beings, those who would not be swayed by employers, landlords, the elite, or husbands. Women were dependent and subordinate and thus not to be trusted to vote with any sense or reason. In 1851 Prussia in fact forbade women, along with children, the mentally ill, and apprentices, from joining political parties or attending political meetings. Despite French women's involvement in the French Revolution, the French Republic of 1848, and the uprisings of the Paris Commune, French women were prevented from full participation by socialist forces which feared women would vote conservative, and the Catholic Church which feared that a woman's vote would break up the family. But the 1800s also offered opportunity. The fight was on, and women's suffrage movements arose, particularly in Britain and the United States, although these were not the first countries to grant women the right to vote in national elections. These movements set out to convince an all-male electorate and governing structure that women should be accorded the same rights as men—no easy task.

In Britain the woman's suffrage movement began to gain momentum in the mid-1800s, despite the fact that Queen Victoria was strongly opposed to women's movements and that Parliament, as such, was very hesitant to respond too favorably to the suffrage movement's demands. However, by 1869 Parliament granted that women taxpayers be allowed to vote locally. Such concessions indicated a measure of progress, but it was by no means close to any form of legal equality with men. Frustrations mounted, generating a more coherent and organized suffrage movement across Britain called the National Union of Women's Suffrage Societies, but also resulting in a more militant and violent wing as successive suffrage bills were defeated in Parliament. It was not until the end of World War I that it was finally recognized across all political parties that women ought to be granted the right to vote. By 1918, all British women over the age of 30 were accorded the right to vote in national elections, and by 1928 the voting age was lowered to 21, the voting age of men.

The British situation was not global—not all countries exhibited the same levels of hostility or resistance to extending the vote to women, nor have all countries been as welcoming of the measure. Whereas by the mid to late-1800s countries such as Britain, Sweden were allowing women to vote in local elections, others such as New Zealand and Australia had granted women full voting rights (1893 and 1899 respectively). Generally speaking, Scandinavian women met fewer barriers to gaining the vote than did their British counterparts. Finland (1906), Norway (1913), Denmark and Iceland (1915) granted women the right to vote prior to the end of World War I. Finland was the first European country granting women the right to vote, and elected nineteen women to its Parliament in 1906. Even though Norway granted women the right to vote in 1913, it already had one female representative sitting in its national Parliament by 1910. Swedish women did not gain full voting rights until 1921. Between the two world wars, women's full enfranchisement, or the granting of full voting rights, was extended throughout the various republics of the Soviet Union, to Canada (most Canadian women got the vote in 1918, although women in Quebec were not granted voting rights until 1940 and Indian women and men got the federal vote in 1960), Austria, Germany, Poland, Belgium, Luxembourg, Czechoslovakia, Poland, Germany, Austria, Hungary, United States, Great Britain, Burma (Myanmar), Ecuador, South Africa (whites only, since black women did not gain full suffrage until 1994), Chile, Spain, Sri Lanka, Thailand, Brazil, Uruguay, Turkey, Cuba, the Philippines, Bolivia, and El Salvador. In Europe, France waited until almost the end of the war before granting women voting rights in 1944. The last European country to grant voting rights was Switzerland, in 1971. Since the end of World War II, most women (but not all) in the world have been granted the right to vote. Ecuador was the first Latin American country to grant the vote, Chinese women only got the vote after the establishment of the People's Republic of China in 1949.

The "privilege" of living in countries that have had relatively long histories of legal equality between the genders has led somewhat to a misguided notion that women have full equality, if not "more" equality than men. For some, the granting of voting privileges and full citizenship makes women "just like men." This should be enough. However it has been recognized that access to the public sphere, both political participation as well as working outside of the home, has nevertheless been restricted. As such a number of countries have implemented programs to increase the numbers of women participating in politics and the work force. Many of these programs have been in force since the 1970s, and have worked reasonably well to increase women's overall public participation. Today, reactions to such programs as employment equity (Canada), affirmative action (United States), "likestilling" (Norway), and the like are varied, with strong criticisms generally coming from conservative-oriented factions, expressing views that range from "employment equity had its time but now is not necessary" to "employment equity has always been about favoritism." Particularly within societies that have been used to these debates since the 1960s and 1970s, it often appears that such measures as employment equity have had their time. Affirmative action has been equated with preferential treatment on the basis of gender, race, and ethnicity. The measure has been seen as a blow to public equality and citizenship—every man is equal. To prefer one group over another, in this case to prefer women over men, endows women with "more" rights. They are already equal under the law, equal citizens. To prefer women is to perpetuate a reverse discrimination that is just as abhorrent as the discrimination the measure purports to rectify.

Within these same societies engaged in these debates are the vast numbers of women who are the "proof in the pudding." Women make up almost half of America's workforce today, possibly demonstrating the efficacy of such affirmative action plans. However, if we compare the numbers of women who were in the workforce in 1960 (33.4 percent) to the percentage in 2004 (46 percent of the American workforce in 2004 was female), the increase does not appear to be so extraordinary. This amounts to a 13 percent increase over a forty-four year period. Where there has been some change is the percentage of the female population which is employed; in 1960 only 38 percent of women were employed, whereas it was almost 60 percent of women in 2004. In 2000, the European Union pledged to make Europe the most competitive region in the world, and increase women's labor force participation to 60 percent. Five years on they have not even achieved their interim target of 57 percent. But bringing more women into the workforce is not the only goal. In Europe, the employment rate is still 15 percent lower than that of men, one third of women work on a part-time basis (as opposed to 7 percent of men), and women need to earn 15–20 percent more to close the wage gap with men. Women are also concentrated in less valued service sectors such as health and education. Two thirds of managerial positions in Europe are held by men, and only eight percent of the corporate boardrooms are occupied by women. Exactly ninety of the Fortune 500 companies in the United States have absolutely no female representation on their boards at all, and only nine of those companies have women as CEOs or presidents (there are nineteen female CEOs if you expand to the Fortune 1000 list). Norway boasts the highest rates of female workforce participation, at 77.7 percent, as compared to 86.3 percent of men. Norwegian women are in the majority as the highest educated in the land.

However they also encompass the vast majority of public employees (83 percent in the health and social sectors), and there is still a significant gender wage gap, low female representation in the private sector, and low female numbers in decision-making positions.

What this suggests is that, despite the various gender equity programs that have been in place for a number of decades, there is still considerable work to be done. These statistics refer to those countries and/or regions which often boast about their gender equality (President George Bush's State of the Union Address in 2004 was a resounding example of making extraordinary claims about the freedoms and "modernity" of American women as compared to the women of Afghanistan), and yet measures continue to be implemented because the gender gap has not disappeared. By the end of 2005 the new leader of the British conservative party voiced plans to increase women's participation, including splitting winning seats 50–50 between women and men.

These measures constitute some of the possible vehicles available to women to move into positions of power and be decision-makers. Access to the public sphere through employment is just one of the many initial steps. Entering low, mid, and high level management positions are equally important toward providing women with the right leverage to continue further into the political realm of public leadership. History shows however that the vehicles and measures implemented to date have not been the most effective, particularly if governments today are still struggling to find effective methods to increase women's political participation. But not only are governments addressing these hurdles, so are many women themselves. There are women, albeit not many yet, who are in positions of power partly because they had the right tools themselves to get there. Whether this means that they have had access to the finances, education, contacts, and/or inner strength necessary to "move up" depends on each particular case. However it must be acknowledged that these women who we will present in this book have all a particular strength to get themselves past the many hurdles they as women have had to face along the way.

WHO ARE THE WOMEN LEADERS?

The quote opening this chapter was written just prior to the start of the twentieth century, noting not only how infrequent it was that women were in positions of power, but also the irony that though very few became world leaders (usually as a result of monarchical succession), the rest of their sex had access to virtually nothing. Has much changed now for women as political leaders in the 100 years that have passed? In many respects, yes, much has changed. Women, almost everywhere in the world, can vote and be elected, no longer dependent upon the "law of succession" to attain power. Now the "singular exceptions" are those countries where women are not accorded these rights, such as the United Arab Emirates (women in Kuwait were granted voting rights in 2005). However the fact still remains that despite the many legal hurdles that women have overcome to acquire rights toward greater political representation within legislatures or as leaders, the proportion of women represented in these bodies falls drastically short of their percentage in the general population. Despite the many criticisms waged against the communist regimes of Eastern Europe, they could at least boast of some of the highest rates of women's representation in politics in the world. The fall of the Berlin Wall in 1989, however, unfortunately heralded a concurrent fall in women's political representation in the former Eastern bloc. In fact, it also heralded a reduced access to employment for women in general, in particular due to, among other things, reduced child care services.

The Geneva-based Inter-Parliamentary Union (IPU) that comprises 139 parliaments, claims that 86 percent of the world's parliamentary representatives are still men, and nowhere have women achieved complete parity, not even in the Scandinavian countries that are often hailed as models of gender equality. There is some sign of encouragement as some studies show that the percentage of women in world governmental bodies rose 2.1 percent from 1985 to 1995. In sub-Saharan Africa, female representation in parliaments rose from 6 to 11.5 percent during this same time.

At the turn of the twenty-first century women occupied 13.8 percent of the seats in national parliaments around the world. The Nordic countries, despite their lack of parity, nevertheless hit the top of the representation list with almost 40 percent of parliamentary seats going to women. The rest of the world pales in comparison, with the Americas, Europe (excluding the Nordic countries), and Asia, seeing approximately 15 percent of their seats occupied by women by the year 2000. The Pacific region was a bit lower at 13.5 percent, and sub-Saharan Africa lower still at just under 12 percent. The Arab states come in last with a small 3.6 percent of their seats occupied by women.[2] This situation could significantly change in the Arab region if Iraq allows for greater representation of women.

There are a few countries where women have at least a quarter of the seats in their respective legislatures. Not surprisingly these are predominantly represented by the Nordic countries, which have already been noted for being the exception to the global rule of limited female participation. In the year 2000, Swedish women had 42.7 percent of the parliamentary seats in their country. Finland, Norway, Denmark, and Iceland roughly ranged from 35 to 37 percent, with the Netherlands and Germany providing some non-Nordic competition at 36 percent and 31 percent female representation respectively. Three African countries are noted for having at least 25 percent female representation in their legislatures, with Mozambique and South Africa following closely behind the Nordic leaders at approximately 30 percent each, and Namibia at 25 percent. New Zealand, a lone representative in the pacific, was recorded as having just below 30 percent female representation in 2000, followed by a few more Europeans: Bosnia and Herzegovina (28.6 percent), Spain (28.3 percent), and Austria (26.8 percent). Latin America can boast that Venezuela, Cuba, Grenada, and Argentina all ensured that between 26 and 29 percent of their parliamentary seats were held by women. Turkmenistan and Vietnam, the only two Asian representatives in 2000, both had at least 26 percent of their parliamentary seats taken by women. The North American representatives, Canada and the United States, were noticeably absent from this list.[3]

There have been inroads made by women around the world to increase political participation and representation, but instead of a steady increase over time of female political representation, the numbers have remained fairly low. The number of women heads of state and/or government or ministers in particular has not seen any significant increase despite there being broad legal access to these participatory channels. When women are chosen to be amongst the ministers of state, they are rarely given the strategic portfolios of finance or defense (although there are, as always, exceptions), but instead are often handed portfolios that reflect stereotypical women's concerns, such as social affairs, family, health, or even environment—all of which come with significantly less political leverage than the higher profile, better funded, and "important" portfolios.

Presently there are twelve women world leaders, meaning heads of state and/or government. They include the president of Ireland Mary McAleese, president of Latvia Vaira Vike-Freiberga, president of the Philippines Gloria Macapagal-Arroyo, prime minister of Bangladesh Khaleda Zia, the prime minister of Ukraine Yulia Timoshenko, president of Sri Lanka Chandrika Kumaratunga, prime minister of New Zealand Helen Clark, president of Finland Tarja K. Halonen, prime minister of Mozambique Luisa Diogo, Germany's Chancellor Angela Merkel, Liberia's newly elected president, Ellen Johnson-Sirleaf, and also newly elected President Michelle Bachelet of Chile. If we think that there are 191 sovereign member states in the United Nations (not including Taiwan or the Vatican), eleven female world leaders is incredibly low. This of course does not include monarchs (or their governor-general representatives) or vice presidents. But we do not have to desperately search for other leadership positions to see the extent of male representation—looking at head of state/government suffices. At least the continents of Africa, Asia, and Europe are represented. North and Latin America are noticeably silent.

If we expand our search and include female members of government in general, participation increases. There are, however, a number of countries that have no female members of government at all, such as Bhutan, British Virgin Islands, Burma (Myanmar), Comoro Islands, Cyprus, Faeroe Islands, Laos, Libya, Niue, Palau, St. Kitts and Nevis, Solomon Islands, Turkish Republic of Northern Cyrus, Tuvalu, Uruguay, and probably North Korea (which is difficult to confirm).[4] There are also those countries that have *never* had any female members of government, such as Monaco and Saudi Arabia. Those nations that have not ratified the Convention on the Elimination of All Forms of Discrimination Against Women (CEDAW) include: Bahrain, Palestine, Qatar, Saudi Arabia, Sultanate of Oman, Syrian Arab Republic, and the United Arab Emirates. The United States is the only industrialized nation that has not ratified CEDAW.

WHO GETS TO BE A LEADER?

The opportunity to become a world leader comes to very few, and amongst those to whom it does, an infinitesimal number are women. When we speak of world leaders in general, we never speak of their gender. News agencies do not purposely report that the world's *male* leaders met at the most recent WTO summit or G8. To write a book about men world leaders of the twentieth century would result in volumes, not one text. World leaders are men, with very little exception. But that these exceptions exist, we find it worthwhile to note this fact. An exercise in identifying "women world leaders" connotes the uniqueness of the position—a woman in the position of a world leader. Some women *have* in fact become world leaders. Since the number of women world leaders as compared to their male counterparts is very low, it begs the question why.

At the local and grassroots levels women have had and continue to have the opportunities to make significant contributions and the capacity to participate in greater numbers. Patriarchal social structures around the world have generally precluded the participation of women at higher levels. Reliance on social change has not yet been sufficient to drive the numbers of women politicians upward, thus extra measures such as quota systems have been implemented, both to increase the numbers faster, as well as make otherwise generally hesitant societies more used to having women at the top.

Most societies in the world have been and continue to be patriarchal societies where men dominate in all areas of life, in private (family) and in public (work and politics). The nature and extent of this patriarchy differs throughout the world, but the dominance of men is generally a shared feature. As such, when women enter public life (when they are usually relegated to work in the family or local community in supportive roles), and particularly public life as the national leader, most of us take notice. This is true even if the nation in question professes "equality of women," and even more so in nations that appear patriarchal to the point of denying women some basic human rights. The following selection of women illustrates not only the uniqueness of women world leaders (in the twentieth century there have been more than fifty women world leaders), but also dismantles some of the assumptions we make about societies around the world—those that have largely appeared to be more open to women in more public roles versus those that appear to have not. The most startling contradiction in this case is the clear lack of women leaders in the so-called Industrialized, Western, Developed world, whereas there has been a significant history of female leaders in societies that are often vilified for their harsh treatment of women, particularly in Muslim societies. Most importantly, however, who are these women and/or what do they have to do have to become the next world leader?

Women are not, despite our gratuitous use of the term "women" to connote an entire group of people, all the same. Their socioeconomic, ethnic, and racial identities, both assumed and imposed, can often separate women from each other just as much as being biologically women might bring them together. Nevertheless, and despite these differences, most women in most societies must overcome important and surprisingly common hurdles before they can enter the domain of the elite. These hurdles are relevant regardless of women's political orientation or affiliation, they are confronted with numerous obstacles that will potentially and realistically hinder their political careers. The hurdles apply to the left as well as right wings of politics. The avenues of possibility for women also exist in both wings. Generally though, women often lack the required time, money, confidence, education and training, and family and institutional support to successfully carry though a successful election. In Africa, for example, more than half of women who are 15 and older are without any income. Such miserable economic conditions not only preclude financial access to political activity but have a large impact on the health and welfare of these women, providing yet one more obstacle to political involvement.

Most cultures around the world have imposed stereotypical roles upon women and men, engendering prejudices either for or against women that are extremely hard to eradicate or overlook. Even in countries where platitudes toward women's legal rights hold sway, women still struggle to convince themselves and others that they do not necessarily belong only in the kitchen, or to tending solely to the home and family. These stereotypes are perpetuated through social and cultural structures, emphasized in the media, reinforcing traditional images of women that conflict with the required role of a political leader, a role that is more often than not associated with the stereotypical physical, mental, and emotional attributes of a man.

A constant issue facing many women is child-care facilities—access, cost, and flexibility. Political party meetings have not been traditionally organized to meet the family demands of their representatives, as these processes have always assumed that there was "someone at home" to look after these things. As far as those who have access and money for child care are concerned, this option is limited to a privileged few. It is also a hidden service in many ways, in that women do not want to admit a dependency upon extra services (extra in comparison to their male counterparts), and have often internalized negative feelings about this dependency. Of course, this assumes that women even find it possible or desirable to have a family while they climb the ladders to the top. Family is still a woman's burden, and to be free of a family means that women can behave more like the men; available at all times, focused on the "important issues" of politics, and not pulled in another direction (such as toward their children). It must be noted at the same time that the demands of family have yet to be respected where political men are concerned also. In the recent election preparation for the British 2005 general election, the leader of the Liberal Democratic Party was heavily chastised in the newspapers for delaying the launch of his party platform because his wife gave birth that same day. In the eyes of some media sources, he should have dropped family considerations (mother and baby were being cared for at the hospital anyway and did not need him), and instead been the leader the Liberal Democrats needed. In the event that women (and maybe even family-concerned men) have the financial capacity to pay for child care, do they have the resources to fund an election campaign? Political campaigns have been and are becoming increasingly expensive. Campaigns are often dependent upon political machinery that is heavily male-oriented, and not interested in sinking funds behind a woman candidate.

Access to finances is also reflected in the ways in which women are represented in the big financial institutions. International financial institutions such as the World Bank, International Monetary Fund, and World Trade Organization have hardly been inclusive where women are concerned, and generally marginalize women, particularly from the global South. As a result, women's issues are not heard in these organizations, or are of such a low priority that they suffer. The relationships between women, the division of labor, trade liberalization, and such issues as HIV/AIDS and access to adequate health care are not adequately recognized in the institutions that control international finance and determine where the wealth in the world will go. Instead, typical "women's concerns" are taken care of by nongovernmental and charitable international organizations; in other words, institutions that are not so heavily financially endowed or well connected are those that are left to treat issues pertinent to over half of the world's population.

This book will take a look at twenty women world leaders who have held top positions of power during the twentieth and the beginnings of the twenty-first centuries. The lessons we can learn from their experiences cannot be encapsulated within a few choice sentences that reveal to us the secrets of attaining the heights of power as a woman, and nor do their experiences necessarily speak to the experiences of all the other women who have been leaders throughout the twentieth century and on into the twenty-first, nor those who have lead communities and nations for the centuries before them. They do, however, provide a glimpse into a world that most of us, women and men, have not and will not experience ourselves. We can learn about their hurdles as well as their advantages, and derive insights about the structures that exist in our own societies regarding the power relations between men and women. We additionally contrast the biographies of these twenty women with accounts of how life generally is for "the average woman" in their respective regions, or for women who are still very much on the margins. This not only demonstrates how impressive the achievements have been for women over the years and around the globe, but also makes plain that those women who become world leaders cannot be assumed to have "done it all" alone. Many of these women have had access to education that other women have not, or finances that others have not. This is not a situation particular to women of course—the many more male leaders of the world are equally if not more privileged. As gender theories (as will be discussed in the next chapter) have argued, the personal is political—and not just the personal of our leadership, but also of the people they lead.

Choosing which women would be in focus in this book was not easy. Once chosen, the available information on each woman was highly variable; whereas there were already an impressive number of biographies available about Angela Merkel even before she became chancellor of Germany, there was precious little to choose from about our two prime ministers from Africa (Rwanda and Burundi), even ten years on. The types of roles represented by the total group of women world leaders over the past century are broad-ranging, from Captain Regent to President. Aside from the current twelve heads of state or government in the world that are women, as noted above, the previous female heads of state and government (since 1900) include the following:

- Sirimavo Bandaranaike, prime minister of Sri Lanka (1960–1965, 1970–1977, 1994–2000)
- Indira Gandhi, prime minister of India (1966–1977, 1980–1984)
- Golda Meir, prime minister of Israel (1969–1974)

- Isabel Peron, president of Argentina (1974–1976)
- Elisabeth Domitien, prime minister of Central African Empire (1975–1976)
- Lucinda da Costa Gomez-Mattheeuws, prime minister of Netherlands Antilles (1977)
- Maria de Lourdes Pintassilgo, prime minister of Portugal (1979–1980)
- Lidia Gueilier, caretaker president of Bolivia (1979–1980)
- Margaret Thatcher, prime minister of Great Britain (1979–1990)
- Vigdis Finnbogadottir, president of Iceland (1980–1996)
- Eugenia Charles, prime minister of Dominica (1980–1995)
- Gro Harlem Brundtland, prime minister of Norway (1981, 1986–1989, 1990–1996)
- Maria Pedini-Angelini, captain-regent of San Marino (1981)
- Milka Planinc, prime minister of Yugoslavia (1982–1986)
- Agatha Barbara, president of Malta (1982–1987)
- Gloriana Rannocchini, captain-regent of San Marino (1984, 1989–1990)
- Maria Liberia Peters, prime minister of the Netherlands Antilles (1984–1986, 1988–1994)
- Corazon Aquino, president of Philippines (1986–1992)
- Benazir Bhutto, prime minister of Pakistan (1988–1990, 1993–1996)
- Kazimiera Prunskiene, president of Lithuania (1990–1991)
- Sabine Bergmann-Pohl, state president of German Democratic Republic (1990)
- Ertha Pascal-Trouillot, acting president of Haiti (1990–1991)
- Violeta de Chamorro, president of Nicaragua (1990–1996)
- Mary Robinson, president of Ireland (1990–1997)
- Edda Ceccoli, captain-regent of San Marino (1991–1992)
- Edith Cresson, prime minister of France (1991–1992)
- Khaleda Zia, prime minister of Bangladesh (1991–1996, 2001–)
- Hanna Suchocka, prime minister of Poland (1992–1993)
- Kim Campbell, prime minister of Canada (1993)
- Patricia Busigani, captain-regent of San Marino (1993)
- Agathe Uwilingiyimana, prime minister of Rwanda (1993)
- Silvie Kinigi, interim president of Burundi (1993–1994)
- Marita Petersen, prime minister of Faroe Islands (1993–1994)
- Tansu Çiller, prime minister of Turkey (1993–1996)
- Renata Indzhova, interim prime minister of Bulgaria (1994–1995)
- Claudette Werleigh, prime minister of Haiti (1995–1996)
- Ruth Perry, chairman of State Council, Liberia (1996–1997)

- Sheikh Hasina Wajed, prime minister of Bangladesh (1996–2001)
- Biljana Plavsic, president of Republika Srpska (Bosnia-Hercegovina) (1996–1998)
- Rosalia Arteaga, caretaker president of Ecuador (1997)
- Pamela Gordon, premier of Bermuda (1997–1998)
- Janet Jagan, prime minister of Guyana (1997–1999)
- Jenny Shipley, prime minister of New Zealand (1997–1999)
- Ruth Dreifuss, president of Switzerland (1998–1999)
- Suzanne Romer, prime minister of Netherlands Antilles (1993, 1998–1999)
- Jennifer Smith, premier of Bermuda (1998–2003)
- Nyam-Osoriyn Tuyaa, interim prime minister of Mongolia (1999)
- Rosa Zafferani, captain-regent of San Marino (1999)
- Irena Degutiene, acting prime minister of Lithuania (1999)
- Mireya Moscoso, president of Panama (1999–2003)
- Maria Domenica Michelotti, captain-regent of San Marino (2000)
- Madior Boye, prime minister of Senegal (2001–2002)
- Megawati Sukarnoputri, president of Indonesia (2001–2004)
- Chang Sang, acting prime minister of South Korea (2002)
- Natasa Micic, acting president of Serbia (2002–2003)
- Maria das Neves, prime minister of Sao Tome & Principe (2002–2004)
- Annelli Jaatteenmaaki, prime minister of Finland (2003)
- Beatriz Merino, prime minister of Peru (2003)
- Nino Burzhanadze, acting president of Georgia (2003)

Of the fifty-eight women world leaders of the twentieth and twenty-first centuries, we chose those who were engaged in politically active roles, and who were not solely figurehead, decorative, or symbolic. From that list we ensured that we had representation from the following regions: five from Asia, five from the Middle East and Africa, five from the Americas, seven from Europe. In some cases we had to choose who would represent each region, in other cases, such as North America, we did not have many to choose from. We tried to include a number of the current women world leaders who have attained their positions after the turn of the twenty-first century, spanning over slightly more than a century therefore. This book provides biographical sketches of the following world leaders:

1. Aquino—Philippines (Asia)
2. Bandaranaike—Sri Lanka (Asia)
3. Bhutto—Pakistan (Asia)
4. Brundtland—Norway (Europe)
5. Campbell—Canada (North America)

6. Chamorro—Nicaragua
   (Latin America)
7. Çiller—Turkey (Middle East)
8. Cresson—France (Europe)
9. Finnbogadottir—Iceland (Europe)
10. Gandhi—India (Asia)
11. Halonen—Finland (Europe)
12. Kinigi—Burundi (Africa)
13. Meir—Israel (Middle East)
14. Peron—Argentina (Latin America)
15. Robinson—Ireland (Europe)
16. Sukarnoputri—Indonesia (Asia)
17. Thatcher—UK (Europe)
18. Uwilingiyimana—Rwanda
    (Africa)
19. Merkel—Germany (Europe)
20. Johnson-Sirleaf—Liberia (Africa)
21. Bachelet—Chile (Latin America)
22. Moscoso—Panama
    (Latin America)

These twenty-two women are among the fifty-eight women elected to top government positions (prime minister or president) in the world during the twentieth and twenty-first centuries. It seems as if political dynasties are important still in getting these women elected (not that this has not been a feature of election for men either), but that may be changing as more women serve in such leadership posts. As mentioned, when Sonia Gandhi was deciding whether or not to run for the post of prime minister in India, the issue was not her being a woman, but her place of birth (Italy). That shows progress. The dynasty theory may have relevance in that women who have been personally exposed to a political life through their husbands or fathers tend to be more prepared to face its rigors and challenges. Another curious phenomenon is that women leaders seem to be emerging more quickly in conflict regions. Rwanda now has the world's highest proportion of female members of parliament, a study shows. Following elections in October 2003, 48.8 percent of Rwanda's members of parliament (MPs) are women, according to the Inter-Parliamentary Union (IPU). The Nordics still prevail as Sweden, where 45 percent of MPs are women, has been the long-standing leader of the IPU ranking of women in parliament. A world record was set on 2 May 2003 when the Welsh assembly became the first legislative body with equal numbers of men and women. Women's rights groups hailed the breakthrough after thirty women were elected to the sixty-strong assembly—an increase of five. In 2002, Sweden, Denmark, Finland, Norway, Iceland, the Netherlands, and Germany had all attained the minimum 30 percent goal of parliamentary seats to be taken by women, along with Argentina, Costa Rica, South Africa, and Mozambique. According to the UNIFEM report "Progress of the World's Women 2002" these states had met the target through quota systems. In the same report by UNIFEM, thirteen developing countries in the sub-Saharan region—the poorest area on Earth—had higher proportions of women MPs than the United States (12 percent), France (11.8 percent), and Japan (10 percent).

Rwanda has 25.7 percent and Uganda, 24.7 percent. Of the Gulf states that have parliaments, the United Arab Emirates is the only one that does not give women the right to vote or stand for election. In May 2003 Qatar appointed Sheikha bint Ahmed Al-Mahmud as the Gulf state's first woman cabinet minister. The appointment followed an 29 April referendum in which Qataris overwhelmingly approved a written constitution recognizing a woman's right to vote and run for office.

The countries that have significant percentage of women in government share these things in common:

1. proportional representation system,
2. some sort of quota system, and
3. separation of church and state.

The United States, ostensibly the bastion of freedom and liberal thinking, seems to be a tough political environment for women to establish themselves beyond a minimal threshold (currently only 14 percent of the U.S. Congress are women). The three main reasons for this are:

1. the significant amount of money needed for campaigning,
2. persistent sexist attitudes exacerbated by religious fundamentalism and the post-9/11 culture of fear, and
3. the winner takes all electoral system (first past the post system).

The secular structure of the U.S. political system (set up by the American founding fathers who were men of the Enlightenment and largely Deists) is being continuously challenged (an uneasy separation of church and state). This tends to hold women back.

Women who hold ministerial positions worldwide remain concentrated in social areas (14 percent) compared to legal (9.4 percent), economic (4.1 percent), political affairs (3.4 percent), and the executive (3.9 percent). And, only 7 percent of the world's total cabinet ministers are women. There are nine women ambassadors to the United Nations. They are from Finland, Guinea, Jamaica, Kazakhstan, Kyrgyzstan, Liberia, Liechtenstein, Somalia, and Turkmenistan. In the United Nations system, women hold only 9 percent of the top management jobs and 21 percent of senior management positions, but 48 percent of the junior professional civil service slots.

ECONOMIC DECISION-MAKING: FACTS AND FIGURES

- Only 1 percent of the world's assets are in the name of women.
- Men in the Arab states have 3.5 times the purchasing power of their female counterparts.

- 70 percent of people in abject poverty—living on less than $1 per day—are women.
- Among the developed countries, in France only 9 percent of the workforce and in the Netherlands 20 percent of the workforce are female administrators and managers.
- Among the developing countries, in Ecuador and the Bahamas, 33 percent of the workforce is comprised of women administrators and managers.
- Women's participation in managerial and administrative posts is around 33 percent in the developed world, 15 percent in Africa, and 13 percent in Asia and the Pacific. In Africa and Asia-Pacific these percentages, small as they are, reflect a doubling of numbers in the past twenty years.
- In Silicon Valley, for every 100 shares of stock options owned by a man, only one share is owned by a woman.

2

Women in Theory and Practice

It is not the prerogative of men alone to bring light to the world.
                    Aung San Suu Kyi, Nobel Peace Prize Winner (1996)

INTRODUCTION

The choice to study women world leaders implies within it that there is
something here to evaluate and to explain. That they are "women" world
leaders, and not "men" world leaders, or just "world leaders" outright,
indicates that a part, probably a substantial part, of understanding the
existence and development of women world leaders will be based on the
fact of their gender—women. It also suggests or implies that there is some
value to knowing more about "women" leaders, otherwise why would
we care whether they are women or not? What is it that we wish to know
then about women, in particular, in their roles as world leaders? And
why? An oft-heard comment is that the world would be somehow better,
safer, more peaceful, if more women lead the world. Is that really the
case? Of course, it is hard to know with so few women leaders as
examples, and given the wide range of political views exhibited by
these few women, their "femaleness" seems to have a variable bearing on
their political efficacy, views, or abilities. Does being female make a
difference in world leadership though, and if so, why? If it does not, that
is important too—why have so few women been elected to positions of
world leaders if there is no discernable difference between female and

male leadership abilities and actions? If men and women behave the same, why would we appear to overwhelmingly choose men? The relative infrequency of women being chosen as national leaders, despite the fact that women make up one half of the global population, does lead a person to wonder. Why are not there more women leaders? Statistically their chances should be relatively good. Nevertheless, the world is very much dominated by male leaders.

To start explaining why, despite their numbers, women do not often make it to the upper echelons of state and global politics is no small task. It has to do with how many women have the ambition to become world leaders, and also the extent to which they have the opportunity to be world leaders. Their opportunities are conditioned by the standards and values of the communities in which they live, and their interests are in part framed by these standards and values. If many women grow up in communities where it is largely unheard of for women to seek positions of power, this in itself can be a hindrance for a woman to pursue such a position herself. She might be dissuaded, or she might be out rightly denied the opportunity altogether as women cannot and should not consider such positions. One might think the latter, more "heavy-handed" approach is most prevalent in undemocratic, authoritarian states and societies, but this is not necessarily so. Even in some of the most democratic, allegedly free states in the world, few women have come to power, and in the most powerful "democracy" in the world, no woman has come to power. The impact of what a woman should and can do is no less powerful in a so-called free state as it is in an authoritarian one.

Why are there so much fewer women in power than men? In large part it has to do with the hierarchical roles we have assigned the genders within the vast majority of human societies around the globe, and the social assumptions these societies hold about women's capacities to lead. As stated in Chapter 1, women have been historically relegated to what we refer to as the private sphere, exemplified by the home and private life of the family. Leadership, particularly on a national scale, constitutes a public sphere activity to which women generally did not have access, not even to the average workplace, let alone the most politically powerful position in the country. This being said, we have nevertheless elected at least some women to the post of a world leader. What reasons might we have for doing this if, broadly speaking, we are socially trained to believe that women are not "cut out" for leadership, or rather, that our nation will not benefit from a woman's leadership?

One of the first questions to ask is whether there actually is a difference between women's and men's leadership, and explore some ideas behind the frequent choice to elect men, versus the occasional choice to elect women to such high and important posts. Thankfully the tools of examination are diverse and well-developed, as the roles and power relations between men and women have been the subject of discussion and theory for centuries. Here we refer to this large assortment of theoretical approaches as gender theories. Gender theories attempt to explore, if not answer, questions regarding the differing attitudes toward the sexes within and across societies. National leadership is a very obvious and pointed example of gender inequality, at least if one looks at it in terms of numbers. That 51 percent of the world's population rarely if ever is adequately represented in the upper echelons of world governments needs examination.

Gender theories approach the question of similarity and difference between the genders or sexes,[1] attempting to arrive at explanations as to why men and masculinist structures have dominated so many societies, but also to generate theories of change based on these evaluations of masculinist society. Masculinism defines patriarchy, rooting itself within the assumed supremacy of male behavior and values. Gender theories include a variety of perspectives, ranging from the vast selection of feminisms, masculism, and bi, hetero, homo, neuter perspectives, where most, if not all, are responding to the dominant masculinist paradigm. All provide different understandings of the world and seek to inform, if not change, the societies in which we live in the interest of achieving greater equality and minimizing, if not eradicating, discriminatory and violent behaviors that have been connected to past and present power relations between genders.

Gender theories are preoccupied with relations of power, and have focused in large part on the inequalities of power between men and women, with an emphasis on women's roles, knowledge, and experiences as the nondominant and/or subordinate group. As such gender theories are very much dominated themselves by women-based or feminist approaches. More recently, however, "masculism" has arisen as an attempt to understand men's experiences in a masculinist society. Masculism examines oppression from the standpoint of men, the vast majority of whom do not fit the mould of the masculinist paradigm. Not all men reap the benefits of masculinist society, although many men have been able to ride on the coat tails of masculinist thinking to, at least, benefit from their physical association of being male if nothing else.

FEMINISM IS DEAD SO SHADDUP ALREADY!!

Despite the advances made on the gender front, gaining and establishing legal if not social equality between the sexes, the subject of gender is still very controversial. In parts of the world a backlash is felt against what is considered to be white, middle class Western dominant Feminism—a liberal type feminism that declares it knows all women's experiences and has a universal solution for gender equality based on legal equality and equal access to the public sphere, particularly the workforce. All women desire a competitive and 9 to 5 job, want to share or even off-load house responsibilities, and need full-time day care. Although this scenario does represent the desires of many women, it cannot be assumed to be a global or universal demand, nor does it reflect global gender issues. We address the response to this briefly below, but it suffices to say that this challenge to the dominant view of Feminism (identified as Feminism with a capital "F," as opposed to the many variants of feminisms that actually exist) has been significant. For the most part Feminism has been positive, as masculinist views require challenge, particularly those that claim an overarching, universalistic application. This is also particularly significant when assessing the accomplishments and challenges of women in world leader positions—have all of them achieved this position on the basis of a desire to be equally powerful as men (or at least the elite few who make it to positions of power), shunning the private for the public, and to demonstrate that "women can have it all" too? Such an explanation is far too simplistic, and frankly irrelevant depending on the cultural and contextual background of the individual and society in question. How and why women make it to positions of power is complex and cannot be encapsulated by one explanatory approach. That being said, however, can the variety of feminisms available to us as tools of analysis say anything about women world leaders? Do they have anything to say at all, in fact, in today's world?

That there may be different points of view about gender and its role in society is one thing, but it is another to suggest that gender perspectives, and feminisms in particular, are no longer relevant or meaningful, or even dangerous. A not-so-compelling but nevertheless oft-repeated argument is that Feminism's objective is in fact the dominance of men by women. In this case, women *should* run the world, as men have demonstrated that they lack the ability for leadership and instead need to be controlled. Both men and women have been known to respond to Feminism with this type of a retort—men out of fear/threat, and women out of solidarity for their male counterparts. That some feminist arguments might be interpreted in this way is possible, but that this particular interpretation represents what feminisms, or more broadly speaking, gender theories are all about is not at all accurate. However, the notion of women taking over the world is not the strongest or most prevalent argument concerning Feminism's irrelevance and/or demise.

Views expressing ambivalence if not outright hostility toward Feminism were most recently expressed on the 30th anniversary of Britain's Sex-Discrimination Act, introduced originally by Harold Wilson's government in December of 1975. Women's equality was won, now it was women's responsibility to ensure that it was kept. According to Carol Sarler however, women messed up big time—what was hard won by the feminists of the 1970s has since been lost, if not destroyed, by countless number of women running to the courts whining about discrimination, looking to state mechanisms to support them rather than standing on their own two feet.[2] While the women of the 1970s were strong, making use of legal abortion, convenient contraceptives, and enjoying hairy armpits, the women who followed are weak and pathetic. Today's gender issues, she argues, are all about how women are so weak that they cannot stand up for themselves—women as victims, women as targets, and women who cannot and will not cope are the result of Feminism. Sarler's argument is fairly extreme in that she equates sexual harassment with being "excessively liked," something with which women should be able to cope with well enough with a witty rebuke. Women who are beaten, moreover, are weak and cannot cope in Sarler's view, as they wait, on average, until they have been beaten thirty-five times before resorting to calling the police. This sort of argument, and similar ones like it, appear to argue that once such legislation as the Sex Discrimination Act and the Equal Pay Act comes into force (this accomplishment in itself demonstrating the strength of women who fought for it), women should not use it; claiming sexual harassment in the workplace is a demonstration of the weakness of women.

Sarler's lament against Feminism, or at least a number of the points she raises, can be often heard in discussions about Feminism. More and more women, at least in parts of the Western world, have greater access to education and jobs like never before. Since the adoption of the Sex Discrimination Act in Britain, the country has witnessed a rapid growth of girls and women excelling in academics, where over 60 percent of applicants to medical and law school are women. Such social change has undoubtedly been assisted by such measures as this thirty-year-old act, and given these social advances for women, many assume that gender equality is now a fait accompli. Barriers to women because they are women no longer exist, and therefore any measures that continue to focus on female inclusion are either unnecessary or reverse-discrimination.[3] It is not uncommon to see younger generations of women in university, for example, bristle at the suggestion that their gender is still at a disadvantage. Part of this can be attributed to the fact that continued legislation allowing women greater access to higher institutions and better jobs are now interpreted as a crutch for women that they do not need. The "merit" argument arises here, whereby no woman wants to be told or allow that she reached the position she has on the basis of anything else than the skill and knowledge she brings to the position. Women wish to break ceilings on the basis of their merit, not on the basis of social programs.

This circles back to Sarler's argument about emphasizing weakness. She argues that women have destroyed their chances at equality by using legislation such as the Sex Discrimination Act and Equal Pay Act to fight for claims based on, and allowing for, female weakness—women's incapability to fight off sexual harassment, their inability to stand up for themselves in the face of spousal abuse, their seeking concessions to make up for their physical weaknesses (hormones, pregnancy), or when women make "mistakes, getting too drunk on a date and having sex."[4] Despite the tenuous nature of some of these arguments (is the fight against sexual harassment really only dependent upon a witty rebuke? Do women now have complete equality in and out of the workplace, making employment equity programs irrelevant?), the overarching message should not be overlooked. That is the problem of the victim—often women are portrayed as victims and only victims. Seeing women as fighters, enablers, able to ensure the security of themselves and others, is not a frequent picture that is portrayed. How do we overcome the vision of the perpetual victim without denying the very real discriminations women have and continue to face?

THEORIES OF GENDER—UNDERSTANDING OR KNOWING THE POWER RELATIONS BETWEEN THE SEXES

The challenges of understanding the impacts and relations of power between the genders are significant, and as such there have been numerous theoretical contributions attempting to grapple with and make sense of the social, political, and legal dictates that result in our treating men and women significantly differently. Since the field of gender studies has been largely focused on the experiences of the nondominant group, that of women, gender theory is often equated with feminist theories. Although gender does not mean "women," it is often associated with women due to this focus. Given our own focus on women, women world leaders specifically, those gender theories that take the female experience as their starting points are most relevant to our analyses. However, the body of literature that is encompassed by feminist theories is vast. We touch on a number of the more well-known feminisms to demonstrate the differences between these approaches and their varying assumptions about gender to provide an overview of what the literature has to offer. We will finally present the approach we will take in this book, which will be the leading analytical theme throughout the following chapters detailing the biographical and political outlines of twenty women world leaders.

Liberal Feminism

Liberal feminism is the feminism many of us are most familiar with (albeit not exclusively). This approach focuses on rights, autonomy (individualism), and reason/rationality. Humans share some basic qualities, such as rationality or the ability to reflect on and choose among conceptions of the good life. In other words, we know how to think. As individuals we have the capacity to rationalize according to our own needs and interests, and as rational, thoughtful individuals we have endowed ourselves with particular rights primarily because we are rational individuals. This presupposes that all those who are members of the human race are first and foremost individuals who share this capacity for rationality, and most importantly, that this capacity is gender neutral. Any possible physiological or social differences associated with gender are not relevant at the level of the individual—all individuals are the same, and operate according to their own interests. Individuals are restricted (by external forces, such as government through policing) only insofar as their behavior can or does cause harm to others. If individuals are restricted in their behavior on any other basis, such as on the basis of their gender, such restrictions are irrational. The measures necessary to mitigate against unnecessary restrictions are legal ones. We require laws that make sure that individuals are not discriminated against on the basis of their gender, or any other physiological feature for that matter.

The freedom of the individual and the ability to choose (therefore they are not restricted), function concurrently with the exercise of rights, and it is this that is the main driving force behind liberal feminism. What is compelling about this approach is the strength of the individual—it is assumed/expected that through legal equality all individuals, women included, would have access to the same opportunities. This also assumes that women would make use of these opportunities. By endowing people with rights—the right to work, the right to nondiscrimination, the right to earn equal pay, and most importantly, the right to be considered an equal member of society, all people will be able to excel according to their own abilities. Rights are currently the central method by which we include women and gender at the moment, and through legal recognition we have managed to increase women's legal equality worldwide. If women are held as equal in the eyes of the law, they should have equal opportunity to seek political office-on paper, at least. Many would and have argued that legal recognition and the endowment of rights does not address societal level discrimination. This is borne out by the results, for example, of the Sex Discrimination Act in Britain. After thirty years, many advances have been made (as mentioned regarding women's access to higher institutions). An important feature of this approach is the acknowledgment of human agency—that individuals have the abilities, if not otherwise hindered, to change their environments for the better. However much still has to be done.

The advances made for women entering higher education have not been matched for those who do not seek the academic route. Occupational segregation, locking nonhighly educated women into low paying jobs such as clerks, cashiers, and cleaners still exists. The thirtieth anniversary of the Equal Pay Act has actually done little to rectify the problem of the gender wage gap—in general terms it has reduced by not been eradicated (lowered from 30 to 17 percent), but the wage differences between part-time women (a very common job position for women, both for familial as well as circumstantial reasons such as reduced access to full-time jobs) and full-time men remains at 40 percent, a wage difference that has hardly moved over thirty years. Legal equality has apparently done nothing to stem the resistance many British firms have toward hiring women of childbearing age. A recent survey demonstrated that 75 percent of British companies actively avoid hiring such women. These companies claim that they cannot cover for the losses sustained during maternity leave. The demands of and access to the workplace, the structure of capitalism, and its dependency upon nonwage labor, and the impacts these all have on gender were instrumental in developing another avenue of gender analysis which attempted to explain why legal devices do not suffice in bringing equality between the sexes.

Marxist Feminism

The critique against capitalism and class discrimination waged by Karl Marx has been taken up by a number of feminists, and is known as Marxist feminism. What makes us human is determined by our activity, and thus the fact that we produce our means of subsistence, in other words, we are productive, is central to understanding our humanity. That our productivity has become segregated on the basis of productive (saleable) and nonproductive (nonsaleable, such as taking care of family) tasks, that we either own the means of production or are the means of production, and that we are valued (or not) on the basis of our rank and position within this system (upper, middle, and lower classes, working/ proletariat and owner classes) has had a significant impact on the development of inequalities worldwide.

Women's oppression is linked to the oppression of the proletariat/ worker, but their oppression functions on two levels, going beyond the discrimination that occurs in the workplace. In some respects women find equality with men in the workplace as they are "equally" oppressed as workers. However there is still the gendered division of labor, where women and men are accorded different tasks according to their assumed abilities as women and men (women as support staff, men as managers). This at least applies in the cases where women are contributing to the public domain and working in the labor force. In many societies women do not work in the public domain, and therefore contribute to the unpaid labor force in the home, upon which the capitalist system depends (caring for the necessary current and future workforce).

Either way, men generally dominate the world of business and industry, at the blue- and white-collar levels (recall the introductory chapter and the still low numbers of women entering the top jobs in industry and finance). Men are also a part of the family, however, and can therefore express themselves in both of these contexts—the public and private domains. This is not the case for many women, particularly those who are restricted to the private sphere or the home. Those who labor in the public domain (male or female) are objectified through the expropriation of their labor, and are thereby alienated, or estranged, from the means of production. Women experience an even deeper sense of alienation and estrangement from their home and society as they are objectified and alienated by the men in the families who exploit their unpaid labor and seek relief from their own oppression in their relations with the women. As such, women are alienated by the relations of production, often keep apart from each other (by the demands of the nuclear family, which dominates the Western model of male/female relations), and are kept ignorant of collective meaning and power.

Women's access to positions of power is quite limited in this model—those in power own the means of production and determine the exploitative relations that produce their wealth. Suffering from oppression on more than one level reduces women's abilities to become informed about their potential political agency (both collectively as women and as individuals) and about opportunities for leadership. Of those who do move past the dominant discourses of the ruling classes, leadership may be possible at local, resistant levels. But the upper echelons of class resistance remain in the hands of men.

Radical Feminism

There is one other variant of feminism that is fairly well known in that it presents the relations between men and women in ways that have been interpreted by some as hostile toward men. This perspective is broadly known as radical feminism, and it emerged through the rise of the civil rights movement, new left politics, and peace movements. Its object was to escape the sex/gender system. It argued that women were, historically, the first oppressed group, and that women's oppression is the most widespread, existing in virtually every known society. Women's oppression is also the deepest in that it is the hardest form of oppression to eradicate and cannot be removed by other social changes such as the abolition of class society, as the Marxist feminists would suggest, or through legal reform, as Liberal feminists would endorse. Women's oppression causes the most suffering to its victims, qualitatively as well as quantitatively, although the suffering may often go unrecognized because of the sexist prejudices of both the oppressors and the victims.

Radical feminism has been effective in making the structures of gender oppression visible. What is often taken as "the way it is" has been explored more deeply by radical feminism. As such, the situation of sexual harassment in the workplace—a phenomenon that was not only a case of "the way it is," considered harmless and generally well meaning (why complain about being "excessively liked?"), but a phenomenon such that in the event a woman *was* to complain, she would be confronting a whole system supporting the established practices and norms. By not recognizing such systems, generally known as patriarchy, one is prone to similar comments such as the following (again, from Carol Sarler):

> Being excessively liked, mind, causes as much grief: vast sums are paid to those propositioned by a sexually uppity colleague, as compensation for the gal being so traumatized that she is forced to retire and spend more time with her stress counselor. Women in the Armed Forces seem especially attracted to this milch cow, with 2,400 of them last year complaining of harassment—in other words, the very women expected to produce super-human effort under enemy fire cannot, apparently, be expected to produce a robust rebuttal of a smutty overture.[5]

In this case, women who seek redress through the courts are weak and whining. What is not addressed in this comment, or within the whole of Sarler's article, is the situation of these women who actually decide to use the courts. What must it have been like for the first woman to do so, particularly in the system of the Armed Forces? Would this have been a pressure-free decision, one in which all of her colleagues, male or female, would have defended and supported her right to be heard on this issue? Or is it possible, even with the existence of a legal act that recognizes the right for everyone, including women, to be free from sexual harassment, that the workplace might have in fact reacted in a hostile manner toward anyone exposing the inappropriate behavior occurring in a supposed prestigious institution? The Armed Forces are still significantly male dominated, stepped in traditions based upon "male warrior" mythologies about strength, courage, and perseverance. There have been all too frequent reports of late on the types of rituals these institutions continue to uphold and (secretly?) endorse—rituals for new recruits entering elite units, rituals that involve acts of sexual submission, among others. Similar acts have also been sadly reported being practiced against prisoners in Iraq. The torture of prisoners with sexual humiliation is just one of the more extreme expressions of how sex is used in fact to harm people. Sexual harassment is yet another such expression, is it not? Sexual overtures—are these appropriate in the workplace, devoid of power relations? Military life for males is all psycho-sexual. It is quite common to refer to other soldiers as "bitches," or some other derogatory term for a female. The use of such language is all about power over the other individual, put into male-female terms in an environment devoid of females. The best illustration of this is in the opening scenes of the Stanley Kubrick Vietnam War film *Full Metal Jacket*.

The identification of patriarchy by radical feminism opened up these questions to full view. It makes visible the barriers that women meet despite the legal avenues available. This applies to invisible (i.e., not just legal) barriers women face in the case of spousal abuse (who would phone the police after the first incident? How does a woman decide that she should have her partner arrested, the person she is sharing her life with, who may or may not be her sole source of economic as well as emotional support? How does a woman decide how many incidents of spousal abuse are enough? How would you decide?) to the barriers against women (and yes, men) to seeking legal redress against sexual harassment, to the barriers (financial, social, etc.) women meet when reaching for political positions that are "legally" available to them. Women's oppression can form the basis of understanding for all other forms of oppression. The notion of patriarchy, or the dominance of masculinist paradigms, played a large role in radical feminist arguments, where they noted that patriarchy socially defined gender differences.[6]

In response, radical feminists argued, for example, for androgyny, and sought out technological methods to eradicate biological difference (reproductive control). Removing the basis for discrimination which lies behind patriarchy—that women are physiologically incapable of power and leadership due to their inclination to succumb to their physiological weaknesses (menstruating, getting pregnant, nursing)—would make women equal players, and no longer could their biology be held against them, and nor could social structures embody assumptions about what women could or could not do or be. Women must be women, however they themselves wished to define that. This meant exposing patriarchy for what it was and working toward social and structural change to finally give women freedom to do what they chose, including the desire to lead. But is this what women have become—androgynous (i.e., equivalent to male once their physiological weaknesses were addressed or out of the way) leadership hopefuls? Do they become "men" when they step out onto the national and international stage as leaders? Do they not, in some respects, perpetuate that very system of patriarchy by "eliminating" their female characteristics?

Difference Feminism

Another feminist approach, which is just one illustration of the dynamics and differences between feminisms, is difference feminism. Unlike the radical feminists who argue that differences are socially constructed (and can, in some instances, be eliminated), difference feminists argue that men and women are coded to behave differently. Females, in this view, are primarily oriented toward life giving, cooperative, nurturing activities, while males are primarily oriented toward death dealing, aggressive, controlling activities. Men are inherently more aggressive, sexually promiscuous, prone to violence, and oriented toward dominating women sexually. Women are inherently more nurturing, more submissive, (particularly to men), sexually less promiscuous, and less driven by sexual urges, while more concerned about care for children and infants. While there is disagreement as to the causes of these differences, there is a remarkable level of agreement on the differences themselves.

On a very simplistic level, a popular culture conceptualization of this approach is offered in the best seller *Men are From Mars, Women are from Venus* by John Gray. Although scientifically tenuous (the research base and the educational background of the author, John Gray, have come under serious question), the response to the work speaks volumes. Why have millions of readers been drawn to this work? It says something about the assumptions many people make about men and women, that men and women are naturally made to communicate differently and therefore we must learn to understand male and female behavior differently. Although critics of this work have noted that John Gray presents his work as "the way it is" rather than a theoretical approach (such as difference feminism), and that his assumptions about women's natural behavior work to encourage women to accept their subordinate position in the patriarchy, it is worth noting the interest this book has generated. We can probably say safely that gender, however one chooses to understand it, is not a dead issue. But if this is one of the most popular ways to view the genders (instead of androgynous, male-like equals), what can it say about women and leadership?

Difference feminism provides a lot of the basis for the "if women ran the world it would be peaceful" arguments. The differences in women's behavior cannot, according to this model, be attributed to mere social structures. Arguments about women's style of leadership, including cooperative and peaceful styles, are well suited to this approach. However, this also raises the question of whether women are naturally inclined toward leadership. Do women even want the job? Again, pointing to the recent anniversary of the British Sex Discrimination Act, some commentators claimed that the reason this act has not had the monumental effects on gender relations that were expected (greater gains in equal pay and social equality) is because women just do not want to pursue the power otherwise waiting for them in the top positions. Women do not want to devote the necessary time to work life that is required when working one's way up the corporate and political ladder. Women are more interested in family, caring, and focusing on their local needs, and if they will "run" for any positions, it will be on the local parent council or school board, where their interests are most directly affected. It would explain the dearth of female world leaders. Is this what prompted Sonia Gandhi to reject the position of prime minister of India?

Postmodern Feminism

There are those who argue not for inherent female differences, nor for androgyny or assumptions of a shared human nature among individuals. Postmodern feminism argues that there is no single formula for feminism. This approach instead deconstructs notions of identity and gender roles, largely through language and our use of language, demonstrating how current constructions are fundamentally flawed. This approach is anti-essentialist, in that gender identities are not reified as "essentially" one thing or another. It challenges notions of truth and reality about both men and women as these are shifting and in flux. "Truths" of other feminisms are a source of problems, as relations between men and women are not the same the world over, women's experiences are not all alike, and forms of oppression are not alike. Criticisms about Western feminism (rooting themselves in relations between men and women in the nuclear family, for example, which is not a relevant springboard for all women, including those from other classes or other cultures) start to arise here. The "feminist movement" is identified as one expression of feminism; one that is white and middle class, and has largely excluded women whose experiences, needs and interests are different. Postmodern feminism therefore provides a critique of the dominant "Feminism" referred to earlier. The problem is in defining "woman" itself—as soon as woman is defined, it becomes exclusionary. Thus postmodern feminism recognizes the complexity of a variety of standpoints, such that the notion of feminist depends on where you are, and who you are.

How this approach assists us in understanding more about women and leadership is more difficult to say, precisely because the approach acknowledges that there cannot be one particular way of knowing. The benefits of the approach are that the social constructs that pose as obstacles to women entering political office are torn apart, revealing the nonsensical basis of these constructs (gender roles), supporting the notion that women, like men, should not face any hindrances. How to export this critical thinking to the society, however, without constructing other concepts that would thereafter be subject to deconstruction is often not clear.

Multicultural/Non-Western/Global Feminism

Capital "F" Feminism is white, middle class, and Western. The multicultural/non-Western or global approach to feminism (which we will call just "global" for simplicity's sake) agrees with postmodernists that the self is fragmented, but on ethnic, racial, and cultural lines. Each woman experiences oppression, but she does so differently, depending on her age, race, class, religion, educational attainment, occupation, marital status, health condition, and so forth. These differing oppressions can occur within one state or across states, meaning that not only are oppressions different when comparing North American women's experiences to African women's experiences, but also between women with in the same state, such as between white and indigenous women in Canada.

This could not be better exemplified than in the recent lambasting received by Canada from the United Nations Human Rights Committee, which slammed the nation for its poor human rights record with regard to indigenous women. The side of Canada that reflects liberal feminist ideals, women making great strides in the academy (at least at the entry level), women jockeying for higher and higher positions in the workplace ... this has no bearing on a complete "otherworldly" experience of many indigenous women, by otherworldly we mean not part of the dominant "Canadian" picture often portrayed by high ranks on the human development index (in the top five of best countries in the world to live). According to the UN Human Rights Committee, Canadian indigenous women are not accorded their rights, including the ability to pass on status and reserve membership to their children and grandchildren, and to adequate police protection. These issues are either of no consequence or no relevance to the white, middle-class Canadian woman and are therefore grossly overlooked by policymakers. If there can be such discrepancies and lack of acknowledgment of differing gender issues between groups within one country, it cannot be expected that gender issues are completely universal between countries and societies. One woman's experience cannot dictate universal gender equality, just as the male experience cannot dictate universal human equality. Situations are different, needs are different, and gender issues are different, depending on where you are.

This perspective celebrates and demands diversity. Notions of a "melting pot," and similar types of assimilationist approaches are oppressive to multicultural standpoints. Colonialist, assimilationist approaches (including many Western feminisms) are oppressive to global insights and perspectives. What makes, therefore, a non-Western woman leader may not be the same circumstances, values, or roles that influence the election of Western woman leaders. The concerns, interests, and needs of non-Western woman cannot be assumed to be synonymous with those of their Western counterparts. This complicates any analysis of leadership, of course, as blanket statements about what it takes for a woman to be a leader cannot apply globally.

If we take these brief looks at feminist theories as our starting point, it becomes clear that there is no one way to approach either the roles of women nor their leadership experiences and capacities. An overriding theme, however, centers on whether we ought to focus on difference or upon sameness, in other words, equality. Generally speaking, there are three approaches we can take to women's leadership:

1. those arguing that women's differences from men should be minimized (emphasizing equality, dominated by the liberal feminist view, but can include Marxist and radical feminisms);

2. those holding that women are essentially different from men (difference feminism); and

3. those who argue that women's experiences are dependent upon their differing standpoints, and moreover differ according to race, class, and ethnicity, such that feminisms as a consequence differ across the globe according to these experiences.

Theoretically speaking, the difference positions dominate, whether they refer to inherent differences between men and women, or differences between women themselves, coming from different standpoints. Practically speaking, however, the equality position prevails, whereby policy supports women's political participation through legal access, including quotas (discussed below). A potential dilemma arises in that one cannot ignore difference for fear that a false sense of neutrality is created; on the other hand, however, difference can also emphasize deviances from the "norm."

Below we will discuss one particularly popular way of ensuring gender equality through legal reforms, in particular through quota programs. However we will first explore some of the arguments made in favor of "difference." Many of the arguments that dominate this discourse emphasize women's "ways" of knowing, thereby informing alternative approaches to power and leadership. Empowerment, popularly conceived as a female model of power, is a shared or cooperative effort as opposed to the domination game of male power. The female model is considered by some feminist theorists to be better than the male model because it is more humane and less destructive. The traditional male "power over" concept captures only the ability to act or compel actions, whereas the female "power to" concept includes the power both to act and to refrain from action.

Many of the assumptions behind what we consider to be the capacities of women, and how these capacities differ from men's, are rooted in women's role as mother. Women are thus endowed with maternal thinking patterns, which emphasize caring, nurturing, and cooperation. It is assumed that this type of thinking, if allowed to flourish, could counter the values and norms of patriarchal society, such as militarism.

Beyond the biological difference, however, some theorists point out that people themselves produce and construct differences (psychologically, socially, and culturally) between men and women. According to this view (recall both radical and postmodern feminisms), gender differences are created and are not permanent. Instead, gender identities are created, imposed, and resisted in the context of differing standpoints. The emphasis on biological difference, however, is especially important as it relates to the question of gender inequality in society. Biological difference arguments, supported by biologically derived social practices and institutions, lead to the notion of the "woman-as-peacemaker" role. Whereas the other feminist approaches may expose these institutions and assumptions to be a distortion of reality, they nevertheless successfully serve to perpetuate the existing patriarchy. The dilemma for women is that few people will listen to them if they do not speak the language of power (male power)—yet the process of learning the language forces them to leave their own identities behind (if their identities in fact embody such "peaceful" tendencies). This is also true for men who do not speak the language of power.

GENDER RESISTANCE

Gender resistance pertains to approaches, experiences, and ways of understanding that break with the traditional notions of what gender is about, and how one ought to "behave" in relation to one's gender identity. Resistance speaks to the critique of victimization—instead of viewing women constantly as victims, unable to respond to oppression, resistance allows for women's agency. Women can experience oppression but also, depending on their circumstances, make use of the resources available to them and respond. Whether women seek political leadership as a career aspiration, a calling based on their motherhood, or whatever, following through on the processes to seek, obtain, and retain political leadership is an act or series of acts of resistance against the general expectations of the female gender.

Resistance speaks to relationships of dominance and nondominance (who is exerting power over whom) as it reflects resistance to that relationship, either positively or negatively. The relationships are intricate, particularly when we speak of resistance to not only identities imposed by our own cultures, but also by others as well, which may impose yet other demands on what gender roles ought to encompass. Women and men are caught in and between competing notions of masculinity that attempt to reduce women to essentialist notions of womanhood, or if one were to include awareness of other identities, reducing women to "hyper-liberated western women" or "excessively repressed Islamic women," for example.

Gender can often be best understood through power and resistance. Dominant discourses or languages—ways of knowing—established through patriarchal society impose identity meanings, particularly through gender, thereby subordinating certain segments of the population. What it means to be a woman, therefore, is created by the patriarchal society. Subordination occurs when the meaning of woman, or any other category, means submissive, pliant, obedient, restricted to particular social roles, etc. Subordinate groups resist these meanings and attempt to create alternatives to identity development.

Seeking political office, and more so seeking the highest office in the land, is an act of contestation; it runs counter to dominant perceptions of women's capacities for leadership and power. Gender resistance pertains to the social construction of gender roles in a given society or within and between societies. "To understand resistance to gender expectations, we must therefore focus on social relations and interaction."[7] If we do gender "appropriately," we do it right, we behave (as dictated by the social construct), we simultaneously sustain, reproduce, and render legitimate the institutional arrangements that are based on the category of sex. In other words, if everyone behaved as good little girls and boys should, according to the dictates of society, those dictates become more firmly entrenched within our societies. If we fail to do gender appropriately, or behave badly as boys and girls, as men and women, we as the resisting individuals—not the institutional arrangements—may be called to account (for our character, motives, and predispositions). In other words, it is not the institution of gender that has failed us, but we who have failed ourselves. We have not met expectations. As such, resistance is not easy—it is a very decided, particular act of human agency that takes on the expectations of whole societies. Recall the discussion of the weak and victimized women of Sarler's commentary, the women who run to the courts seeking redress against sexual harassment because they are too weak to handle the situation themselves. The invoking of the legal system in this case can also be interpreted as an act of resistance—resisting the dominant expectation that women accept that sexual harassment in the workplace is "the way things are," and that women should either just put up with it or be witty about it. This applies as well to women seeking public office. The infrequency of women engaging in highly public behavior, such as seeking a post either in parliament or as the leader of a nation, demonstrates the constraints placed upon women through the socially acceptable expectations of their behavior. Women refrain from seeking office because it is not what women do. However they can resist, and some do. Political activism can also be seen as a moment of identity choice, on the part of both women and the societies in which they find themselves.

REACHING FOR EQUALITY: THE QUOTA SYSTEM

Given that women comprise upward of 52 percent of the world's population, one would think that the equivalent percentage of parliamentarians or legislative representatives would also be women. This might be the case "all other things being equal." However, all other things are not equal. For women to take their place amongst the leaders of the world, certain strategies have been and continue to be implemented. Of course, this assumes that there is a benefit to having more women world leaders, or that equality for women amongst the leaders of the world, ministers, heads of state, and the like, is important. This assumption, that there is some sort of value behind increasing the representation of women in positions of power, is one that is reflected in the writing of this book, but also by many states that have opted to implement particular strategies toward increasing female representation. These measures have been implemented but not without controversy— should we construct representation to reflect high ideals of equality, or should our legislatures merely reflect the interests and tastes of the voting public, which has not previously demonstrated a need or interest toward increasing female participation?

Quota systems have been implemented within a number of countries, particularly in the Nordic countries, which have led to increasing numbers of women holding seats in the legislature. Over time these quotas have been raised, resulting in near parity in some circumstances. The reception of quota policies is mixed however; a number of left-wing parties have adopted these policies whereas others continue to reject the idea, as Portugal did in 2000. We cannot say that the use of quota systems has any particular attraction amongst certain types of countries over others, such as Western democracies. Whereas Canada and the United States have yet to take the notion of quota systems seriously, a number of so-called developing countries such as Angola, Burkina Faso, Cape Verde, Chile, Guatemala, India, Namibia, the Philippines, South Africa, and Sri Lanka have either seriously discussed the idea, announced intentions to implement, or have actually implemented quota systems.

Quotas

Quotas refer to a method used to recruit women to positions of leadership, but this system does not, of course, speak of leadership style. Styles of leadership will be taken up later in this chapter. But we first have to see how we get women to those positions where their leadership style will actually matter. Some have expressed concern saying that use of quotas could be abused by political parties to retain or usurp power.

Quota systems are in fact in widespread use, probably much more than most suspect. As mentioned in the introductory chapter, women are making their way into parliaments around the world, although very slowly and without the increases that one might expect or hope for. At present women constitute approximately 15 percent of the legislative members around the world. Given the slow speeds by which women are gaining access to the halls of global power, particular measures have been considered and implemented in the interest of achieving gender balance, with quota systems being one of the most popular mechanisms. That the quota system is in widespread use does not mean it is not a controversial move. Despite the efficiency of this approach in that more women are very quickly introduced into the political system, there is considerable resistance against it.

First and foremost quotas give the impression that women are actually favored over men, and that any potential equality between them toward attaining a seat in the legislature or parliament is eradicated in favor of women. It also mitigates voting for the "best person" on the basis of their qualifications—we end up voting for women because they are women, not because they are the best for the job. In this respect the electoral process appears undemocratic because "the system" determines who gets elected (which women), as opposed to the electorate itself. These arguments are often raised, and are equally effective upon men as upon women, particularly women who intend to run for office. With all the baggage of being provided "special treatment" and the like, many women resent being part of a quota system where it becomes even easier to sling derogatory comments their way—"she's only in office because she is a woman." On balance, it becomes more palatable to overcome the many extra hurdles women face on their own, instead of participating in a system where no one will recognize your talents because you are only one of many who came into office because of a quota.

To try to meet some of the arguments that resist the implementation of quotas to achieve gender balance, we ought to consider some of the reasons why such a system would be adopted. First and foremost, of course, is to increase the sheer number of women in the political system.

To ensure proper representation of women means ensuring proper representation of the greater population as a whole. It also allows for a diversity of views from the women who benefit from the system. Instead of obtaining a token few women who "tow" the right party line or feel pressured to be the one voice that represents all women, we can ensure that a variety of views are represented from a variety of women. What becomes easily forgotten when quotas are introduced, supposedly "favoring" one group over another, is that the quotas are trying to compensate for barriers that the nonquota group do not face. The quota system ensures that by assisting in overcoming these hurdles, women can participate more fully as citizens and in public life. Barriers to women's full participation in politics are real and persistent. Such barriers come from cultural prohibitions dealing with women being with men and speaking their minds in front of men. In a study by The Center for Women in Politics at Rutgers, 68 percent of the women surveyed said that participation in politics would create problems with their spouse, their children, and would require large sums of money to run which they did not have and could not raise. Many women said that their primary role was to deal with their families to the exclusion of all other activities. Girls are not given equal schooling since their role is to eventually find husbands who will support them.

Some of these barriers pertain to the qualifications women have—are the right qualifications the ones that traditionally men have held, such as a particular education, social background, financial support, and so forth? Or can women now enter the system with their own brand of diverse qualifications, better representing the population as a whole while receiving support for the qualifications they do hold, whether they fall into traditional male qualifications or not (a stay-at-home mother, for example, may not have the qualifications of her male peers, but can nevertheless represent a substantial portion of the population). Thus the diverse experiences of women are needed in the political context to adequately represent the population and articulate the needs of diverse groups. In this respect plurality is accomplished, as opposed to the limited perspectives of male elites. Finally it ought to be remembered that the voters themselves do not have the opportunity to choose who runs for election—that is up to the party. The voters just validate or reject these choices.

The type of quota system determines the extent of "variety" one gets; a party-based quota system ensures that a minimum number of women can stand for election on behalf of the party in question. On the other hand, the legislature or parliament itself might require that a specific number of seats is held by women, regardless of party affiliation. Thus quotas can be set regarding how many women (what percentage) hold seats within a particular legislative body, from candidate lists to actually holding a seat in parliament itself. Quotas are not limited to women, of course, as there can be quotas to ensure representation of various minorities based on ethnicity, region, language, and the like.

According to Drude Dahlerup, political scientist at Stockholm University, there are at least four different types of quota systems:

1. Constitutional Quota for National Parliament: These are quota provisions that are mandated in the constitution of the country. Examples are Burkina Faso, Nepal, the Philippines, and Uganda.

2. Election Law Quota or Regulation for National Parliament: These are quotas that are provided for in the national legislation or regulations of the country. Legislative quotas are widely used in Latin America as well as for instance in Belgium, Serbia, Bosnia and Herzegovina, and Sudan.

3. Political Party Quota for Electoral Candidates: These are rules or targets set by political parties to include a certain percentage of women as election candidates. There might also be quotas for internal party structures, but these are not included in this Web site. In some countries there are many political parties that have adopted some type of quota provisions (e.g., Argentina, Bolivia, Ecuador, Germany, Norway, Italy, and Sweden). But in many other countries, only one or two parties have adopted quotas. However, if the majority party in a country uses quotas, as the African National Congress in South Africa, this may have a substantial effect on the overall representation of women. Yet, most political parties in the world do not apply any quota system at all.

4. Constitutional or Legislative Quota for sub-National Government: These are quotas that are provided for in the constitution or legislation that require or set targets for women to constitute a certain percentage of candidates at sub-national government level (including local, district, or state/provincial levels). Examples are India, Pakistan, Bangladesh, France, and South Africa.[8]

The quota system seems like a lot of effort to go through just for the sake of women, or so it may seem. In this respect it might be easier to understand, if not accept, the quota system if we first examine it in light of regional representation. In many countries quota systems are adopted to ensure that adequate representation is obtained from all the regions within a country. This mitigates against a "tyranny of the majority" by extensively populated regions over less populated regions, whereby the interests of the less populated regions are never represented in parliament. The argument can be made that a country, if reasonably democratic, ought to follow the wishes of the majority of the population, even if that majority is concentrated within one or a few regions of the country (this does not alter the fact that they are the majority). However it has been noted frequently that the circumstances that would dictate the interests and wishes of say, a heavily urban population, do not reflect the interests and wishes of the rural population. As such, to truly represent the population, the wishes of the "minority" (as many rural folk are becoming) ought to still be taken into consideration. Thus particular regions are protected through a quota system to ensure that their voices are heard and their needs considered along with those of more powerful or populated regions.

The same argument applies to women. In parliaments dominated by men, it is not a given fact that the interests that may be relevant to women as women will be addressed, because the parliamentary representatives have no connection to those interests and needs. This is not to suggest all women have the same interests or needs, but there are concerns, often labeled "women's issues," that most if not all countries face, such as adequate day care, parental leave, education, health, and so forth. It is also crucial to obtain the most diverse possible views on the highest matters of state, such as security. To leave such decisions to a select few who may not necessarily reflect the diversity of the population would be irresponsible at best, and dangerous at worst.

To obtain the required breadth of perspective one needs to address these concerns, it is necessary to have representation that reflects the population, not unlike regional representation. Part of the dilemma is that even when women do enter politics, they are outnumbered by men and find it extremely difficult to sponsor and pass progressive legislation that addresses women's issues such as divorce law, domestic violence, and reproductive rights. Women will have to reach a critical mass in government before needed change begins to occur.

At the present time, quota systems designed to increase female representation in parliament have more modest goals than attempting to reflect equally the gender balance of a country. These quota systems are presently after a "critical mass," meaning that enough women hold seats in parliament so that their voices are heard, they constitute a far more substantial group than a token few, and they have a reasonable chance of effecting policy. This critical mass would consist of around 30–40 percent of the representatives in the legislature. Ideally a "true" gender balance could be achieved, and Sweden is coming ever closer to this ideal. However it can be considered an accomplishment that other legislatures around the world are at least attempting to reach a critical mass. Quotas are not isolated to women however—some are gender neutral, meaning that they stipulate a minimum and a maximum representation for both genders (i.e., neither men nor women should have less than that 45 percent representation or more than 55 percent, for example).

We have focused here on the quota system because it appears to be one of the more used, if not effective, systems available within electoral processes. Of course, it is dependent upon an electoral process and some semblance of democracy. If women are not elected, then they assume positions of power through hereditary right or some familial association.

Since the women that we are examining here have been actually elected to office, we will limit ourselves to measures that encourage women's participation in these contexts. Hereditary or family contacts as a means of attaining office have less to do with a country's choice to have a woman in power and more to do with maintaining a questionable legitimate hold on power.

The social structures of the societies in which we live have a great deal to do with these tensions pulling men and women in particular social and political directions, but these structures can also be very complex as explanatory tools. It would not be possible to cover all the possible factors that impact women and their choices/opportunities to reach for the top political position in the land. Thus we would like to focus on some features that appear to play a role in the decision for women to vie for positions of world leaders. Two such features are:

1. the role of social structures such as patriarchy (what is a woman's relation to the state and her society), and

2. gender resistance (both on the part of women and on the part of the societies accepting her role as their leader).

Each woman world leader we examine will have been affected in one way or another by social structures, the expectations of her society. And each will have also had to, despite any other benefits (familial connections) or disadvantages (lack of finances) she may have, make the personal decision to break a barrier and move to the top of the world.

3
Africa and the Middle East

We do not want wars even when we win. We do not rejoice in victories. We rejoice when a new kind of cotton is grown and when strawberries bloom in Israel.

Golda Meir

INTRODUCTION

Women are marginalized both in the public and private spheres throughout the world, although their marginalization and oppression differ according to their location, ethnicity, race, and class. Women in Africa and the Middle East face oppressions that are particular to their own regions, due to cultures, economies, and religions that dominate the region's politics.

In addition to the varying legal statuses of women in Africa, they are subject to social, patriarchal structures that are often quite oppressive. They are subject not only to the demands of repressive governments, but also to international economic institutions such as the World Trade Organization, the International Monetary Fund, and the World Bank, wrestling with the demands of structural adjustment programs, trade liberalization, the enormous costs of HIV/AIDS treatment, and the like, even though they are not represented in these institutions, and their voices largely go unheard.

This does not make African women helpless, however. Despite these hurdles, women have accomplished and continue to accomplish a great deal, playing instrumental roles in, for example, the peace process (even

though they were not "at the table" so to speak) through various women's and peace organizations in Sierra Leone. Women's equity commissions are expanding throughout sub-Saharan Africa, demonstrating that women's rights are coming more and more to the forefront. A comprehensive protocol on women's rights was passed by fifteen African nations in December 2005 (although whether this will translate into any meaningful domestic policy has yet to be seen).

Kenyan Wangari Maathai, the most recent winner of the Nobel Peace Prize, is also the first woman in East and Central Africa to obtain a doctoral degree. She has been applauded for her work with African women's and environmental groups, starting the Green Belt Movement in Africa as well as working for the cancellation of the enormous debts burdening poor countries.

African women have been on the international stage infrequently, but they have been there. Today's prime minister of Mozambique, Luisa Diogo, has been preceded by female prime minsters in the Central African Empire (now Central African Republic), Senegal, Rwanda, and Sao Tome and Principe; an interim president in Burundi, and a chairman of State Council in Liberia. Africa has seen the election of its first female president—more than North Americans can boast about. Women also hold one in six parliamentary seats, keeping up with the global average. The work of politically active and successful women demonstrates what is possible, but there are still many hurdles for the vast majority of women in Africa.

The concerns of women are predominantly filtered through local and civil society organizations, and customary law still dominates the lives of many women, limiting what they can do and subjecting them to the men in their lives (fathers, husbands, brothers) and to traditions such as virginity tests and female genital cutting. As well, and as mentioned before, women do not fight a unified fight against universal oppressions. Women have different standpoints from which they make their claims. Recently hundreds of Ugandan Muslim women fought legislation that would have banned polygamy and female genital cutting, and would have raised the legal marrying age to 18 and guaranteed equal rights to women and men in marriage. The Ugandan government withdrew the bill. Another issue facing many African women, or more to the point girls, is early marriage. Girls are sent by their families to "marry" men, often decades older than they, prior to reaching puberty. They are the price paid for family debts, or the price for families that do not have enough resources to sustain the whole family. The results are too-early pregnancies, hazardous births, and recently an increased incidence of AIDS amongst younger girls. Some countries such as Ethiopia and Malawi are attempting new measures such as bans against marriages with girls aged from 12 to 15, or raising the marrying age to 18. How does one combat traditions that both women and men wish to uphold but which infringe the individual human rights of the same people who endorse them?

The solution lies with African women themselves, not without the support of women and men outside of Africa as well. They, as has been expressed in African feminist writings themselves, need to speak with their African sisters to find the best way in which to protect women without completely infringing on the traditions or values that they wish to uphold, that reflect their identities and give them strength as women, as members of their communities, and as Africans as a whole. The task is not an easy one however. Women and girls compose half of the population in Africa according to estimates by the Development Bank of South Africa (49.9 percent in 2001).[1] In sub-Saharan Africa women compose less than 45 percent of the workforce, and this has not changed since 1980.[2] However, in northern Africa and the Middle East, women make up only 27 percent of the total labor force, even with an annual growth rate of the total labor force at 3 percent.[3] Economic deprivation amongst African women is generally quite high, and as in many other parts of the world, women are often poorer and have less access to work opportunities than do men. This applies also to access to education and the political process. The catch-22 is that women need access to the political process to effect any change on their behalf. However, the statistics do show a positive side; in sub-Saharan Africa, for example, rates of illiteracy are going down, amongst both men and women. In 2001, rates of illiteracy amongst women 15 and older was 45.7 percent, down from 60.2 percent in 1980. More encouraging, however, are the illiteracy rates for female youth, which were 27.5 percent in 2001, down from 40.3 percent in 1980. As well these female youth are now roughly at par with their male colleagues, who were recorded as having an illiteracy rate of 25.0 percent in 2001. It is also the young women of sub-Saharan Africa who are bearing the brunt of the HIV/AIDS epidemic. One can only hope that increase in literacy will not only possibly politically mobilize more women, but also save more lives through education.

Women experiencing the hard circumstances of early marriages to older men, virginity tests, hazardous births, and overall subordination to male interests might find it difficult becoming local leaders, let alone national ones. That African, Asian, or any other regionally based women have had and used the benefit of familial or other connections to work up the political ladder (for example, had access to education) should not be surprising, given the obstacles they might otherwise have faced. And of course they are not alone. Most women, and men for that matter, around the world do not have the resources to become world leaders—this is still a privilege of the elite. As such those who do make it to the top, even with "connections" demonstrate a particular fortitude in doing so.

This is equally so for women in the Middle East. If one of the crucial steps toward national leadership is the step into the public sphere, usually the workplace for most women, then employment numbers can be used to indicate the degree to which the public sphere is accessible and available to them, let alone aspirations for global leadership. The numbers on employment for women in Middle East are unfortunately not all that surprising when examined in the social context in which many Middle Eastern women live. In a region struggling to form its own identity against external interests, particularly those interested in securing access to natural resources (oil), women are both participants and pawns in the development of socio-political-religious structures that can be guides to independent development in the Middle East. That these structures are often influenced by leading religious dogma does not help the gendered struggle for equality. This is the case in any part of the world where fundamentalist and essentialist notions of what is truth, particularly about men and women and how they ought to behave according to their essentialist characteristics (which is a feature of many fundamentalist religious approaches), dominate the discourses or the language of the day. American Christian fundamentalism has its own brand of inequalities imposed upon the roles of men and women, not unlike Islamic or Judaic. However it is the Middle Eastern, particularly Islamic fundamentalism that appears to be playing a central role in both the identity formation of the region, as well as determining who can participate politically. According to the Programme on Governance in the Arab Region, a part of the United Nations Development Programme, women's gains are balanced against the dictates of Islamic law. In Algeria for instance, women are subject to the Personal Code which is based on Islamic law, whereas the rest of the legal system is based on French civil law. Women in Algeria must all have a male guardian, in the United Arab Emirates Muslim women are not allowed to marry non-Muslim men (whereas Muslim men can marry outside of the religion) and require the permission of a male guardian to leave the country (the same applies to Yemen), in Syria women cannot marry without the consent of a male guardian, and in Saudi Arabia a women needs written permission from a male family member to receive medical treatment. Many of the Islamic nations of the Middle East have signed the Convention on the Elimination of all Forms of Discrimination Against Women (CEDAW), but always with a reservation that if the convention comes into conflict with Islamic law, then the latter rules over the former.

Remarkably, women have nevertheless been making some gains in these countries insofar as greater access to political and social equality defines "gains." Kuwait, despite it granting voting rights only this past year (2005) to women, has been one of the most progressive when it comes to rates of employment participation, social equality, and reduced discrimination against women. A very strong women's movement has resulted out of the Palestinian struggle in the West Bank and Gaza, taking advantage in part of the social upheaval of the national struggle, but also finding strength in its identity politics. In this respect, women's resistance has found a voice on two fronts. Sudan, which has seen the violent deaths of countless women and children (let alone the men), has also provided women with the chance to become more active in the public sphere. Sudanese women, forced into refugee camps and lacking resources, have often resorted to prostitution to survive, but the demand on women to be the sole breadwinners for the family has also led to increased workforce activity on behalf of women. The struggles of war have offered a tension-filled space to women, hanging between new opportunities due to social and political upheaval, and the catastrophic threats of conflict.

This dynamic is reflected even in the case of Iraq, which is moving in fits and starts toward a type of democracy (and the success of this still needs time to be determined), and has women represented in its parliament. As people jockey for position in this newly forming government, women and men of significantly opposing views are making their presence known. Members of the assembly include women in Western-style suits demanding 40 percent reserved seats for women on party slates, guarantees that women will run at least ten of the thirty or so Iraqi ministries, and most of all, respect for women's rights.[4] It also includes women dressed in black *abayas* who are demanding that Shariah law be the foundation of the legal system, that men be allowed at least four wives, and that the amount of money allotted to women in inheritances be reduced. The battle is between the perceptions that Iraq is adopting "western" style law and values, and the perceptions that women are the pawns of the religious extremists who use them to increase their power. It is probably fair to say that neither set of perceptions are true; secular women want to increase and protect their freedoms, which includes the freedom to assert a non-Western identity, whereas those espousing greater reliance on Shariah law want protection for women as well, allowing women to be part of greater families instead of living alone (multiple wives), and be assured economic security as men are obliged to take care of poorer relatives.[5] How these different sides will reach a compromise will be a part of the political process, but at least the women are there.

The opportunity to represent one's community is not afforded to all Middle Eastern women, however. The Arab Human Development Reports of 2002 and 2004, written by an independent group of Arab scholars, have noted that women's rights are severely lacking in the region.[6]

According to the reports, women are doubly excluded in that they are discriminated against both in law and in practice. Many women still do not have adequate access to the political process, and are inadequately protected against gender violence such as domestic violence. Positive signs are visible, such as the reformed family laws in Morocco where women are accorded far more protections and freedoms, such as equality in the family, right to divorce, and custody of children. A quota was introduced in Jordan for the first time in 2003, reserving seats for women in parliament. Women are very slowly inching their way toward more powerful positions, either as legislative representatives, ministers, or senior executives. The process is painfully slow, however, and the societal attitudes toward women still greatly hinder access.

A note about Israeli women should also be mentioned. Women have in recent years been accorded more rights, and presently represent 12 percent of the Knesset. They account for nearly half of the workforce, but dominate in those jobs that earn minimum wage.

AGATHE UWILINGIYIMANA

Agathe Uwilingiyimana was minister of education from 1992–1993, and prime minister of Rwanda from 1993–1994. She was shot, along with her husband, the day before she was to step down. Her assassination, in conjunction with that of President Habyarimana the day before, was the catalyst for one of the worst genocides in world history.

Life Before Politics

Agathe Uwilingiyimana was born in 1953 in Gikore, in the village of Nyaruhengeri, approximately 140 km south-east of Kigali, the capital city of Rwanda and 5 km from the Burundian border. She moved with her family to the Belgian Congo before returning to Gikore in 1957 to begin her primary school education. She came from modest beginnings as her parents were peasant farmers, but she excelled despite this. She earned her certificate in teaching humanities in 1973, and after teaching mathematics for a while in Butare, she continued her studies and obtained a degree in chemistry, teaching in high school until 1989. Thereafter Uwilingiyimana was director for small and medium-sized industries in the Ministry of Commerce and Industry. Uwilingiyimana married Ignace Barahira in 1976 (a fellow student at university), and had five children.

Political Career

Agathe Uwilingiyimana's political career was intimately tied to the ethnic strife pervading Rwandan politics in the 1990s and before. Rwanda's two major ethnic groups, the Tutsi who compose approximately 10 percent of the population and the Hutu who account for over 85 percent of the population, have dominated the dynamics of ethnic struggle in the region. The Tutsis, despite the fact that they are greatly outnumbered by the Hutu, had been the traditional monarchical rules of Rwanda prior to colonization by the Germans and later the Belgians. Rwanda gained independence from Belgium in 1962 and the previous ruling Tutsi minority (of whom the Tutsi men were favored by the Belgian colonial government) was overthrown by the Hutu majority, leading to the massacre and flight of thousands of Tutsis. Periodic massacres of Tutsis continued until 1990 when a Tutsi led rebel group, the Rwandan Patriotic Front (RFP), invaded Rwanda from Uganda. An agreement to end the war was signed by the RFP and President Juvenal Habyarimana toward the end of 1993, but it amounted to nothing. Uwilingiyimana was herself Tutsi, and became a central pawn at a crucial time in Rwanda's history.

Uwilingiyimana's brief tenure in politics occurred at the time of these negotiations. Uwilingiyimana was a member of the opposition party called the Republican and Democratic Movement (MDR). She was appointed as minister of education despite the fact that she was not a member of the president's party, as however a power-sharing agreement between the parties was in effect.

Agathe Uwilinigiyimana became the first woman prime minister of Rwanda on 17 July 1993, and among other things, she was accorded the task of bringing the rebel RFP and the government toward a peace accord. However her position was not acquired without controversy. Members of her own political party suspended her membership within their party. She nevertheless succeeded in leading all the concerned parties to an agreement with President Habyarimana on 4 August 1993, whereby the president would form a new government within a one-month period, sharing cabinet posts with the RFP and MDR. As a part of the negotiated plans toward this agreement, the president removed Agathe Uwilingiyimana from her post as prime minister, however Uwilingiyimana remained as logistical support (also under controversy, as she was accused at one point as being a "political trickster"). Uwilingiyimana was to step down once the agreed parties were ready to take over the new multiparty democracy on 25 March 1994, but the RFP did not participate; it was agreed however that the transition would take place shortly thereafter. The opportunity was forever lost, as President Habyarimana was killed on 6 April 1994 when his plane was shot down in its approach to Kigali airport (Burundian President Cyprien Ntaryamira was also on board and killed), some arguing that he was shot down by his own presidential guard which feared a loss of Hutu power.

Agathe Uwilingiyimana lost her life early the next morning. A Belgian escort came to her house to take her to Radio Rwanda to broadcast a message of calm to the Rwandian people following the death of the president. Her house was guarded by UN troops on the outside, and the Rwandan presidential guard on the inside. The latter shot and killed Prime Minister Uwilingiyimana and her husband. The Belgian escort was disarmed, removed to a military compound and massacred.

These events led to the genocide that reached the eyes and ears of the general world public far too late. Over one million Rwandans were killed in the space of a few months.

Legacies

Despite her brief moment on the national and international stage as Rwanda's prime minister, Agathe Uwilingiyimana was a participant in some of that country's most pivotal and brutal moments. The political life of Rwanda's first and Africa's second woman prime minister was indeed short and rife with hurdles and tragedy, but that did not make her accomplishment any less significant. She was chosen as prime minister by the same people that ultimately willed her to step down (including the president), and was shunned by her own party, making it easy to question the motives of those who were around her. To what extent was this former education minister used or manipulated? What benefits did Uwilingiyimana see or gain in playing the roles that she did, and what were her hopes? These questions we cannot answer here, and though they are important, they do not diminish the fact that she broke through the glass ceiling in Rwanda and set a precedent for women, as well as played a role in the attempt to bring peace to her country, particularly while so many others stood by, watching the events unfold and reacting only when it was much too late. Many Rwandan women have followed in Uwilingiyimana's political footsteps, becoming ministers in various portfolios including minister of justice, minister of state economic planning, and minister of state of lands and environment, to name a few. In October 1994 it was announced that a shrine would be built to honor Agathe Uwilingiyimana as a hero of Rwandan history.

SYLVIE KINIGI

In 1994 Sylvie Kinigi had the role of acting president after the death of Burundian President Melchior Ndadaye. Later Cyprien Ntaryamira, who died in the same plane crash (shot down) as Rwandan President Juvenal Habyarimana, took over the role of president. During the interim period Kinigi was the highest ranking person in Burundi.

Life Before Politics

Sylvie Kinigi was born in 1952 and was of Tutsi origin, not insignificant in the ethnic-torn country of Burundi. She was a graduate of economic management from Burundi University, and was afterward engaged with economic civil service work until 1991. Sylvie Kinigi chose to marry a Hutu man—a move that significantly departed with tradition but which demonstrated the ability to bridge the ethnic divide—with whom she had five children. Her husband died in 1993.

Political Career

Sylvie Kinigi began her political career in 1991 in the prime minister's office as a senior consultant responsible for economic reform. The job posed an enormous challenge as Kinigi was responsible for meeting the increasing demands of foreign donors expecting significant economic change in the region, cutting back the heavily financed Tutsi-dominated army, finding a place for an economy dominated by tea and coffee exports, and ensuring that the already poor people of Burundi did not bear the negative brunt of the potentially harsh economic measures. In 1993 Kinigi's career took a significant swing upward when the newly elected Hutu president of Burundi, Melchior Ndadaye, appointed her prime minister, a measure which was meant to contribute toward reconciliation between Hutu and Tutsi factions, as Kinigi was a Tutsi in a predominantly Hutu government.

As such, Sylvie Kinigi became the first woman prime minister of Burundi in July 1993, entering a politically charged environment where such reconciliatory measures as shared power between the Hutus and Tutsis in government would not be accepted easily. However Kinigi saw hope in this measure such that with the possible reductions of ethnic strife, greater economic and social development could result.

On 21 October 1993, President Ndadaye was captured and killed by rebel Tutsi troops, along with other members of his cabinet. Burundian Hutus fled to Rwanda to escape massacres in the rural areas. Prime Minister Kinigi sought shelter at the French embassy with some of the surviving cabinet ministers, and from there Kinigi tried to restore calm through radio broadcasts. Public support for the coup was low, and as such the overthrow faltered. Kinigi was suddenly in charge of the Burundi nation.

Eleven days after the coup attempt, Prime Minister Kinigi left the French embassy to restore both order and justice in the country. She refused to give way to the coup leaders and grant them amnesty from prosecution, and arranged for a new election. Although she was not an elected president, she now had de facto control over the country. She managed to restore a semblance of order, but her government could not control the ongoing carnage that took place in the countryside, killing upward of 100,000 people. In January 1994 the Burundian parliament decided to elect Cyprien Ntaryamira, the agriculture and livestock minister, to the post of president to complete Ndadaye's term. Ntaryamira was also Hutu, and his election caused anger amongst some Tutsi groups. Kinigi stepped down as prime minister in February 1994, as she was replaced by Anatole Kanyenkiko, also Tutsi, and a member of her party. April 1994 would see the assassination of President Ntaryamira, shot down in the same plane as the president of Rwanda.

Legacies

Kinigi moved on after her brief foray in the limelight as the interim leader of Burundi, taking a job in the banking industry at Burundi's Commercial Bank. She has been reported as saying that she thought Burundi was not prepared for democracy or a multiparty system given the ethnic turmoil that still enveloped the politics there. Despite the infrequency, however, of women reaching the heights of political office in Africa, it would be difficult to claim that Kinigi was merely a token or puppet in her role. She could not bring resolution to the struggles of her country, but she did her utmost to restore order and was not swayed off track in trying to bring the coup leaders to justice nor to initiate proceedings for a new election. Her role is an important one for women in Africa, as Kinigi can be counted amongst the few women who have attained such a high political position, and who had to deal with enormously difficult circumstances during a pivotal time in Burundian and African history.

TANSU ÇILLER

Prime Minister Çiller's tenure in politics was characterized by much potential, controversy, and in some respects mystery. She was the prime minister of Turkey from 1993 to 1996, transformative years for Europe and important to the potential of Turkey winning the acceptance of her European neighbors. The "iron lady with a smile," made her husband adopt her own last name.

Life Before Politics

Tansu Çiller, born in 1946 in Istanbul, grew up amongst middle-class means and upper-class ambitions, and demonstrated no particular religious predilections. Her parents struggled to ensure that their daughter attended Robert College, a private American College in Istanbul. She met and married her husband, Ozer Çiller, who also attended Robert College, and they left for the United States so that Tansu Çiller could pursue her studies. She obtained her Master's and then Ph.D. in economics, the latter from the University of Connecticut, followed by post-doctoral work at Yale University. Çiller and her husband became American citizens in

1970, however they moved back when Ozer Çiller was offered an attractive position in Turkey. They also had two children. Tansu Çiller began to teach economics at Bosphoros University (previously Robert College), became an associate professor in 1978 and full professor in 1983. She has published nine works on economy. She has also served on a number of academic boards. A clearly cosmopolitan woman, Tansu Çiller exuded confidence, intelligence, and could function well amongst those in "higher circles," speaking fluent Turkish, English, and German.

Political Career

Çiller started her political career with the True Path Party (DYP) in November of 1990 and became deputy chairperson. A year later Çiller was elected to Parliament on the DYP ticket. She was appointed minister of the economy in the resulting coalition government. She ran for party leadership in June 1993, winning on the first ballot. She became, as a result, the first female prime minister of Turkey.

Çiller's stint as prime minister was not without controversy. On the one hand she presented a charisma and attractiveness that many wished to emulate, copying her fashion statements with scarves and perfumes. Her cosmopolitan approach seemed to be a winning formula with the Europeans. However, during the years she was in government, she demonstrated varying positions on the role of religion, particularly Islam, in the development of Turkey. Early on she appeared quite secular, but when her government appeared to be entering troubled times, her devotion appeared to increase, including potential cooperation with Islamic political groups. Her honesty in declaring her wealth was called into question as she neglected to divulge that she and her husband had accumulated equity in the United States after her political career in Turkey began. Her role as minister of the economy was also suspect as she was alleged to have been rather careless in fronting facts and figures, interpreting data in ways that did not accurately portray the government's financial situation. Her use of government funds was called into question, paying for extravagant perks such as travel, exotic foods, flowers, and the like. An investigation began to find out what had happened to a secret slush fund that was subject to a large withdrawal shortly before Çiller stepped down as prime minister.

Çiller's ties to the police department and secret police were also called into question. She took a hard line against the Kurdish groups. By the time of the 1995 general elections her undeclared wealth in the United States was discovered and making headlines. Çiller tried to woo voters on a campaign focused on EU membership, subduing Kurd separatism, and denouncing Islamic bids for power. The result of this election was a coalition between the Motherland Party lead by Mesut

Yilmaz, and Çiller, who persuaded Yilmaz not to build a coalition with the Islamic Party (even though they won the highest number of votes). The coalition dissolved in the spring of 1996 after Çiller had to remove herself from government altogether as she had multiple parliamentary investigations against her.

However, Çiller managed to negotiate with the very party that was heavily investigating her, the Islamic Party. By agreeing to a coalition with the Islamic Party, Çiller managed to convince her new colleagues to stem any further investigations. In June of 1996 a new coalition was formed with the leader of the Islamic Party as prime minister, and Çiller as minister of external affairs, as well as assistant to the prime minister. She demonstrated a new found devotion to the Islamic religion, suddenly praying in public and covering her head.

It was not enough, however, as inquiries into Çiller's connections to mafia and police forces continued to plague her. Members of her party began to leave.

Legacies

Tansu Çiller was attractive to Western allies with her cosmopolitan charm and intellectual style. However her use of the highest office in the land was too rife with controversy for her successes in the West to have any beneficial effect. If her time in office could have at all sold the Turkish people upon either a secular but Turkish style of government, or the benefits of having a woman in power, the effects appear to have been minimal, given the increased interest in the Islamic Party.

GOLDA MEIR

Golda Meir was already heavily involved in the politics of Israel for more than forty-five years before she became prime minister in 1969. Often stereotyped as a tough example of a woman leader, one who does not balk at the idea of going to war, her interest was more in furthering peace: "We do not want wars even when we win. We do not rejoice in victories. We rejoice when a new kind of cotton is grown and when strawberries bloom in Israel."

Life Before Politics

Golda Meir was born on 8 December 1898 as Golda Mabovitch in Kiev, Ukraine. With her parents Moshe and Blume Mabovitch, Golda experienced severe anti-Semitism in her first eight years, living among Cossacks and peasants who hated Jews. By 1906, however, she moved to Milwaukee, in the United States, with her mother and two sisters, following her father who had moved there earlier. Meir was introduced to Zionism, the right of the Jewish people to have their own nation, while staying in Denver with her sister. Although she trained to become a teacher, she did not pursue that career goal, instead working for a socialist Zionist group called Poale Zion by 1917. At around the same time she married Morris Meyerson and moved to a kibbutz in Palestine, immigrating in 1921. Morris's health could not tolerate the life on a kibbutz, and the couple moved first to Tel Aviv and then to Jerusalem. Meir focused on raising their two children, quitting her job at the Histadrut, a Jewish labor organization and instead taking in laundry. The toll this took on Golda Meir was heavy; she found the work meaningless. She joined the Histadrut again in 1923, separating from her husband Morris ten years later. In 1956 Morris Meyerson changed his name to the Hebrew version of "Meir."

Political Career

Golda Meir actively pursued support, mostly financial, for Israel. She traveled extensively, was a delegate to the World Zionist Congress, and took on more and more tasks, adding to her work of administrating health and aid programs, and the tasks of the political department and foreign affairs. She was driven.

Meir was one of signatories to Israel's declaration of independence on 14 May 1948. She was an active part of the Israeli government immediately, first appointed as minister to the Soviet Union, and in 1949 elected to the Knesset where she served as minister of labor from 1949 to 1956 under Ben Gurion's government, then foreign minister. In 1969 she became Israel's fourth prime minister.

Despite Meir's efforts to mitigate conflicts between the now disposed Arabs and the Israelis, by 1973 Israel was at war with its neighbors. Golda Meir resigned her post as prime minister after the end of the war, having been the target of blame for the war.

Legacies

Golda Meir died in 1978. She was awarded the Freedom of Jerusalem in 1971, and is fondly remembered by many Israelis and non-Israelis alike. She is probably one of the best remembered women world leaders of the twentieth century.

ELLEN JOHNSON-SIRLEAF

The nation of Liberia was founded by African-American settlers who were ex-slaves. They established a colony of "free men of color" in 1822 with the help of the American Colonization Society, in the hope of settling freed American slaves in West Africa. Those who descended from the original African-Americans who settled the country amount to only 5 percent of the current Liberian population, but they have dominated the country's intellectual and ruling classes. The majority of Liberians today have descended from sixteen indigenous tribal groups of Africans whom the African-American settlers came to dominate and control.

The Republic of Liberia was declared independent in 1847. The settlers did not integrate into African society; in fact, hostility between the African-American settlers of the coast and the indigenous Africans of the interior has defined much of Liberian history. Unfortunately, the ex-slaves set up a hierarchy, not unlike the antebellum South in America, where Africans were considered inferior to African-Americans. The U.S. government has played a role in Liberian politics and economics since Liberia's inception. In 1926 the American-owned Firestone Plantation Company made a land concession to the Liberian government thereby moving the nation toward economic modernization. During World War II, the United States began providing technical and economic assistance that enabled Liberia to make economic progress and introduce social change.

In 1980, a successful military coup was staged by a native African named Samuel Kanyon Doe. This coup brought an end to Liberia's "first republic." Doe forged strong ties with and was backed by the United States in the early 1980s, receiving more than $500 million for pushing out the Soviet Union from the country, and allowing exclusive rights for the United States to use Liberia's ports and land (including allowing the CIA to use Liberian territory to spy on Libya). Doe, however, continued his authoritarian policies, banning newspapers, outlawing opposition parties, and holding rigged elections. His regime was corrupt and brutal.

In late 1989, a civil war began, and Doe was killed. Charles Taylor, a former Doe aide and a prominent warlord, the man who led the rebellion was now perceived by the international community to have been fairly elected as president in 1997. Taylor's brutal regime targeted several leading opposition and political activists. Taylor's autocratic style of government led to a new rebellion in 1999. More than 200,000 people were estimated to have been killed in the civil wars. The conflict intensified in 2003, when the fighting moved closer to Monrovia. As the power of the government shrank and with increasing international and American pressure for him to resign, President Charles Taylor accepted an asylum offer by Nigeria. The country of Liberia was then governed by a transitional government until a run-off election on 8 November 2005 between soccer legend George Weah and former Finance Minister Ellen Johnson-Sirleaf. Johnson-Sirleaf won and, when allegations of voting fraud came to nothing, she became the first female elected head of state in African history (president as opposed to prime minister who is only head of government).

Life Before Politics

Ellen Johnson (Sirleaf) was born on 29 October 1938 in Monrovia, Liberia, the daughter of descendents of the original colonists of Liberia (known as *Americo-Liberians*). From 1948 to 1955, Ellen Johnson studied accounts and economics at the College of West Africa in Monrovia. After she married at the age of 17 to James Sirleaf, she traveled to America in 1961 and continued her studies, earning a degree from the University of Colorado. From 1969 to 1971 she studied economics at Harvard, gaining a masters degree in public administration. Ellen Johnson-Sirleaf then returned to Liberia and began working in William Tolbert's government.

Political Career

Johnson-Sirleaf became involved in government when she became assistant minister of finance in President William Tolbert's administration in 1970. While running for Senate in 1985, she spoke out against the military regime, and was sentenced to ten years in prison. Released after a short period, she lived in exile and returned in 1997 as an economist, working for the World Bank, and Citibank in Africa. The years in exile until returning for the elections of 1997 gave her considerable international experience at the Citibank in Nairobi, the UNDP, and the World Bank. She held the post of director of the Regional Bureau for Africa at the UNDP, formulating development strategies for African economies, and was Senior Loans Officer at the World Bank.

Initially supporting Charles Taylor's rebellion against Sergeant Samuel Doe, she later went on to oppose him, and ran against him in the 1997 presidential elections. She managed only 10 percent of the votes, as opposed to Taylor's 75 percent. Taylor charged her with treason. She helped remove President Taylor from office and played an active role in the transitional government in the run-up to the 2005 elections.

In the first round of 2005 voting, she came second with 175,520 votes, putting her through to the run-off vote on November 8 against former footballer George Weah. On November 11th, the National Elections Commission of Liberia declared Johnson-Sirleaf to be president-elect of Liberia. On November 23rd they confirmed their decision saying that Johnson Sirleaf had won with a margin of almost 20 percent of the vote. In spite of allegations of election fraud, independent international, regional, and domestic observers have all declared the vote was free, fair, and transparent.

Johnson-Sirleaf supporters call her the "Iron Lady," borrowing the nickname of former British Prime Minister Margaret Thatcher.

Legacy

"It's clear that the Liberian people have expressed confidence in me," Johnson-Sirleaf told The Associated Press. "They have elected me to lead the team that will bring reform to the country and that will deliver development." She added that she would lead "a government of inclusion" and said she would offer Weah a post in the government— perhaps the Ministry of Youth and Sports. "We hope that Mr. Weah will get over his disappointment that has led to his rejecting the results, and that ultimately he'll accept it and we'll find a way forward together," she said. Weah's supporters included many former warlords, rebel leaders, and young men who fought in Liberia's fouteen-year civil war that killed up to 200,000 people and plunged the country's 3 million residents into abject poverty. While international observers who monitored the poll said it was a fair election. David Carroll, leading a twenty-eight-person team from the Atlanta-based Carter Center, said that while "minor irregularities" had been noted, "none of our observers saw any serious problems." Observers from the Economic Community of West African States, which played a key role brokering peace in Liberia, also deemed the vote fair.

As the winner, Johnson-Sirleaf will have to govern a country left in ruins by war, its buildings smashed and nearly one-third of its people in relief camps. She has pledged to end corruption. During the election campaign, this small-statured grandmother was often dwarfed by her party officials and bodyguards. Despite her diminutive stature, she has definitely earned her nickname, the "Iron Lady." She was imprisoned in the 1980s for criticizing the military regime of Samuel Doe and then backed Charles Taylor's rebellion before falling out with him and being charged with treason after he became president. She twice went into exile to escape her legal problems with the governments of the day. In 1997, she came a distant second to Taylor in elections following a short-lived peace deal. One veteran of Liberia's political scene said Johnson-Sirleaf's nickname comes from her iron will and determination. Her supporters say she had two advantages over the man she faced in the run-off election—former football star George Weah—she is better educated and is a woman.

Given Johnson-Sirleaf's experience in a string of international financial positions, from minister of finance in the late 1970s to Africa director at the United Nations Development Program, she is well-equipped to rebuild Liberia's shattered economy. "We know expectations are going to be high. The Liberian people have voted for their confidence in my ability to deliver … very quickly," she told Reuters news agency.

Many educated Liberians—and members of the old elite, who descended from freed American slaves—gave Johnson-Sirleaf their backing. Women and some gender-sensitive men in the city are also quick to blame men for wrecking the country. "We need a woman to put things right," said one waitress. Johnson-Sirleaf said she wants to become president in order "to bring motherly sensitivity and emotion to the presidency" as a way of healing the wounds of war. She has pledged to work toward reconciliation by bringing her former opponents into a government of national unity—if they want to join her. "We are going to reach out to them and assure them the country is also theirs," she said.

Throughout her campaign, she has said that if she won, it would encourage women across Africa to seek high political office. But in rural areas, where male-dominated traditions remain strong, there may be some resistance to the idea of a female leader. Even one well-educated man said: "Only a man can be strong enough to deal with all the ex-combatants. Liberia just isn't ready to have a woman leader yet." Some are wary of her because of her previous support for Taylor—currently facing seventeen charges of war crimes for his alleged ties to rebels in neighboring Sierra Leone.

After spending a generation in politics, she comes with considerable baggage and has made many political enemies. She constantly stresses her commitment to the fight against corruption and after returning from exile she served as head of the Governance Reform Commission set up as part of the deal to end Liberia's civil war in 2003. She resigned that post to contest the presidency, criticizing the transitional government's inability to fight corruption. She has also promised to "revisit the land tenure system" in order to remove a potential source of dispute between Liberia's rival ethnic groups. At present, much of Liberia's land is controlled by local chiefs.

Johnson-Sirleaf, whose ex-husband died a few years ago, is the mother of four sons and has six grandchildren. Like her other high-ranking female colleagues in Africa and the Middle East, Johnson-Sirleaf is a well-educated, seasoned politician. All of these women had access to education, which appears to have been crucial in their personal fights for power. Claiming an education is in itself an act of resistance in societies that attempt to hinder women at every turn. To do so required at least some financial, if not moral/emotional support from families or other support units. Given the regions these women represent, parts of the world rife with poverty and massive women's rights violations, their accomplishments are very significant.

What is interesting is noting the countries in which they were able to reach the positions they attained. Women are not filling political positions in Saudi Arabia or sub-Saharan Africa. It may be too much to hope that these regions would see representation by more women in the near future. However, the countries that these woman have or do represent have not been trouble free, either ideologically (dealing with the tensions of fundamentalism or secularism) or ethnically (Rwanda and Burundi are two sad cases in point). Part of their success has to do with the abilities of each individual woman in becoming a part of the political process. However another part has to do with the dynamics of the regions or countries they represent—what is it about these countries and societies that they have been willing to front the first female prime ministers? That the societies were open to it, and that the women were ready for it, is the combination that made these women enter the history books as women world leaders.

It is also worth noting, however, that even the women are not free from condemnation or accusations of corruption. They are not images of perfection, as Uwilingiyimana of Rwanda was at one point called a political trickster,Çiller could not run fast enough from her questionable financial transactions while in office, and Johnson-Sirleaf's questionable election rumors, although largely laid to rest, demonstrate the fallibility of women leaders. Such insights are not restricted to the women of Africa and the Middle East however—the tensions faced by women at the top appear relevant to other leaders around the world, to whom we shall now turn.

4

Asia

Jai Durga!

　　　　　　　　Hindu battle cry to the warrior goddess Durga

INTRODUCTION

Between 1960 and 2006, a total of fifty-eight different women have been prime ministers or presidents around the world. The first was Sirimavo Bandaranaike of Sri Lanka in 1960. There is geographical diversity in this pool of fifty-eight leaders. Europe claims the most women leaders with nineteen. The Americas (including the Caribbean) have had sixteen leaders and the Asia-Pacific region has had thirteen. Africa and the Middle East have had only eight leaders. It should be noted that although the Americas have had sixteen women leaders, only one has come from North America.

It is amazing how many governments or opposition movements in Asia have been, or are, led by women given the fact that the countries in Asia are largely patriarchal and paternalistic in character. These ambitious women have risen to power in Asia where politics, the economy, and the social order have been traditionally dominated by men. Despite the Christian, Muslim, Buddhist, and Hindu cultures dividing them, these women shared a common political start. They were widows or daughters of powerful men who, with one exception, were removed by force in the political violence that has marked Asia for half a century. Women leaders have emerged in Asian countries with different levels of economic development, cultures, and political systems. However, most female leaders in Asia have come from developing countries.

Women leaders are found in predominantly Buddhist (Burma and Sri Lanka), Christian (the Philippines), and Hindu (India) countries. Female leaders have also emerged in Muslim states in Southeast and South Asia. Except for Afghanistan and Brunei, women lead, or have led, governments or opposition groups in all predominantly Islamic countries in this region (Bangladesh, Indonesia, Malaysia, and Pakistan). Women have both led struggles against dictatorships, and participated in competitive, democratic elections. These differences in economic development, culture, and political systems provide an opportunity to discover the common root to the ascendancy of these women to positions of power.

PATHS TO POWER
Family Dynasty

All of the women who have come to power in Asia have been in the role of victim at one time or another. The assassination or imprisonment of their father or husband generates a very strong "victimization sentiment" which can be used by these women politicians in order to mobilize their political followers. It can also be interpreted as a starting point of resistance—demonstrating the capabilities of these same women who have also had tragedy define a part of their lives. For Corazon Aquino (Philippines) and Wan Azizah (Malaysia) the victimization sentiment became their political capital. Even when political "martyrdom" did not serve as a primary catalyst for a political career, the injustice suffered by the male predecessors could be used to campaign for support of the descendants or the surviving dependents. Benazir Bhutto of Pakistan, and Aung San Suu Kyi of Burma are examples, although Kyi is herself a victim of the Burmese regime.

These women are not really seen as traditional politicians because they did not come up through the political ranks. Most came from prestigious families and have been well-educated, often in the West or in Asian schools influenced by the West. Although their prominence is inspiring and has helped to open doors for women, the majority of Asian women are only slowly emerging from poverty and have very limited access to the world of politics.

In spite of the family dynasty connections, these women leaders should not be seen as simply replacements for their dead husbands and fathers, but rather as natural leaders who only needed an opportunity and a door to open for them to be engaged in national politics. It is often forgotten that many men around the world have come to power because of family connections and name recognition. India's Sonia Gandhi, whose story opens this book, is an Italian-born heir to the Nehru-Gandhi dynasty, who met Rajiv Gandhi, son of Prime Minister Indira Gandhi, when they were students at Cambridge in England. Her story is unfortunately not an uncommon one for many wives of world leaders. When Rajiv Gandhi was assassinated by terrorists during a political campaign in 1991, Sonia Gandhi left the public sphere to raise their two children. As the years passed, she was repeatedly urged to enter politics by members of the Congress Party who sought to use her family name. She finally consented, but was unable to lead the party to a clear-cut victory. However, she did become president of the Congress Party, and later could have been prime minister had she not backed out at the last moment in May 2004.

The rise of female leaders is often linked to their being members of prominent families—they are all the daughters, wives, or widows of former government or opposition leaders. These women all came from political dynasties and inherited political power. In general, political dynasties are not uncommon or unusual. What is unusual is women being the beneficiaries of their family's political connections. It is not just a shortage of men that leads to women being selected as political heirs within the family, but also their ability to symbolize nonpartisan alternatives to corrupt (male) leadership.

Women are considered to be less threatening to potential rivals, who lend their support without having to sacrifice their own ambitions. Although women benefit from their respective political dynasties, men still maintain real control of the political parties for the most part, although Sonia Gandhi demonstrates that this fact too is changing. Otherwise, many see female leadership as largely symbolic, with their ability to unite the party being considered more important than their actual political skills.

Burma's Nobel Peace Prize winner Aung San Suu Kyi is one woman who would be a great national leader, and was elected on her own right, but is not allowed to assume her rightful position. Kyi was placed under house arrest by the military junta that prevented her from taking office when her National League for Democracy won the elections of 1990. Suu Kyi is the daughter of General Aung San who helped win Burma's independence. He was assassinated six months before independence was declared in 1948.

Mother Figure/Female Purity/Goddess Power

Another reason for the rise of some women leaders is that traditional female stereotypes proved to be a political advantage. The role of women as caregivers and with their lives rooted in the family can serve both as a hindrance and as an advantage in politics. This approach reflects one of the dominant feminist perspectives addressed in Chapter 2. Women have, according to this view, a natural inclination to care for others, a trait that is perceived by some to be politically beneficial (mostly for those backing the woman in question though). Because of this selfless family-centered role, women leaders were often perceived as apolitical. They were best suited to lead a moral struggle against male "Machiavellian types."

Some women leaders portrayed themselves as fresh, uncorrupted alternatives to the male-dominated political network. It enabled them to achieve the apparently paradoxical: while they were the heirs to a political dynasty—which in few cases was renowned for its commitment to good governance or its upholding of lofty political morals—they appeared to be politically virtuous with a sincere commitment to reform.

Women leaders might attempt to capitalize on the mother image as well. The mother image brings with it power derived from being the caretaker of the family, the one who brings a life into the world. Her role as leader of the nation is seen as equivalent to being the mother of the nation with all that implies. This limits the female leader's policy options since any behavior that would be considered political in nature would cause people to question the image of mother and could cause a deeper sense of betrayal than with male politicians.

It is ironic that men in Asia treat their sons better than their daughters, yet are prepared to elect and worship women political leaders like goddesses. In India, Nepal, and Sri Lanka, soldiers dedicate their weapons to a beautiful demon-slaying goddess named Durga. In battle, this warrior deity is invoked through the battle cry: "Jai Durga!" Women presidents and prime ministers in Asia may be tapping into this feminine power.

Belief in goddess power may have helped elect Indira Gandhi, Chandrika Kumaratunga, Sirimavo Bandaranaike, and Benazir Bhutto. These women used all of their resources in gaining power, including their family names. Often their male family members had been killed, raising sympathy for a grieving widow or daughter. But this dynastic connection alone does not explain the ascendancy of women in South Asia, and it certainly does not keep them in power. Perhaps goddess power may be partly responsible for their ascendancy and grip on political power.

Indira Gandhi did not shy away from comparisons to Durga. But invoking goddess power along with a mother image is risky and can deepen the sense of betrayal in politics. Indira crushed her opponents after she was first elected. After being defeated and returning again, she was assassinated by her own bodyguards.

TROUBLE WHILE IN POWER

Women who come to power based on family connections, goddess power, martyred fathers or husbands, or as mothers of their countries, must then govern their respective countries just as men do, but under a different set of standards. The voters do not consider the experience and abilities of these women when they elect them, yet they expect them to perform better than male leaders once in power. Of course, most of the criticism comes from men.

Because women leaders are perceived as offering a moral alternative to male leaders, any indication of mistakes once in office leads rapidly to disillusionment among the electorate. This is exactly what happened to Benazir Bhutto in Pakistan. Grave accusations of massive corruption against her administration (directed primarily against her husband) contributed to her downfall.

Women political leaders often receive unfair criticism from men because women leaders are looked at as representing the purity of motherhood. Not only are these women expected to be perfect people while in office, but they must also be perfect political leaders. We do not hold such high standards for male leaders. The number of women who come to power in Asia is still small, yet on the surface it appears as if Asian countries are ahead of the West in terms of gender equality (e.g., no woman has served as president of the United States). This picture equality based on political power is misleading since it does not so much reflect increasing female empowerment and grass roots representation as it does Asia's infatuation with dynastic politics and the symbolic roles of women.

While strides have been made in terms of the participation of women in politics since the first International Women's Day thirty years ago, women remain severely underrepresented in parliaments across Asia. Currently, Asia has three women leaders: Prime Minister Helen Clark in New Zealand; President Gloria Arroyo in the Philippines and Prime Minister Khaleda Zia in Bangladesh.

Until October 2004, Megawati Sukarnoputri was Indonesian president and Sonia Gandhi nearly came to power in India. Pakistan has had a female prime minister in the not too distant past, and, as for the current countries in Asia that have women leaders—Bangladesh, Sri Lanka, the Philippines, and New Zealand—they are not the first women to head their respective nations. Yet, it is important to note that in all but the case of New Zealand, these women leaders have been the widows or daughters of former rulers and founding fathers, some of whose families have maintained a grip on power off and on over several decades. Family background takes precedence over gender, but this leadership by women does not translate into empowerment of women in their countries, where levels of female education and social, political, and economic development remain low. And the grip these women have on power is tenuous at best, based on an electorate that sees them not as normal political leaders, but as symbols and icons. Real change in terms of gender equity needs to follow the ascendancy of these Asian women leaders.

What does the future hold for Asia? Afghanistan is presenting a fascinating and tenuous flirtation with democracy, including electing women into their parliament. During the first parliamentary elections in thirty years, women ran for election and will sit in 68 of the 249 seats in the lower house. It is a cause for celebration and a cause for skepticism. Although women will occupy a quarter of the seats in the lower house and are considering to create a woman's party, the parliament is still overwhelmingly dominated by members of the old, if not dangerous, guard—including Mujaheddin commanders, ex-Taliban fighters, old communists, technocrats, and tribal chieftains. On the other hand, there are also many urban progressives and even poets. A number of parliamentarians are illiterate and the vast majority of members have no experience in this Western style of governance they now find themselves employing. In addition, the Taliban pressure has not let up. A teacher was recently shot in front of school children for refusing to stop teaching girls at a coed school. Such reactions by the Taliban since the U.S. invasion in 2001 have been increasingly common place, often starting with warnings, beatings, or the burning down of schools. Some of the women who ran for the parliamentary elections had one or multiple threats made on their lives. These are the women of the future, however. Side by side with women of Asia who may or may not represent mothers, victims, or take over where their family dynasties have left off, women on this continent have only just begun their climb to power.

CONCLUSION

Some of the women are "politicians by chance" such as Aung San Suu Kyi of Burma. Other women leaders had to be strongly persuaded to become political leaders. In democratic systems, being a victim is of less importance. Women in democratic states have often developed their own political base, which is often different from that of their fathers or husbands, such as Chandrika Kumaratunga in Sri Lanka.

By categorizing the women leaders of Asia, one can see patterns:

1. Established tradition of female leadership: Chandrika Kumaratunga of Sri Lanka and Sonia Gandhi of India.

2. Leaders emerging in progressive industrialized countries: Tanaka Makiko of Japan, and Park Geun Hye of South Korea.

3. Leaders emerging from democratic revolutions: Corazon Aquino of the Philippines and Sheikh Hasina/Khaleda Zia of Bangladesh.

4. Leaders of opposition movements to authoritarian regimes: Aung San Suu Kyi of Burma, and Wan Azizah of Malaysia.

5. Leaders from democracies emerging after the fall of a dictator: Benazir Bhutto of Pakistan, and Hasina Wajed/Khaleda Zia of Bangladesh.

6. Leaders in predominantly Islamic societies: Bangladesh, Indonesia, Malaysia, and Pakistan.

One can see from the foregoing discussion that the dynastic factor alone does not explain the rise of women leaders in Asia. Political skills and political resources do play a strong role as well. But it is not enough to ask why there are so many women leaders in Asia, but also what difference they make once in office.

1. Have female leaders' efforts to bring about social, economic, cultural, and political changes transformed gender relations in any meaningful sense?

2. In particular, have women leaders put emphasis on strengthening female involvement in economic development?

3. Is there a link between female leadership and the promotion of democracy/democratization?

4. Does the example of female leadership and their political agenda promote increased political participation by women generally?

These questions require substantial analysis, beyond what we are capable of providing here. But the questions are important nevertheless, and worth thinking about as we look more closely at some examples of woman leadership in Asia. Afghanistan again raises itself as an example—women in Afghanistan have not been raised in a void, nor are devoid of resources and skills and capacities that enable them to pursue politics in one shape or another. Whether they are particularly inspired by their sisters across the continent is very difficult to say. However it is our guess, maybe hope even, that increasing female representation across Asia does amount to something for women, and possibly can make a difference over time. Of course, what sort of difference it will make, and how fast this difference could be made (here referring to advances in gender equality, at the very least), cannot be overestimated. If societies that preach gender equality cannot manage to support female leadership (such as the United States), how can anything the same be expected in allegedly more patriarchal societies?

CORAZON AQUINO

Life Before Politics

Corazon "Cory" Aquino was born in the Tarlac province of the Philippines on 25 January 1933. Aquino received her education at the Assumption Convent in the Philippines, Ravenhill Academy in Philadelphia, Notre Dame Convent School in New York, College of Mount Saint Vincent in New York, and Far Eastern University in the Philippines. She married a young politician named Benigno S. Aquino in 1956. Benigno became the chief political opponent to strong-armed President Ferdinand Marcos.

Political Career

Cory Aquino did not at first seem like the type of woman who would come to lead her nation. She did have some political experience from working on Thomas Dewey's 1948 presidential campaign while living in New York and from coming of age during the Philippines independence after World War II. But it was her marriage to Benigno Aquino that really gave her firsthand political experience. Her husband's 1983 assassination on his return to Manila from exile in the United States brought her out of his shadow and into the spotlight. But she seemed to lack the self-confidence to take up his fight to restore democracy on her own. After her husband's funeral, she planned to return to her old life and fight Marcos from the sidelines. She did not realize, at first, the power she had in the role of the widow of a martyr. As her influence grew, she still did not see herself as a political leader and turned down many appeals to run for office.

When President Marcos called for a sudden presidential election in 1985 to catch the opposition off-guard, Aquino realized that she alone could unite the anti-Marcos forces and remove the dictator from power. Aquino felt that God was on her side. The military sent signals that they would support her if Marcos tried to rig another election.

Defense Minister Juan Ponce Enrile and Deputy Chief of Staff Fidel Ramos turned against Marcos, claiming massive electoral fraud. When Marcos threatened to retaliate, the Archbishop of Manila, Jaime Cardinal Sin, broadcast an appeal for "people power" to protect the opposition to Marcos. Marcos's tanks that were dispatched to quell the rebellion were met by hundreds of thousands of Filipinos who had gathered to pray the rosary and to stop the tanks in their tracks. Cory swept into power with the backing of the victorious rebels who then whisked Marcos off to exile in Hawaii.

Aquino faced severe challenges after assuming power as disgruntled pro-Marcos members of the military attempted seven coups. Her makeshift coalition was tested to its limits and she was forced to make decisions that were unpopular. Enrile, her defense minister, threatened to overthrow Aquino if she carried out the promise she made to negotiate with the communist guerrillas. She announced a ceasefire with the insurgents and fired her defense minister. Defying her core supporters in the liberal community and the Catholic Church, she endorsed Ramos, an architect of martial law and a Protestant, as the candidate best equipped to restore stability and promote economic recovery.

Legacies

A little over two years after her husband's assassination, Cory Aquino, a widowed homemaker, took over the leadership of one of the world's most volatile nations. She did this with little or no political experience.

President Aquino's awards and distinctions are numerous, some include: Woman of the Year in *Time* magazine, the Eleanor Roosevelt Human Rights Award, the United Nations Silver Medal, and the Canadian International Prize for Freedom.

Aquino restored the democratic institutions Marcos had destroyed, freed political prisoners, launched a peace process that eliminated communist and Muslim insurgencies as major threats to national stability, and laid the foundations for economic recovery.

The concept of People Power defines her place in history. Her determination to lead by example helped restore Filipinos' faith in government—and themselves. Cory Aquino was like so many other modern women leaders such as Violeta Chamorro, Benazir Bhutto, Chandrika Kumaratunga, Khaleda Zia, Megawati Sukarnoputri, and Aung San Suu Kyi, who were thrust into public life by the violent fates that befell their husbands or fathers and were asked to heal their respective countries.

SIRIMAVO BANDARANAIKE

Life Before Politics

Sirimavo Bandaranaike was born Sirimavo Ratwatte on 17 April 1916 in Sri Lanka. She was the eldest daughter among six children and came from a wealthy, aristocratic land-owning family. Although a Buddhist, she was educated at a convent in Colombo run by Roman Catholic nuns. In 1940, when she was 24, she married Solomon Bandaranaike, who formed the nationalist Sri Lankan Freedom Party and led it to election victory in 1956. The family dominated Sri Lankan politics for most of the second half of the century. But in 1959, Mr. Bandaranaike was shot by a Buddhist monk. After her husband's assassination, Sirimavo became the first woman in the world to serve as prime minister.

Political Career

Bandaranaike was dubbed "the weeping widow" for frequently bursting into tears as she pledged herself to continue her husband's vaguely socialist policies. She led the Sri Lanka Freedom Party, which her husband had founded, and headed two coalition governments (1960–1965, 1970–1977).

A year after her historic 1960 election victory she declared a state of emergency after continuous civil disobedience by the minority Tamil population. The Tamil population was upset because Bandaranaike had replaced English with Sinhala as the official national language.

In 1964, she and her cabinet were defeated in a confidence vote, and lost the general election that followed. But in 1970, she again became prime minister, after an electoral landslide victory by her left-wing coalition. Her politics moved to the left, thanks to her strong personal ties with China and the then Indian prime minister, Indira Gandhi. She declared the country a republic in 1972, changing the name from Ceylon to Sri Lanka. She also nationalized some companies in the plantation sector and restricted some imports.

The coalition broke up in 1975, and her government was defeated in 1977. She was expelled from parliament in 1980 and stripped (1980–1982) of her civil rights because of abuses as prime minister. She reentered politics in the late 1980s and was an unsuccessful candidate for president in 1988.

Legacy

Her daughter, Chandrika Kumaratunga, became president of Sri Lanka in 1994 after leading the left-wing People's Alliance to an election victory, and reviving the fortunes of the Bandaranaike family. She appointed her mother prime minister, a position that has become largely ceremonial.

But observers believed that Sirimavo Bandaranaike and her daughter did not always see eye to eye—largely over issues of leadership rather than policy. Bandaranaike, having returned to the post of prime minister, reluctantly gave up the reins of power on 10 August 2000. Shortly thereafter, Sirimavo Bandaranaike suffered a fatal heart attack while driving home after casting her vote in the general elections.

BENAZIR BHUTTO

Life Before Politics

Benazir Bhutto was born on 21 June 1953, in Karachi, Pakistan, as the daughter of a land-owning family prominent in politics. Her father,

Zulfikar Ali Bhutto, served in various government posts. She was tutored by an English governess and enjoyed a pampered, upper-class life.

When Benazir was only 16 years old she came to the United States and attended Harvard's Radcliffe College. Bhutto received a degree in government in 1973, and then went on to England and studied politics, philosophy, and economics at Oxford.

Benazir Bhutto returned to Pakistan in 1977 in the midst of political turmoil. Her father was removed from power by the military regime of General Zia and later hanged. She was arrested by the military regime and repeatedly detained between 1977 and 1984. Finally in 1984, after being held for three years, she was allowed to leave Pakistan and settled in London.

In 1985, after her brother (who had organized antigovernment organizations) died under mysterious circumstances, Benazir took part in antigovernment political rallies, and was again arrested. She was released in early November 1985. Martial law ended in Pakistan in December 1985. Political demonstrations resumed and Bhutto then demanded that General Zia step down. Bhutto was named cochair of the Pakistan People's Party.

Political Career

Bhutto was elected prime minister in 1988, the first woman elected prime minister of an Islamic country. Her objective was to return Pakistan to civilian rule and oust the men who executed her father. She was taken out of office by President Ghulam Ishaq Khan in 1990, but she ran on an anticorruption campaign and was reelected prime minister in 1993.

Benazir was removed from office a second time in late 1996 after her government was charged with corruption, mismanagement, and the purging of political rivals. Bhutto's husband, Zardari, was often the target of criticism. She had appointed him investment minister and he was accused of taking bribes and stealing from government accounts.

Benazir Bhutto's political platform was leftist in that it called for hunger relief, health care, job creation, slum clearance, and increases in minimum wage. Islamic fundamentalists were suspicious of Bhutto's leftist leanings. To make matters worse, the military was always standing by to impose martial law. Bhutto ran in the national elections of February 1997 and was defeated.

Legacies

Throughout the years in opposition, she pledged to transform Pakistani society by focusing attention on programs for health, social welfare, and education for the underprivileged. As prime minister, Benazir Bhutto emphasized the need to heal past wounds and to put an end to the divisions in Pakistani society—including reducing discrimination between men and women. Bhutto also launched a nationwide program of health and education reform. Her legacy is mixed. Her ambitious social political agenda was compromised by an unstable and violent mixture of politics in Pakistan and her often heavy-handed attempts to hold on to power and eliminate rivals.

Bhutto is the author of *Foreign Policy in Perspective* (1978) and her aptly named autobiography, *Daughter of Destiny* (1989). She received the Bruno Kreisky Award for Human Rights in 1988 and the Honorary Phi Beta Kappa Award from Radcliffe in 1989.

INDIRA GANDHI

Life Before Politics

Indira Gandhi was born on 19 November 1917, in Allahabad, India, to Jawaharlal and Kamala Nehru. Her family was forever changed when they met Mohandas Gandhi in 1919. Gandhi had just returned from South Africa and had formed the pacifist Indian Freedom Movement and proceeded to convert Indira's family. Her wealthy family gave up their luxuries and set up their home as a center for Gandhi's movement. Members of her family were often jailed for their activities.

Indira was insecure growing up in such a tumultuous environment but resolved early on that she would not to be held down by Indian social customs that repressed women. She was active in the fight against British authority as a child and remembered visiting Mohandas Gandhi in prison. He had a huge impact on her development.

Indira lost her mother to cancer when she was 17. She spent the next five years studying abroad. She was married in 1942 to a man not of her Brahmin class. She was criticized by her family and the public and later jailed. Following her release from prison, she became involved in politics. She also gave birth to two sons, Rajiv and Sanjay. Gradually she and her husband drifted apart and although they never divorced they lived separately until his death in 1960.

Political Career

When India achieved independence in 1947, Gandhi's father became the nation's first prime minister. Because Nehru was a widower he needed his daughter to act as hostess at official government functions. Gandhi lived in her father's shadow for years, but she eventually began to speak out during her own campaigns and at functions her father could not attend. By 1959 she was president of the India National

Congress. Influenced by Nehru's socialist leanings, she brought a fresh perspective to the party and sought to increase women's participation in politics.

When Jawaharlal Nehru died of a stroke in 1964, his daughter Indira was not seriously considered as a successor. However, when the new prime minister, Lal Bahadur Shastri, also died two years later, Gandhi was chosen to fill the leadership void in India. Overnight she became the leader of the world's largest democracy and perhaps the most powerful woman in the world.

Indira had problems immediately after taking power. The right wing challenged her and forced compromise. Her reelection by a very narrow margin in 1967 led to her having to accept the right wing leader Moraji Desai as her deputy prime minister. She was a nervous person and did not trust fellow politicians.

Gandhi won by a large margin in the 1971 election and India began to make great progress in both food production and industrialization. She gave military support to the people of East Bengal to secede from Pakistan. This led to the formation of the state of Bangladesh. The high court accused her of violating election laws in 1972 and began the process of removing her from power.

Instead of accepting the High Court's decision, Gandhi declared a state of emergency, imprisoned her political rivals, and suspended civil liberties. In 1977 her party was swept from power. She regained her seat in Parliament and in 1979 she was elected again as prime minister. Her two sons became close political advisors as she was grooming them both for party leadership. After Sanjay died in a plane crash in 1980, Rajiv took over as the heir apparent.

During the 1980s several of India's states sought independence from the central government. The most violent were the Sikh extremists in the Punjab province. After sending the army to capture Sikh guerrillas, a violent conflict ensued wherein 600 people died. As a result, in October 1984, Gandhi was assassinated by two of her Sikh security guards. Rajiv became prime minister after her mother's death. He himself was assassinated at a 1991 reelection campaign rally.

Legacies

India had been ruled by England for over a century prior to its independence in 1947. Although the British had built many roads, schools, and hospitals, they had also acted as a superior colonial power. The Indians greatly resented British control. The organized struggle for freedom began early in this century and grew until after World War II, which ended in 1945, when the British finally realized they could no longer hold India. The ascension of a woman, Indira

Gandhi, to the highest position in the world's most populous democracy was especially significant for Indian women, who had traditionally been subservient to men. In addition, she was also an inspiration to people in other Third World nations. Her legacy is mixed, based on her ambitious social goals and the inevitable nondemocratic measures she employed in order to keep order in a violent and volatile Indian political landscape.

MEGAWATI SUKARNOPUTRI
Life Before Politics

Megawati Sukarnoputri was born on 23 January 1947 in Jakarta, Indonesia (which had gained its independence from the Netherlands in 1945). She grew up in luxury as the second child and eldest daughter of Sukarno, then the president of Indonesia. Her mother Fatmawati was one of Sukarno's nine wives.

Megawati went to Padjadjaran University in Bandung to study agriculture, but dropped out in 1967 when her father was succeeded by a military regime led by Suharto. Her family was not bothered by the new regime as long as they agreed to stay out of politics.

In 1970, the year Sukarno died, Megawati went to the University of Indonesia to study psychology but dropped out after two years. Megawati is not an intellectual, and she has little knowledge of the world outside Indonesia. She is a Muslim who also follows traditional Javanese beliefs and astrology.

Megawati's first husband was killed in a plane crash in 1970. She remarried in 1972, but the marriage was annulled shortly thereafter. She married Taufik Kiemas, her present husband, in 1973. They have three children.

Political Career

Megawati avoided politics for nearly twenty years and described herself as a simple housewife. In 1987, however, Megawati and her husband joined the Indonesian Democracy Party (PDI), a government-sanctioned party which provided a façade of democratic choice in Suharto's "New Order" regime. As a reward for her apparent acceptance of the regime, Megawati was elected to the rubber-stamp Indonesian parliament. Then, in 1993 Megawati became the leader of PDI. She took this opportunity to begin her challenge to Suharto. This increased her popularity that was already strong because of her father.

In 1996 the regime forced her removal from the leadership of the PDI. This triggered rioting in Jakarta. This only increased her popularity. She formed her own party, PDI-Perjuangan or PDI-P—*Perjuangan* means "Struggle." During this period Megawiti displayed great courage in opposing the regime and became a symbol of hope for democratic reform.

The Asian economic crisis in 1997 and increasing public anger at pervasive corruption brought the end of Suharto's regime—he resigned in May 1998. In the 1999 elections, the PDI-P emerged as the largest party, but did not win an absolute majority of votes, or a majority of seats in the Parliament. Under Indonesia's new constitution, the president was chosen by the legislature, and Megawati appeared to have the strongest claim to the presidency. But the other parties united to block her, partly because of Muslim opposition to a woman president. Her friend and ally, Abdurrahman Wahid, was chosen as president and Megawati agreed to become vice president. After a series of strokes and charges of corruption, Wahid was ousted and on 23 July 2001 Megawati was duly installed as president of Indonesia.

Legacies

Under Megawati, the process of democratic reform continued, but slowly. Megawati appeared to see her role mainly as a symbol of national unity, and she rarely actively intervened in government business. The military, disgraced at the time of Suharto's fall, regained much of its influence. Corruption continued to be pervasive, though Megawati herself was seldom blamed for this.

Although Indonesia's economy has partly recovered from the 1997 crisis, unemployment and poverty remain high, and there is considerable disappointment at Megawati's presidency. The Indonesian Constitution has been amended to provide for the direct election of the president, and Megawati's term expired in 2004.

She rarely gives interviews or makes political speeches—some say her silence is evidence of political cunning, others that she has nothing to say. One of the most frequent criticisms is that she is rather limited intellectually. But her supporters point to other qualities—she is a good listener, and a team player who can get things done.

5

Europe

If you want something said, ask a man. If you want something done, ask a woman.

Margaret Thatcher

INTRODUCTION

Despite higher rates of education and a tradition of waged labor, women still face discrimination in Europe in their workplaces as they pursue their careers. Women often rise to middle management, but few reach the highest levels of management in either private or public institutions. A common lament is that women perform and men lead.

Even in Scandinavia where women are integrated into the political system and hold more than one-third of both parliamentary and cabinet positions, the actual decision-making is still mostly in the hands of male party leaders and inner circle male ministers. Gender parity is seen as the only solution.

European women enjoy much greater freedom and equality in society than do women in other regions of the world. Even though Asia, Africa, and Latin America have had women leaders, the rights of everyday women in the developing world lag behind those of women in Europe or in America. So, it stands to reason that women who come to power in Europe may be coming to power for different reasons than in the developing world.

Not all of Europe is as enlightened in terms of gender equality as Scandinavia. Women in France, for instance, are largely underrepresented in government. Many French women believe that a constitutional reform is necessary to achieve political equality in France. Male politicians openly discriminate against women and the media is often sexist. Women make up only 5 percent of the French parliament. Citing concerns over gender equality, many male politicians are strongly opposed to any measures to get more women into government. But the male electorate diverges from the political parties on this issue. Many male voters trust women and elect them when they are on the ballot. Consequently, there would be more women in power in France if there were more female candidates on the electoral lists.

On 17 June 1997, at the European Council Summit in Amsterdam, the governments of the fifteen EU member states concluded the Intergovernmental Conference (IGC) with the aim of reforming the European institutions and adopting the new Union Treaty. As far as women are concerned, Articles 2 and 3 now include the promotion of equality of rights between women and men in the EU. This advancement was the result of the hard work by European MPs (both men and women), members of the Commission for Women's Rights, and various NGOs. The member states, unfortunately, did not go as far as to include both equality as a fundamental right and parity as a basic principle of the Union. They also rejected any action to compensate for discrimination against women.

Article 2 of the European Commission (EC) Treaty stipulates that promotion of equality between men and women is a task of the European Community. Article 3(2) states that it should aim to eliminate inequalities, and to promote equality, between men and women in all its activities (also known as "gender mainstreaming"). There are three legal bases in the EC Treaty for EU legislation on equal treatment of men and women: Article 141(3) in matters of employment and occupation; Article 13(1) outside of the employment field; and Article 137 in the promotion of employment, improved living and working conditions.

Gender mainstreaming is the integration of the gender perspective into every stage of policy processes with a goal of promoting equality between women and men. It calls for assessing how policies impact both women and men and calls for modifying policies if necessary. It is hoped that gender mainstreaming will make gender equality a reality in the lives of women and men.

In order to succeed, gender mainstreaming needs to be embraced by the highest political levels and needs to permeate the whole organization, and should not be dependent on a few dedicated individuals. Ultimately, at the policy level, the issue of gender equality should become a visible and central concern in all policy and planning.

It is not enough to call for gender mainstreaming, there must be a way to measure progress against the goals. Gender statistics, indicators, and benchmarks play an essential role in promoting gender equality. They are a tool for gender mainstreaming and are needed to monitor progress in implementing the gender dimension in different policy fields, and toward the goal of equality between women and men. They make policy makers accountable toward citizens.

The EC first started work on gender mainstreaming in the early 1990s, developing a more consistent approach following the UN Women's Conference held in Beijing in 1995. Since then, gender mainstreaming has steadily grown in importance. It is at the heart of the thinking behind the European Commission's Framework Strategy on gender equality 2001–2005.

Equality between women and men is reinforced by the new treaty establishing a Constitution for Europe. In addition to the provisions of the current treaty on gender equality, the Constitution states that equality is a value of the Union, which should be promoted not only inside the Union but also in its relations with the rest of the world. Demographic changes, with an aging population and a shrinking working population continue to be a major challenge in the EU. Difficulty in balancing family and professional life, partly due to lack of child care and insufficiently flexible working conditions, appears to be contributing to the postponement of having the first child and to low fertility rates in most member states. However, experience shows that member states having comprehensive policies to reconcile work and family life for both men and women show higher fertility rates as well as higher labor market participation of women.

There is a need for new initiatives to increase employment in order to meet the challenge of an aging society, including providing adequate pensions for women and men. Particular attention must be paid to mobilizing the full potential of female employment and to boosting labor market participation of older women and immigrant women who have the lowest employment rates.

Reports on the progress toward the goal of gender mainstreaming by the European Council point to the following recommendations:

1. strengthen national machineries for gender equality;
2. ensure correct and rapid implementation of equal treatment for men and women as regards access to employment, vocational training and promotion, and working conditions;
3. continue cooperation with social partners in order to avoid gender segregation in the labor market and to reduce the gender pay gap, in particular with regard to immigrant women;
4. increase women's labor market participation, which will not only strengthen the financial sustainability of pension systems, but also allow women to become economically independent and earn better pensions of their own;

5. guarantee and respect the fundamental rights of immigrant women and promote employment for immigrant women by recognizing their important role in the integration process;

6. strengthen efforts to prevent violence against women;

7. examine how well pension systems meet the needs of both women and men;

8. increase the provision of care facilities for children and other dependents; and

9. reinforce strategies for reconciling work and private life for both men and women.

CURRENT STATUS OF WOMEN IN EUROPE
Paid Work

Paid work is a precondition of economic independence during the active ages as well as a basis for pension in older ages. It is measured by the employment and unemployment rates, and the share of part-time work. In 2003, there was an employment gender gap of 15.8 percent in the EU, while the unemployment gender gap in 2004 was equal to 1.7 percent. Women form the majority of those working part-time. The share of women employees working part-time was 30.5 percent in the EU in 2004. The corresponding figure for men was 6.6 percent.

Income and Pay

In 2003, in the European Union the estimated gender pay gap was 15 percent. The risk of poverty was higher for women compared to men in seventeen of the member states.

Decision-Making

Balanced participation in decision-making is looked at in the political and economic fields. Around 23 percent of parliamentary seats in the EU are currently occupied by women. Some member states experienced a substantial increase in the number of women in parliament since 2003 while others saw a slight decrease. The percentage of women in managerial positions in the EU has increased by 1 percentage point since 2002, to reach 31 percent in 2003. Very few women hold executive positions in the top fifty corporations.

Knowledge

Development toward a knowledge-based society makes high demands on the educational level of the labor force. Women present higher educational attainment than men: the gap between women and men aged 20–24 attaining secondary educational level was 5 percentage points in the EU in 2004. Traditional patterns remain in the research field where men represented 86 percent of academic staff who are full professors (or equivalent) in the EU in 2002. More women than men participate in adult education and training (life-long learning) in twenty-one member states.

Working Time

The gap between average hours worked by women and men with children shows that women with children work eleven hours per week less than men with children in the EU in 2003.

Healthy Life Years

Women are expected to live longer in absence of limitations in functioning/disability than men in most member states (except in Germany, Sweden, Denmark, UK, the Netherlands, and Finland.

The Average Age of Women at Birth of First Child

The average age of women at birth of first child has increased by at least 0.5 years in fourteen member states during the past few years.[1]

The draft EU Constitution, signed by the Heads of State and Government on 29 October 2004 in Rome, can only replace the EC Treaty when it has been ratified by all the member states. The draft EU Constitution contains similar provisions to the EC Treaty as regards equality between men and women, but it also contains references to equality and non-discrimination in the values of the EU, and in the Charter of Fundamental Rights.

In the EU member states, poverty mainly strikes women. Women comprise:

1. 70 percent of the 36 million Europeans living in poverty,
2. 55 percent of the long-term unemployed,
3. 90 percent of single parents, and
4. 80 percent of part-time workers (mostly employed in flexible and insecure jobs not eligible for employment protection and social benefits).

Increased participation by women in decision-making is a key factor in the much-needed democratization of European institutions. Only parity can achieve a balanced participation of women and men in the government of human affairs. Parity both affirms and extends the recognition of equality.

The Nordic countries are far above any other nation in terms of women representation in the government. It would be worthwhile to focus a bit more on the Nordic region and find out what would explain the ascendancy of women.

WOMEN IN THE NORDIC REGION

The Nordic countries—Norway, Denmark, Sweden, Finland, and Iceland—are small, largely homogeneous societies with high standards of living, common historical tradition and culture, with emphasis on Protestantism, and social democracy. Slightly more than 20 million people live in the Nordic region or Scandinavia.[2]

The post–World War II era economic expansion shifted the economic base from fisheries and agriculture to industrial and service-based sectors. By the 1970s women had emerged in politics. Although women entered rapidly into political life throughout Scandinavia, their position in the family and in the workplace did not progress as rapidly. The proportion of women in Nordic parliaments is high compared to world standards (see Table 5.1), but as impressive as these percentages are, the majority of decision-making bodies in the Nordic countries are still dominated by men. Additionally, women are underrepresented in private sector management in Scandinavia.

One factor in women attaining political power in Scandinavia was that women were better educated by the 1960s and 1970s. Also, the number of women working outside the home has increased dramatically due to rapid economic expansion after World War II and labor shortages. Declining marriage and birth rates and the rise in the divorce rate also contributed to more women being in the workplace. Public policy has supported the move of women into the workforce through expanded educational opportunities and child-care facilities.[3]

Women's political participation tends to be highest in social democratic societies—where the government's role is to equalize social and economic

Table 5.1
Percentage of Women in National Parliaments

Nordic countries	38.8
Americas	15.3
Asia	15.3
Europe (excluding Nordic countries)	14.1
Pacific	13.5
sub-Saharan Africa	11.7
Arab States	3.6
World	13.8

Source: Inter-Parliamentary Union, April 2000

inequalities. Norway, Sweden, Iceland, Finland, and Denmark lead the world in terms of percentage of women in parliament, but how do women affect politics in the Nordic region?

Most women politicians in Scandinavia want to make a difference, but they do not want to act too differently. They tend to avoid conflicts with their male counterparts and do not seriously challenge the party line. Despite increasing numbers of women in politics, they are still fearful of being singled out as women politicians. A sharper focus is needed to really understand how women came to power in Scandinavia and what impact they have had. Let us take Norway's political system to be representative of the Scandinavian political culture.

There are a number of reasons for Norway's success in promoting female leadership in politics (these hold for the rest of Scandinavia as well):

1. a deep appreciation for democracy and equity,
2. a well-organized women's movement,
3. Lutheran religion,
4. women who belong to left-wing or socialist parties,
5. high education level for women,
6. high percentage of women in the workforce,
7. electoral system based on proportional representation, and
8. party lists or ballots with many candidates.[4]

Two major factors have contributed to the advancement of women's rights in Norway. The first factor is women entering the workforce in large numbers in the 1960s and 1970s. In 1965, only 1 out of 10 Norwegian mothers worked outside the home. By 1993, more than 7 out of 10 worked outside the home. The other major factor was the growth of women's education. Currently, more women attend university and college than men in Norway.[5] Economic independence and education lay the foundation for the growth of women's rights and representation in government. But other factors are important as well.

Norway's multiple-party system creates greater consensus than the U.S. two-party system, which tends to produce more conflict than consensus. Class differences are not as pronounced in Norway, because of their strong sense of social democracy based on having been dominated by stronger European countries and marginalized. Due partly to the promotion of women in politics, Scandinavian countries lead the world in foreign aid. Scandinavians have a sense of duty to help the oppressed and underprivileged peoples of the world. As shown in Table 5.2, Norway leads the world in terms of official development assistance (ODA) as a percentage of GNP at 0.92, with Denmark a close second at 0.84, and the United States well in the rear at 0.14.[6]

Table 5.2
Official Development Assistance (ODA) 2003

Country	Percentage of GNP
1. Norway	0.92
2. Denmark	0.84
3. Netherlands	0.81
4. Luxembourg	0.80
5. Sweden	0.70
6. Belgium	0.61
7. Ireland	0.41
8. France	0.41
9. Switzerland	0.38
10. United Kingdom	0.34
11. Finland	0.34
12. Germany	0.28
13. Canada	0.26
14. Spain	0.25
15. Australia	0.25
16. New Zealand	0.23
17. Portugal	0.21
18. Greece	0.21
19. Japan	0.20
20. Austria	0.20
21. Italy	0.16
22. United States	0.14

Source: Organization for Economic Co-operation and Development
(http://www.oecd.org/)

GRO HARLEM BRUNDTLAND
Life Before Politics

Brundtland was born in Oslo, Norway, on 20 April 1939. Politics and medicine were fixtures of her life from the earliest days of her childhood. Brundtland's father was a doctor who specialized in rehabilitation medicine. When Brundtland was 10 years old, her family moved to the United States after her father received a Rockefeller scholarship to study. She was influenced by her father and became fixated on starting her own career in medicine. When her father accepted a position in Egypt as a United Nations expert on rehabilitation several years later, his family went with him.

After her family returned to Norway, Brundtland remained dedicated to pursuing medicine. Her father, who was also a prominent member of the nation's Labor Party, was appointed defense minister of the Norwegian cabinet. Brundtland's father had already convinced his daughter to join the party's children's organization: young Gro had been a member of the Labor Party since age 7. Brundtland's parents encouraged their daughter to believe that women can achieve the same things in the world as men.

Brundtland received a Doctor of Medicine degree from the University of Oslo in 1963. In 1965 she received a Master of Public Health degree from Harvard University in Massachusetts. From 1968 until 1974, she worked for Oslo's Department of Social Services as the assistant medical director of the Oslo Board of Health. There, her career focused on children's health issues.

Brundtland is married to Arne Olav Brundtland, a prominent member of Norway's Conservative Party, the opposition to Brundtland's Labor Party. The Brundtlands have four children and eight grandchildren.

Political Career

Brundtland reflected a new style of politics in Norway. She was an ambitious intellectual and was quick to learn the world of male politics. The 1972 European Community vote politicized Norway and spurred interest in two movements: the feminist and the environmental movements. Academics were also making headway into party politics. The stage was set for Brundtland.

Brundtland became Norway's environment minister in 1974. In this position, she received a lot of attention for her deft handling of an oil platform fire in the North Sea. The resulting spill cost the country a great deal of money, and, as a result, offshore drilling was indefinitely postponed. Brundtland handled the situation very effectively in an emotionally charged atmosphere.

Brundtland took a little-known Ministry of the Environment and elevated it into the political mainstream during her five-year tenure. However, a power shift in the Labor Party in the late 1970s shifted the party's focus from growth to defense. Her presence in the party and in Norwegian politics was growing, so it was natural for her to assume that she would be put into a more important ministry. The Conservative Party came into power in the latter 1970s as Norwegians began to favor less regulation.

Brundtland ran for Parliament in 1977 and won, but her seat had to be held by a proxy as she was still in the cabinet. In 1979 she resigned from the cabinet and took her seat in the Storting (the Norwegian parliament). Political support from respected politicians (i.e., former Prime Minister Einar Gerhardsen), combined with her grassroots appeal and will to power, brought Brundtland into the prime minister's office in 1981. Brundtland was the first woman prime minister in Norway and Scandinavia.

Brundtland's path to power was short. It took her six years in state politics before she became prime minister. She had both ambition and the will to power. There were those in the party who thought her rise to the top was too fast. But the grassroots of the party wanted her. She knew of the criticism, but she made up for her lack of experience with an incredible work ethic and energy for the job.

Brundtland was the first Norwegian prime minister to go by a first name—Gro. Many feminists thought that this was a form of discrimination, since she was a woman, and no male prime minister had been called by his first name. Brundtland said that she did not mind.

Brundtland built a cabinet that included seven women. The cabinet addressed broader issues once in power. These included an expansion of day care and an extension of paid maternity leave from 18 to 26 weeks. Since 1981 the Labor Party required that 40 percent of its candidates for public office be women.

By 1991 half of the major political parties in Norway had chosen women as leaders. Norway's percentage of women in Parliament grew to more than 36 percent, compared to below 10 percent in the early 1970s. Yet, in the private sector, little changed in terms of women's sharing positions of leadership.

In September 1989 she was voted out of office again, in spite of her rising international popularity. She remained out only until November 1990, when she came up with a new compromise with the oil producers and a favorable position on EC membership for Norway. There was even talk late in 1991 that Brundtland would become the UN secretary-general.

Brundtland holds that feminism is the promotion of real female interest, including women being able to bear children if they want. Brundtland carries with her a strong sense of social responsibility that transfers to the foreign policy of Norway. She believes that the advantaged have an obligation to the disadvantaged.

Legacy

As prime minister and as party leader, she enforced a strict quota established by the 1978 Act on Gender Equality that stipulated that 40 percent of candidates on her party's ballot must be female and 40 percent of candidates must be male. Brundtland never had fewer than eight women in her eighteen-member cabinet. Norway has the highest proportion of women in top government positions in the world.

Brundtland combined feminine and masculine styles of leadership. She was very much on her own level, unique, and even those who opposed her views respected her highly. Hers was a personality-driven success. She listened well and was open-minded. Brundtland's emotions were a problem at first but became less problematic later. She was definitely willing to use her power when necessary and could be very durable. She was very confident; she could cry at funerals and during her Christmas speeches, but she was powerful as well. She mixed her femininity with strength, redefining the common notion of strength perhaps. On the negative side, she could be an elitist, arrogant, short-tempered with reporters, and a poor public speaker. She had to balance environmental concerns with economic growth in Norway and was severely criticized by environmentalists. By 1995 she was untouchable politically in Norway. The problem with Brundtland, according to some Norwegians, was that there were no opposition to her and too much consensus.

Brundtland announced her resignation on 23 October 1996 after dominating Norwegian politics for more than fifteen years. The 57-year-old prime minister gave no reason for stepping down but apparently had made the decision more than a year earlier.

EDITH CRESSON
Life Before Politics

Edith Campion (Cresson) was born on 27 January 1934 in the Paris suburb of Boulogne-Billancourt. Her father was a senior civil servant. Raised by a British nanny, she became fluent in the English language. Cresson attended the School of Advanced Commercial Studies, earning a degree in business and later a doctorate in demography. She later became a consultant in private industry.

A successful businesswoman, she added a second career in politics when she met François Mitterrand in 1965. For the next twenty-six years the future president helped Cresson advance through the ranks of what is now the French Socialist Party, calling her "my little soldier." Cresson is married with two daughters.

Political Career

Active in the Socialist party, Cresson became national secretary of the party for youth in 1974 and was elected to the European Assembly in 1979. She then held a series of ministerial appointments, including agriculture and forestry (1981–1983), trade and tourism (1983–1984), and industrial redeployment and foreign trade (1984–1986). From 1986 until her resignation in 1990, she was a member of the national assembly. In April 1991 she became France's first woman prime minister. She replaced Michel Rocard as prime minister and held office until May 1992.

Cresson was well-known for making outspoken and often controversial comments. She was very critical of Anglo-Saxon nations and often condemned the culture and people of the United States, Germany, and Great Britain. She often described homosexuality as being a largely Anglo-Saxon problem that had little relevance in France. Her strong criticism of Japanese trade practices likewise prompted her to use harsh rhetoric that some considered borderline racist. From 1995 to 1999, she was the EU Commissioner for Research, Science and Technology.

Legacy

Edith Cresson is no stranger to controversy. While serving as France's first female prime minister in 1991–1992, she made headlines by claiming that one in four British men was homosexual and attributing the economic success of the Japanese to their "ant-like" qualities. Her erratic tenure, marked by ineffectual leadership and record low poll ratings, ended after only ten months. With her characteristic lack of self-criticism, Cresson blamed her downfall on what she called "a macho plot."

In fact, she owed her career rise largely to her friendship with one man, the late President Francois Mitterrand, under whom she served in a variety of positions. Cresson's stumbling performance as prime minister left a cloud over her political career. In 1994 Mitterrand named Cresson as one of France's two delegates to the European Commission.

She arrived in Brussels with a bad attitude. As a former prime minister of France, she demanded one of the two vice presidencies as the only suitable position for someone of her standing and notoriety. She was snubbed and was given the job of overseeing Research, Education and Training. Arrogant and abrasive, she annoyed colleagues by showing up unprepared and using commission meetings to catch up with personal correspondence.

Cresson was also responsible for the Leonardo Da Vinci program for vocational training. Since the commission did not have the staff to administer the program itself, it was bid out to a private company, Agenor. Numerous internal audits raised concerns about Agenor fixing bids for lucrative contracts, paying on fraudulent invoices, and hiring family members at lavish salaries. Cresson failed to inform the Parliament about any of this.

When word of these and other irregularities began leaking in the press, Cresson threatened to sue for defamation, thereby fueling what might have remained a private squabble but became the public scandal that ultimately brought down the whole commission. She seemed to attract hostility and enemies everywhere she went.

Edith Cresson learned two lessons from Francois Mitterrand. First, never admit or apologize for wrongdoing. Second, always prize friendship and loyalty over competence. Neither precept is good for democracy or the rule of law. Today, Cresson claims to have no regrets. Yet, she blames the French media for much of her troubles while in office.

VIGDIS FINNBOGADOTTIR
Life Before Politics

Vigdis Finnbogadottir was born in Reykjavik, the capital of Iceland, on 15 April 1930. Her father, Finnbogi Rutur, was an engineer and professor, and her mother, Sigridur Eiriksdottir, was the chair of the Icelandic Nurses' Association.

She left Iceland in 1949 to study French language and literature and drama at the University of Grenoble and at the Sorbonne in Paris. She later studied theater history in Denmark and French in Sweden. She rounded out her education at the University of Iceland. She was married in 1954 and divorced in 1963. She took a job as a teacher and used summers to guide tourists through Iceland. She eventually moved to the University of Iceland to teach French drama and later became a television personality. She was appointed director of the Reykjavik Theater Company in 1972. She was also named chair of the Advisory Committee on Cultural Affairs in the Nordic Countries.

Political Career

In 1975 the women of Iceland organized a general strike called "Women's Day Off," which nearly paralyzed the country. In the capital city of Reykjavik, there were more than 20,000 women in the main square who had left their homes and told their husbands to take over. Men had to organize day care. Women's issues were spotlighted, and many Icelanders felt that it was time to have a woman leader. Finnbogadottir was persuaded in 1980 to pursue the presidency. Although she had never been active in politics, she was such a well-known television personality and cultural expert that many people supported her nomination. It was time, many supporters said, to prove that a woman could hold the office of president. She ran against three men. Many believed that her divorce and being a single parent might hurt her chances of being elected. She spent her four-month election campaign period talking about cultural identity, history, and ecology. She was proud to claim that Iceland was the least polluted country in the world.

Finnbogadottir was elected president with 33.8 percent of the vote. The Constitution of Iceland does not grant political responsibility to the president, and she had only limited governmental authority. Among her duties was the signing of all bills passed in the parliament. "The President of Iceland is not a political person," she explained. "I've never been involved in politics or even belonged to any political party."

Finnbogadottir was inaugurated in August 1980 for a four-year term. She was the first popularly elected woman head of state (in contrast to heads of government such as Thatcher and Gandhi). Icelandic presidents are required to sign all legislation passed by the Allthing, or Parliament (the oldest one in Europe). Although she had veto power, she never exercised it. Unlike many political leaders, Finnbogadottir had an open door to the public. Twice a week, Icelanders were given ready access to her to discuss problems or just to talk. Her ability to bridge cultural differences was valuable in a meeting with British Prime Minister Margaret Thatcher in 1982. Previous to their meeting, England and Iceland had engaged in a fishing rights dispute known as the Cod War.

Legacy

She decided to run for reelection in 1984 and had no real opposition. In 1986 Iceland received international attention when U.S. President Ronald Reagan and Soviet leader Mikhail Gorbachev chose Reykjavik for their summit. The summit was successful and only two years later Communism would fall in the Soviet Union. Finnbogadottir was reelected again in 1988 and 1992. She left office in 1996. Her legacy as the president of Iceland is as a cultural ambassador, unifier, and eternal optimist.

TARJA KAARINA HALONEN
Life Before Politics

Tarja Halonen was born in Helsinki on 24 December 1943. She lived for most of her life in the Helsinki working class district of Kallio. She earned a law degree in 1968 at the University of Helsinki. Halonen's professional career started in the National Union of Finnish Students, where she worked as the Social Affairs Secretary from 1969–1970. She became a lawyer with the Central Organization of Finnish Trade Unions in 1970. Halonen is married to Pentti Arajärvi and has one daughter. She is interested in theater, history of the arts, painting and drawing, rhythmic gymnastics, and swimming.

Political Career

Halonen joined the Social Democratic Party in 1971. Her political career began in 1974 when she was appointed parliamentary secretary to the prime minister, a post she held until 1975. Halonen was elected to the parliament in 1979 and held her seat in five consecutive elections until she assumed the office of the president of Finland. In the parliament she served as Chair of the Social Affairs Committee from 1984 to 1987,

Deputy-Chair of the Legal Affairs Committee from 1991 to 1995, and Chair of the Grand Committee in 1995. An integral part of Halonen's political activity has been her five terms in the Helsinki City Council from 1977 to 1996.

Halonen has served in three cabinets: minister of social affairs and health from 1987 to 1990, minister of justice in 1990–1991, and minister for foreign affairs from 1995 to 2000. She was also minister responsible for Nordic cooperation in 1989–1991. During her time as foreign minister Finland held the EU presidency for the first time in July–December 1999.

Halonen has also played an active role at the Council of Europe, first as Deputy-Chair of the Finnish Delegation to the Parliamentary Assembly from 1991 to 1995 and later in the Ministerial Committee. She was also a member of the Committee of Wise Persons of the Council of Europe in 1998–1999.

Tarja Halonen, the eleventh president of Finland and the first woman to hold her country's highest position, was inaugurated for a six-year term on 1 March 2000. She defeated the non-socialist candidate, former Prime Minister Esko Aho, in the second round of the popular vote. A member of Parliament since 1979, she was also the first woman to become foreign minister.

Tarja Halonen has a reputation as an independent spirit who goes her own way. As an unmarried mother she raised and educated her daughter Anna, who is studying international politics in England. Despite concerns that her church membership had lapsed and the fact that she lived with a man without being married, opinion polls supported Tarja Halonen as president.

The relationship between the head of state and her partner did cause a minor headache where protocol was concerned. At official functions, however, Pentti Arajärvi—a senior civil servant at Parliament—was received naturally in the same way that a spouse would have been. Then, in late August, the two married in a simple and very private ceremony conducted by an official from the Helsinki registry office.

As a leader, Tarja Halonen has been described as generous and possessing a sense of humor, but also as demanding and exact. Indeed, she describes herself as demanding. Anecdotes about her colorful language are still told in the corridors of the Foreign Ministry, where people are accustomed to more formality.

President Halonen avoids unnecessary ostentation, and there is no doubt that this will have an effect on life at the Presidential Palace. The nation had a foretaste of the new style already during the inauguration ceremonies. Having raised her glass in a toast with Speaker of Parliament Riitta Uosukainen, the new president was horrified at the stiffness of the people all around her. "Couldn't we get into a somewhat looser formation?" she asked. Uosukainen, herself a highly charismatic character, immediately got into the spirit and barked the order "Spread out!" to the officials.

In keeping with tradition, the president's first state visit was to Sweden. Accustomed to their royals, the Swedish media were interested enough in the president as a woman, but did not give her many marks for style. The headlines about her hats and bags seem at most to amuse the president, whose profile and the respect she commands are founded on solid expertise. Already during the election campaign she highlighted her most important values: democracy, a welfare society, and the rule of law. She can contribute to defending these values on a level above that of day-to-day politics.

Legacy

President Halonen has paid close attention to issues of human rights, democracy, and civil society. Issues concerning social justice and promotion of equality have been central themes throughout her political career. She has likewise long played an active role in the international solidarity movement.

ANGELA MERKEL

Life Before Politics

Angela Dorothea Kasner was born on 17 July 1954 in Hamburg. Her father was a Lutheran pastor and her mother was a teacher. In 1954 the family moved to the countryside only 80 km (50 mi) north of Berlin, in the village of Templin in the communist German Democratic Republic (GDR). She went to the University of Leipzig where she studied physics (1973–1978). Merkel worked and studied at the Central Institute for Physical Chemistry of the Academy of Sciences (1978–1990). After graduating with a doctorate in physics she worked in quantum chemistry.

For the first three decades of her life, Merkel disguised her inner thoughts and feelings—an essential skill for survival in the GDR. The State Security Police (Stasi) had informers everywhere. Her father, although committed to socialism, was regularly rebuked by the Stasi secret police. Consequently, Merkel quickly learned to never talk in public about things that were better discussed at the family dinner table. Public reticence over personal matters, suspiciousness, and demands for loyalty appear to be Merkel's legacies from growing up in the former East Bloc.

Merkel was not a dissident in the GDR, in fact, she joined the communist Free German Youth movement in order to ensure admission to the university. Merkel did not enter politics without experience. Merkel, through her father's church, maintained close links with leading government figures in the GDR. Since the 1950s, the church had played an important role in the GDR by ensuring that political opposition to the communist regime was kept under control. As the GDR collapsed in 1989, the church helped temper the mass protests and eventually brought about the restoration of capitalism in East Germany and its *Anschluss* (annexation) by West Germany. Merkel began seeking a political identity as the GDR collapsed.

Political Career

The German parliament elected Angela Merkel, the leader of the conservative Christian Democrats, as the country's first woman chancellor. She heads a coalition government with the former governing party, the Social Democrats. Merkel is also the first chancellor to have grown up in the former East Germany. Her foreign policy orientation is more pro-U.S. than that of her predecessor, Social Democrat Gerhard Schroeder. He opposed the war in Iraq and proclaimed emancipation from the United States. She has pledged to revive the faltering German economy. The parties have agreed to work to cut Germany's budget deficit with spending cuts and moderate tax increases. Merkel hopes to restore relations with the United States, boost Germany's role in NATO, and promote fair dealing in the European Union.

Merkel, a Protestant East German, is not a typical leader in the CDU, which has been traditionally dominated by Catholic West German men. She first came to prominence five years ago during a CDU party slush fund scandal. Some members of the press have labeled her as Germany's Margaret Thatcher. Others say she is a bit like Margaret Thatcher and a bit like Tony Blair.

In 1989, she got involved in the growing democracy movement after the fall of the Berlin Wall. In 1994, she was made minister for the environment and reactor safety, which gave her greater political visibility and a platform on which to build her political career. When the Kohl government was defeated in the 1998 general election, Merkel was named secretary-general of the CDU. In this position, Merkel oversaw a string of Christian Democrat election victories in six out of seven provincial elections in 1999. Following a party financing scandal which compromised many leading figures of the CDU (even Kohl himself). Merkel criticized Kohl and advocated a fresh start for the party without him. She became the first female chair of her party on 10 April 2000. Her election surprised many observers, as her personality offered a contrast to the party she had been chosen to lead.

Merkel supported a substantial reform agenda concerning Germany's economic and social system and was considered to be more pro-free market than her own party. She advocated changes to German labor law, such as increasing the number of work hours in a week to make German companies more competitive.

Merkel advocated a strong transatlantic partnership and German-American friendship. In the spring of 2003, defying strong public opposition, Merkel came out in favor of the U.S. invasion of Iraq, describing it as "unavoidable" and accusing Chancellor Gerhard Schroeder of anti-Americanism. This led some critics to characterize her as an American lackey. She criticized the government's support for Turkish membership in the European Union and favored a "privileged partnership" instead. Many Germans agreed with her since it might stimulate more immigration from Turkey and many Germans already feared too much Islamist influence within the EU.

She is a centrist on social issues such as abortion and legal rights for gay couples. While opposing abortion, Merkel insists her aim is to convince women not to terminate a pregnancy, rather than seeking a German abortion ban.

Legacy

In the English language press, Merkel has been compared by many to former British Prime Minister Margaret Thatcher because both are/were female politicians from center-right parties, as well as former scientists. Some have referred to her as "Iron Lady" or "Iron Girl." Despite the moniker, there appears to be little similarity between Thatcher's and Merkel's agenda.

1. Merkel is of the opinion that the EU has failed to define its common interests "for the (commercial) battles of the future" now that Europe's Cold War priorities of keeping "peace and freedom" have been achieved: "This is where I think Europe needs to learn a lot, not to concentrate too much on whether bicycle paths are built the same way in Portugal and north-west Germany."

2. Domestically, Merkel has advocated change in the country's consensual model: "In Germany, we are always facing the danger that we are a little bit too slow. We have to speed up our changes."

3. "The state has to be the gardener, not the fence."

4. After reaching a deal with the SPD to form a Grand Coalition, Merkel stated: "I am absolutely certain—I know—that the success of this coalition will be measured by the question: Are there more jobs?"

5. Merkel urged her party to approve the deal at a conference in Berlin, saying: "Germany stands at a crossroads where it is about whether we will preserve what makes this country strong—a social market economy in times of globalization."

Seen by some as Germany's answer to former British leader Margaret Thatcher, Merkel, 51, rose in the space of a decade from being an obscure physicist in East Berlin to leader of Germany's main center-right party.

As chancellor, she will have to make tough decisions if she is to cure Germany's 11.2 percent unemployment and lead the country out of economic stagnation.

MARY ROBINSON

Life Before Politics

Born in Ballina, County Mayo, Ireland on 21 May 1944, Mary Robinson was educated at Trinity College, Dublin, where she received a Master of Arts degree in 1970. She also earned a Barrister-at-Law degree from the King's Inns, Dublin, and a Master of Laws degree from Harvard University.

At the age of 25, Robinson was appointed Reid Professor of Constitutional and Criminal Law at Trinity College, where she also served as lecturer in European community law and, simultaneously, she had become a member of the Irish Senate, a position she held for twenty years, until 1989. With her husband Nicholas, Robinson founded the Irish Centre for European Law in 1988. They have three children.

Political Career

From 1969 to 1989, Mary Robinson was a member of Seanad Éireann, the upper house of Parliament. She has also served on the Dublin City Council and the International Commission of Jurists. In December 1990, Mrs. Robinson was inaugurated as the seventh president of Ireland. As president, she represented her country internationally, developing a new sense of Ireland's economic, political, and cultural ties with other countries and cultures. Linking the history of the Great Irish Famine to today's nutrition, poverty, and policy issues, she articulated a special relationship between Ireland and developing countries.

The Robinson presidency was characterized by inclusiveness and a concerted effort to use the office not only to improve the situations of marginalized groups within Ireland but also to draw attention to global crises. Robinson was the first head of state to visit famine-stricken Somalia in 1992 and also the first to go to Rwanda in the aftermath of the genocide there. In recognition of her efforts in Somalia, Robinson received the Special CARE Humanitarian Award in 1993.

It was characteristic of Mary Robinson that her first public engagement on becoming president of Ireland in November 1990 was to open a conference on homelessness. Her last official function, when she relinquished the presidency, in September 1997 was to open a housing project for homeless people. In the interim, she had put her own individual stamp on not only the presidency, but also on public life in Ireland in general. Even before her election, she traveled the country, addressing small gatherings of people in factories, shopping precincts, community centers, and even in people's homes. Yet it was not just a case of showing herself to the electorate: she also listened to the people, heard their complaints, and learned about their concerns and aspirations. From being an outsider, she emerged from the final round of voting for the presidency with 53 percent of the vote on a higher-than-average turnout. Over the next six years she both molded and reflected the life of a country that was experiencing an exciting and formative phase of its historical development.

Prior to Robinson's election to the presidency, there had even been talk of abolishing that institution. In any case, it was fairly unusual for there to be a contested election. But her success in 1990 made Ireland only the second European country (after Iceland) to elect a woman as head of state. But if anyone believed that Mary Robinson would rest content to serve as merely a decorative president they were in for a shock.

In 1971, as a Senator, she presented her first Private Member's bill to the Seanad Éireann, introducing an amendment designed to remove the ban on the sale and use of contraceptives. Later that year, she presented a bill on adoption. These were followed by a second adoption bill and the introduction of the Illegitimate Children (Maintenance and Succession) Act. As a lawyer she was part of a team that won a case in the Supreme Court establishing the right of women to serve on juries and a few years later she won a case that forced the state to tax married couples as two single persons. Another case that she won forced the state to provide legal aid to those who would otherwise have been denied access to the courts. And later, in the 1980s, there came a court judgment that ended the status of illegitimacy in Ireland, a cause that she had first raised in the Senate in the early 1970s. Two years after that, in 1988, the European Court of Human Rights ruled that Ireland was in breach of the Human Rights Convention because of the criminal status of homosexuality there—the legal case was argued primarily by Mary Robinson.

The same thread of human and civil rights ran through Mary Robinson's presidency. But her role extended far beyond that. She successfully projected a new, modernizing image of Ireland internationally, giving immense encouragement and satisfaction to what she herself called the Irish "Diaspora" overseas. She had tea with Queen Elizabeth at Buckingham Palace and invited her to visit Ireland. Two months later, she shook hands publicly with Gerry Adams in Belfast, an act that, with hindsight, might be seen as one of several precursors of the peace process in Northern Ireland. Nor were these gestures intended merely to suggest an even-handed approach to problems that have plagued Anglo-Irish relations for so long.

Legacy

In her seven years as president of Ireland Mary Robinson achieved a worldwide reputation. Her State visits, her humanitarian journeys to areas such as Somalia, her speeches on justice and human rights, to the UN and other forums, have made her a respected and admired diplomat. Through her status as first woman president and her emphasis on "writing back into history" those women who have been marginalized, she has created a new focus on women and a new confidence among women wherever she has visited.

In September 1997, Mary Robinson stepped down as president of Ireland after what is universally acknowledged as the most successful presidency in the history of the state. She elevated what was a figurehead role into a means of highlighting the needs of the disadvantaged and of raising Ireland's international profile. She opened the doors of Áras an Uachtaráin (The Presidential Residence) to people from all walks of life and created a special emphasis on Ireland's Diaspora—the many thousands of Irish people living abroad.

Mary Robinson carried the same wisdom, lightness of touch, sincerity and dignity of office to her next appointment, that of United Nations High Commissioner for Human Rights, the post that she occupies today. Now the need for diplomacy is even greater and her visibility on the world's stage even more prominent. As High Commissioner, Robinson is responsible for overseeing the human rights activities of the United Nations, including promoting universal enjoyment of human rights, responding to human rights violations, undertaking preventive human rights action, and providing education and assistance in the field of human rights. Taking every opportunity to speak out on human rights abuses as they occur, she has recently expressed urgent concern about conflicts in East Timor, Kosovo, and Sierra Leone, among others.

MARGARET THATCHER
Life Before Politics

Margaret Thatcher is the second daughter of a grocer and a dressmaker who became the first woman in European history to be elected prime minister. She then went on to become the first British prime minister in the twentieth century to win three consecutive terms and, at the time of her resignation in 1990, the nation's longest-serving prime minister since 1827. Some people have seen her as a true political revolutionary in that she broadened the base of the Conservative Party to include the middle class along with the wealthy aristocracy.

Thatcher was born Margaret Hilda Roberts on 13 October 1925 in Grantham, Lincolnshire, England. Her father was active in local politics. She was educated at Somerville College and at Oxford University, where she was the first woman president of the Oxford University Conservative Association. She earned a Master of Arts degree from Oxford in 1950 and worked briefly as a research chemist. In 1950 she ran unsuccessfully for Parliament, although she did increase the Conservative Party vote by 50 percent in her district. The following year she married Denis Thatcher, the director of a paint company. After her marriage she passed for the bar and specialized in tax law.

Political Career

Elected to Parliament as a Conservative in 1959, she held junior ministerial posts (1961–1964) before serving (1970–1974) as secretary of state for education and science in Edward Heath's cabinet. After two defeats in general elections, the Conservative Party elected her its first woman leader in 1975.

After leading the Conservatives to an electoral victory in 1979, Thatcher became prime minister. She had pledged to reduce the influence of the trade unions and combat inflation, and her economic policy rested on the introduction of broad changes along free-market lines. She attacked inflation by controlling the money supply and sharply reduced government spending and taxes for higher-income individuals. Although unemployment continued to rise to postwar highs, the declining economic output was reversed. In 1982, when Argentina invaded the Falkland Islands, a British colony, Britain's successful invasion contributed to the Conservatives' win at the polls in 1983.

Thatcher's second government privatized national industries and utilities, including British Gas and British Telecommunications. Her anti-union policies forced coal miners to return to work after a year on strike. In foreign affairs, Thatcher was a close ally of President Ronald Reagan and shared his antipathy to communism. She allowed the United States to station (1980) nuclear cruise missiles in Britain and to use its air bases to bomb Libya in 1986. She forged (1985) a historic accord with Ireland, giving it a consulting role in governing Northern Ireland.

In 1987 Thatcher led the Conservatives to a third consecutive electoral victory, although with a reduced majority. She proposed free-market changes to the national health and education systems and introduced a controversial per-capita poll tax to pay for local government, which fueled criticisms that she had no compassion for the poor. Her refusal to support a common European currency and integrated economic policies led to the resignation of her treasury minister in 1989 and her deputy prime minister in 1990.

Disputes over the poll tax, which took effect in 1990, and over European integration led to a leadership challenge (1990) from within her party. She resigned as prime minister, and John Major emerged as her successor. In 1992 Thatcher retired from the House of Commons and was made Baroness Thatcher. In the mid-1990s Thatcher was publicly critical of Major's more moderate policies, and she has continued to criticize publicly Conservative and Labor positions she disagreed with.

When the Conservatives won a decisive victory in the 1979 general elections Thatcher became prime minister. Upon entering office she advocated measures that would limit government control, such as giving individuals greater independence from the state, ending government interference in the economy, and reducing public expenditures. Although her conservative philosophy met with approval, during her first two terms unemployment nearly tripled, the number of poor people increased, and bankruptcies resulted from her efforts to curb inflation. Thatcher became known as the "Iron Lady" because of her strict control over her cabinet and the country's economic policies. Extending her firm approach into foreign relations, she helped Zimbabwe (formerly Rhodesia) establish independence in 1980 and two years later she oversaw the successful British seizure of the Falkland Islands from Argentina. This victory led to her landslide reelection in 1983.

During her third term Thatcher continued the "Thatcher revolution" by returning education, health care, and housing to private control. She also supported the campaign to keep Northern Ireland within the United Kingdom, a position that could have been fatal: in 1984 terrorist bombers nearly succeeded in killing Thatcher and several members of her administration in Brighton, Sussex. The bombing was allegedly the work of members of the Irish Republican Army, a nationalist organization devoted to uniting Northern Ireland with the Republic of Ireland. In 1990, when a split within the Conservative Party was costing Thatcher political support, she resigned from office. During her tenure as prime minister, however, she set historic precedents and, according to political observers, she brought long-needed changes to British government and society.

Legacy

Many United Kingdom citizens remember where they were and what they were doing when they heard that Margaret Thatcher had resigned and what their reaction was. She brings out strong responses in people. Some people credit her with rescuing the British economy from the stagnation of the 1970s and admire her committed radicalism on social issues; others see her as authoritarian, egotistical, and responsible for the dismantling of the Welfare State and the destruction of many manufacturing industries. Britain was widely seen as the "sick man of Europe" in the 1970s, and some argued that it would be the first developed nation to return to the status of a developing country. By the late 1990s, Britain emerged with a comparatively healthy economy, at least by previous standards. Her supporters claim that this was due to Margaret Thatcher's policies.

However, critics claim that the economic problems of the 1970s were exaggerated, and caused largely by factors outside of any UK government's control, such as high oil prices caused by the oil crisis which caused high inflation and damaged the economies of nearly all major industrial countries. These problems were not the result of socialism and trade unions, as Thatcherite supporters claim. Also the Thatcher period in government coincided with a general improvement in the world economy, and the high tax revenues from North Sea oil, which critics contend was the real cause of the improved economic environment of the 1980s, not Margaret Thatcher's policies.

A clear illustration of the divisions of opinion over Thatcher's leadership can be found in recent television polls: Thatcher appears at Number 16 in the 2002 List of "100 Greatest Britons," she also appears at Number 3 in the 2003 List of "100 Worst Britons," narrowly missing out on the top spot, which went to Tony Blair.

6

The Americas

In a democracy, government isn't something that a small group of
people do to everybody else, it's not even something they do for
everybody else, it should be something they do with everybody else.

Kim Campbell

INTRODUCTION

North America is often heralded as a region that applauds, supports,
and encourages women's rights and advancements. George W. Bush's
2004 State of the Union address was riddled with comparisons between
the liberated American woman and the victimized Afghan woman.
American women and men were fighting side by side to enhance
global freedom and security. Afghan women would have no chance
without these noble efforts by their liberators. A recent op-ed piece in the
New York Times also exemplifies the image of the American, if not North
American, woman—she is dominating in higher education, earning high
wages, and getting pretty darn choosy about potential mates.[1] The crux of
this chapter's argument is that America's misapprehension about
women's inequality (how can they possibly be unequal now as they
outnumber the men at universities and colleges?) is leading institutions to
continue the preferential treatment for women at the expense of men. The
end result is that all of these well-educated women and high-earning
women will find themselves alone at the end of the day, as their male
counterparts have not been granted similar advantages to advance and

match the high salaries of the women. The picture painted in this chapter suggests that American women have the world by the tail. They are becoming far more picky about their potential mates—despite her own high wages, she is still looking to "move up" and not down (a high school educated guy has no chance anymore). Women have the power to make choices, now that they are well educated and well financed. Sounds like we should have a wealth of new and savvy political candidates here then. Why have women made the choice to *not* be more active politically, and be more visible at the top? Is it because their main preoccupation is nevertheless finding the right mate (which appears to be uppermost in the minds of the women mentioned in this chapter)?

North America has lagged behind the rest of the world in both the number of women who have held the position of prime minister or president and the percentage of women in parliament or congress. Only Kim Campbell has served in such a capacity in North America, and only for a short while. The United States has not had a woman president nor is there any indication that this may change soon (although there is increasing talk about the chances of Hillary Clinton or Condoleezza Rice, a possibility we will come back to in our concluding chapter). Only 15 percent of the national legislative bodies in North and Latin America are women. This is only slightly ahead of the worldwide average of 12 percent. American women have made their presence known in many arenas previously closed to them, such as sports, space exploration, the corporate world, and even the Supreme Court. So why has a woman not become president of the United States?

Early in its history, the United States emphasized gender over class as the basis for political rights and made the white male the empowering category in the culture. America made a successful experiment in enfranchising men without property well ahead of Great Britain, where the class system was much stronger. Even black men gained the right to vote fifty-five years before all women gained the right to vote.

Throughout the nineteenth century, American women were active participants in political culture through their leadership in abolitionism, prison and labor reform, and temperance. During the Victorian Era, women exercised greater influence in American society. Women had fewer children since Victorian Era morality allowed women to use sexual abstinence as a form of birth control. Women were educated so as to enhance their role as nurturer. More educated women with fewer children lead to the growth of powerful organizations such as the Women's Christian Temperance Union (WCTU).

As the Progressive Era began in 1900, these educated, socially conscious women dealt with labor issues. Women of middle-class America rallied for fundamental labor rights. The Republican Party told women to lose their social reform agenda in 1920, as a result, younger women aligned themselves with the Democratic Party. It is no surprise that the first woman appointed to a cabinet position, Frances Perkins, was made secretary of labor, since women had embraced labor issues. Since World War II, America has seen the slow dismantlement of the New Deal and the rise of political conservatism. And, in spite of progress on many fronts, it has remained difficult for women to get elected.

Although there is now a record number of women serving in Congress—60 out of 435 in the House, and 13 out of 100 in the Senate—there's still nothing resembling gender parity. The redistricting of Congress in 1992 made more seats available to female politicians. During times of voter frustration, when people want change in politics, women become attractive candidates because they bring hope and, perhaps, a different perspective on problem solving.

In spite of their relatively small numbers, women legislators have been successful in pushing issues onto the national agenda. In the post–Cold War era, so-called women's issues, which focused on health, education and employment, have become mainstream voter concerns. Although small in numbers, women legislators have also been successful in pushing issues related to health, education, and employment (so-called women's issues). Women are effective national legislators, but getting elected still requires substantial fund-raising. Women appear to prefer to accept a call to politics whereas many male politicians are self-promoters. This may also influence fund raising effectiveness. Women politicians are still the primary caregivers and many potential candidates are unwilling to sacrifice family for career.

A poll conducted by the Siena College Research Institute and sponsored by Hearst Newspapers found that 81 percent of people surveyed would vote for a woman for president and 53 percent think New York Senator Hillary Rodham Clinton should try for the job. Other polls have identified the former first lady as the voters' favorite for the Democratic presidential nomination. On the Republican side, 42 percent of voters said Secretary of State Condoleezza should run for the White House and 33 percent named North Carolina Senator Elizabeth Dole.

The pollsters found about 60 percent of voters said they expect a woman to be the Democrats' nominee for president in 2008. In contrast, they found 18 percent expected the Republican ticket to be headed by a woman. About 67 percent of those polled said a female president would be better than a male on domestic issues, but only 24 percent said a woman president would do better on foreign policy issues.[2]

Times appear to be somewhat more ripe for a female candidate, however. Of course, the candidates in question face a tough electorate—they need to defray any suggestion of female stereotype such as "too emotional" or not strong enough for tackling the hard issues of war and defense. The current female hopefuls, Condoleezza Rice and Hillary

Rodham Clinton, are making sure these sorts of claims cannot be waged against them.[3] Both are without a doubt clever, articulate, well-educated, and politically astute. These attributes do not guarantee access to the Oval Office, of course, nor appear to be such stringent requirements for the position of president, at least for more recent male candidates. Such is undoubtedly not the luxury of any alternative candidates, either women or, for that matter, candidates of color. The "alternative" will have to be smarter, faster, and more strategic than the mainstream.

The Canadian example should demonstrate more promise, given that this country has had at least one female world leader since confederation in 1867. Kim Campbell, as discussed below, led the Canadian State in 1993, and one would hope that her breaking through one of the toughest "glass ceilings" in Canada, if not *the* toughest, would have heralded greater advances for women in politics generally, as well in top political positions in Canada. Such hopes have not translated to any meaningful reality however. There have been female political party leaders—Audrey McLaughlin and Alexa Mcdonough have both been leaders of the New Democrats, one of the leading political parties, but always playing a distant third to the more center and right-wing parties of the Liberals and Conservatives respectively. But when a woman has come close to leadership, it has been terribly difficult to stay on track and not fall in some sort of sexist trap.

One of the more startling examples of this was in relation to the political aspirations of Belinda Stronach, first a leadership hopeful for the Conservative Party in 2004 and later raked over the coals for changing political parties in May 2005. When she was a leader hopeful, she was often portrayed as a person of little substance—a comment which was not necessarily gendered in and of itself, as any male candidate can equally lack substance (although a deeper analysis might demonstrate that this female candidate may have very well received the "substance" comment more often, and in more subtle, gendered ways, than have male candidates, but this analysis has not been taken up here). It was that these comments were often followed by the rather unsubtle comments on her looks (young, blond), and she was often referred to in the media as "the blond bombshell." This "bombshell" created quite an explosion a year later. The spring of 2005 witnessed a remarkable public exchange of comments coming from the Canadian political elite when this conservative member of Parliament crossed the floor to the other side, joining the Liberal Party. Granted, the switching of political allegiances is not a popular move, not least amongst those remaining in the party that has been abandoned. However such political moves are not unheard of—many a politician has decided to make such a move, probably more so for strategic rather than principled reasons, but that can be a matter for debate, which is fair enough.

A former Canadian prime minister had also crossed the floor earlier in his career (Brian Mulroney). What was surprising about the exchange in 2005 was that unlike Mulroney, Belinda Stronach was called a whore, a harlot, and an "attractive dipstick." In addition, her love life (she was apparently involved with another Conservative Party member) was splashed across the newspapers as her love interest was "devastated." Photos of a spurned Conservative man back at the family farm mending his wounds were more than over the top for an account of a relatively common political, albeit opportunistic, maneuver. If anyone questioned the gendered baggage in Canadian politics, the differential treatment between women and men, it laid itself bare in this case. Is this the picture of a modern, twenty-first-century state? What chances do women have if sexual politics impacts a woman's ability to be a part of the body politic?

Belinda Stronach is now Human Resources minister for the Liberal minority government (although her position may well change as Canada is headed toward yet another general election as we write, only a year and a half since the last general election in June 2004). She recently commented that she still gets as many inquiries about where she buys her shoes as she does regarding her human resources policies. Is Stronach the exception? Sheila Copps, a parliamentarian who was once told to "quiet down baby" by a fellow parliamentarian, was at one point fronted as a possible Liberal leader candidate. She did not receive the same type of comments as Stronach when rumors were flying about her potential candidacy, but the sound of her "grating oratorical style similar to any suburban Tupperware lady" was all too regularly raised.[4] The sound of her voice? Is that a sound issue?

As in earlier chapters, we also take a look at some of the conditions women face in their regions. Here, Canada can be shown as an example of how women are not all subject to the same discriminatory structures, or all share the same levels of access (or not) to opportunities and a more secure life. Canada is generally taken to be one of the best places to live on the planet—women, despite the sexual hang-ups with blonde bombshell politicians, are thought to have it pretty good in Canada in general. As in most cases, this really depends on who that woman is. Many women do have it very good in Canada—access to education, employment, career advancement, and to some degree political clout and influence. As such, it makes it harder to see those who have no hope in achieving anything like even basic education and employment, let alone top political leadership. However, even in late 2005, Canada was being chastised by the UN Human Rights committee regarding its treatment of aboriginal women. At present, the vast majority of aboriginal women are not adequately protected from violence, from poverty, nor from overt discrimination. A report issued in 2004 focused on levels of poverty and starvation among Inuit women in a Nunavut community which is generally and otherwise quite affluent. The report indicated that upward of 65 percent of the women and children in this community were either "officially" starving, or coming very close to those standards, due largely to inadequate access to traditional foods, and moreover inadequate access to financial resources for which women could buy market-economy foods.

The UN report noted that Canadian aboriginal women in general had limited to no access to decision-making in their lives. This is particularly acute on the reserves, where provincial family and matrimonial property law, which would normally serve to protect women fleeing abusive homes and/or wishing to divorce, often has no jurisdiction. Women who have the ability to leave abusive and/or bad unions often must leave without any financial support, and without their children. This is not to reduce the accomplishments of those aboriginal women who in fact have been able to have their voices heard within the upper echelons of politics—in fact, they very much bring home our over-arching point about resistance. Aboriginal women in Canada meet with a great deal of structural limitation demonstrating that those who break through these limitations are very good examples of resistance against a system that both consciously and unconsciously attempts to limit basic life necessities and opportunities. These women may in fact have more to share with their non-North American cohorts in Africa, Asia, and Latin America in their fight against greater systemic discrimination than do the white, and generally more affluent portions of the female North American population. This also demonstrates the ways in which discrimination functions and how deeply it runs. As the Canadian example shows, the often more privileged groups of women who do make it to Parliament (if not to positions of leadership) still face hurdles and must exercise resistance toward gender discrimination that their male counterparts do not.

The tensions between granting more liberal, equality-endowing laws and the patriarchal systems in which women live exhibit themselves in their own ways in the Latin American context. Some politicians throughout Latin America began to advocate neoliberal economic and progressive reproductive rights policies in the 1990s, even though they had little initial support. Over time these policies gained some level of acceptance and the politicians that supported them gained office. The tensions between political issues and patriarchal structure are however very present. A portion of the electorate in Latin America, both women and men, have remained unwilling to vote for women candidates. Most Latin Americans are concerned primarily with food, jobs, shelter, and performance of the economy in their respective countries, and a female candidate, in the past at least, may have represented for many a "one issue" candidate such as a candidate focused just on gender issues. However, the times seem to be changing. In contrast to their generally more affluent counterparts to the north, Latin Americans are rapidly opening doors to female candidates.

Women who have been successful at reaching the upper echelons of politics have generally focused on issues that are not traditionally considered part of a gender program. Although domestic violence, divorce, and day care are certainly becoming more visible as political issues in Latin America, these do not resonate with the electorate in the same ways that wages and employment are important political issues. In fact, some typically "gender" based issues such as abortion are still very difficult to raise within cultures dominated by the Catholic Church, and those who have attempted to front this issue have not been successful in changing criminal codes in any of the countries in question. Many women candidates are also very much bound to their parties as well—regardless of their own views on gender issues, they are more likely than not to rally around their party policy, rather than rally around a gender issue that may contradict their party.

But doors are opening to women nevertheless. Throughout the 1990s, twelve Latin American countries introduced the quota system, requiring a minimum level of women's participation in national elections, ranging between 20 and 40 percent. This has not jettisoned a critical mass of women to the very top—not yet anyway. But it is a start. Although some of the countries have experienced minimal effect, the overall growing presence of women in Latin American legislatures grew significantly throughout the 1990s. This growth occurred not solely due to quota systems, but also due to increased opportunities and abilities of women in general, as their life expectancies have increased. More and more girls are attending secondary and postsecondary school, and birth rates have declined.

KIM CAMPBELL

Life Before Politics

Avril Phaedra Douglas Campbell was born on 10 March 1947, in Port Alberni, British Columbia. Her parents' marriage was not successful and her mother left the family when Avril was only 12. She changed her name to "Kim" shortly after her mother left. Campbell went to the University of British Columbia, earning a B.A. in Political Science in 1969, an LL.B. in 1983, and started at the London School of Economics on a scholarship in Soviet Studies but left with her thesis unfinished. She married Nathan Divinsky in 1972 and divorced him eleven years later. She remarried Howard Eddy in 1986 but the marriage only lasted until 1993. She served as a Political Science lecturer at the University of British Columbia, 1975–1978, and as a Political Science and History lecturer at the Vancouver Community College, 1978–1981.

Political Career

In 1980 Kim Campbell entered the world of elected public office as a trustee of the Vancouver School Board, serving as its chairperson in 1983 and vice chairperson in 1984, while completing her law degree at the University of British Columbia.

After an early run for the Social Credit Party in the provincial election of 1983 she worked in the office of Premier Bill Bennett before running again and winning in the 1986 provincial election. In 1988 she accepted an offer from the federal Progressive Conservative Party to run for the nomination in the running of Vancouver Centre, where she was elected.

In the cabinet of Prime Minister Brian Mulroney, as her political career progressed, she accumulated many "firsts": first woman minister of justice and attorney general of Canada; first woman minister of national defense (and first woman defense minister of a NATO country); first woman leader of the Progressive Conservative Party of Canada (14 June 1993 to 14 December 1993), culminating as first woman prime minister of Canada.

When Brian Mulroney announced his retirement, Campbell was encouraged to run for the post of party leader. Her strongest competition was Jean Charest, whom she beat in a very close vote at the PC Leadership Convention.

During the 1993 election, Kim Campbell hired an American advertising company to create a commercial for her campaign. The commercial, which mocked Jean Chrétien's facial disability (paralysis on one side), was not well received in Canada.

Unfortunately for Campbell, the Conservative mandate to govern had expired and she was obliged to call an election for October 1993. Nine years of dissatisfaction with the Conservatives, in which Canadians found themselves suddenly saddled with NAFTA (North American Free Trade Agreement), the Goods and Service Tax (GST), constitutional fiascos (Meech Lake and Charlottetown Accords) and a serious recession, were simply too much for Campbell to overcome, and the Conservatives suffered an extraordinary and unprecedented defeat in which Conservative seats in the House of Commons were reduced to only two. Campbell even lost her Vancouver seat.

Kim Campbell served as prime minister of Canada from 25 June 1993 to 4 November 1993, and remains the only women to have served as head of government or state in North America.

Legacies

Kim Campbell was the first woman to serve as prime minister, minister of justice, attorney general, minister of national defense, and leader of the Progressive Conservative Party in Canada.

Campbell called her own style the "politics of inclusion" and she spoke up for what she believed were issues of the day, such as abortion and free trade, and as minister of justice she led major changes in gun control and sexual assault legislation.

Kim Campbell left politics for a while and returned to teaching when she was offered a fellowship at Harvard University. Since then, however, she has returned to politics, having been appointed by Prime Minister Jean Chrétien to the post of Consul General in Los Angeles, California.

On 1 January 2004 Kim Campbell assumed the position of secretary general of the Club of Madrid, an organization of former heads of government and state who work to promote democratization through peer relations with leaders of transitional democracies. The Club of Madrid was incorporated in Madrid in May of 2002, and Ms. Campbell is a founding member and also served as its vice president from 2002 to 2004. She continues her long-standing relationship with Harvard University as an Honorary Fellow of the Center for Public Leadership at the Kennedy School of Government.

In October of 2003 Campbell assumed the presidency of the International Women's Forum, a global organization of women of significant and diverse achievement. Campbell also chaired the Council of Women World Leaders (CWWL) from 1999 to 2003. The Council's membership consists of women who hold or have held the office of president or prime minister in their own country.

Campbell speaks widely on issues relating to international politics and conflict resolution, democratization, international trade, gender, leadership, and Canadian/American relations. She makes frequent appearances on radio and television in North America and abroad.

Campbell is a Senior Fellow of The Gorbachev Foundation of North America in Boston, a member of the International Council of the Asia Society of New York and serves on advisory boards of numerous other international organizations. She is a director of several publicly traded companies in the hi-tech and biotech industries. Her political memoir *Time and Chance* was published in 1996 by Doubleday Canada.

VIOLETTA CHAMORRO

Life Before Politics

Violeta Chamorro came from a wealthy family and was sent to school in the United States in order to learn English. Not being terribly excited about school, she returned and married Pedro Joaquin Chamorro, the editor of the prominent anti-Somosa newspaper *La Prensa*. They were married for twenty-seven years until his violent death in 1978. After his assassination in 1978, Violeta took over as editor of the paper. When the government of Anastasio Somosa fell to the Sandinistas in 1979, she served as the only woman member of the civilian junta that had provisional rule over Nicaragua after the revolution. Daniel Ortega was one of the other prominent members of the junta. She later said that she served because "they needed me...they needed the name of my husband, and the name of *La Prensa*....I wouldn't have been patriotic to refuse." Chamorro served on the junta for only a short time. Although she left the junta, officially citing health reasons, she later confided that she did not agree with the course the Sandinistas were taking—excessive militarism, increasing Cuban pressure, and a loss of interest in democratic ideals.

The Sandinistas faced a serious challenge in consolidating their power in Nicaragua. The spirit of Somosa lived on in an opposition army made up of members of his former National Guard. Contras planned a counter-revolution from staging sites in Honduras. They were then heavily supported by the United States under the leadership of U.S. President Ronald Reagan. The civil war waged on in the 1980s. The Sandinistas finally consolidated power in 1984, when Ortega was elected president, but the U.S.-supported contras kept the pressure on. Chamorro, in her position at *La Prensa*, protested the Sandinistas' press censorship. Yet, despite her opposition to the Sandinistas, Chamorro was not a puppet of the United States or a contra supporter.

Political Career

Throughout the 1980s, Chamorro continued her attacks against the human rights record of the Sandinistas. She insisted that Western democracies should demand a civilized government in Nicaragua, free elections, and human rights. Moreover, she began calling for a national dialogue and reconciliation between the warring contras and Sandinistas. Chamorro often called on the image of her martyr husband in her *La Prensa* editorials. After the Sandinistas shut down the paper in 1986, Chamorro came out with an article in the U.S. journal *Foreign Affairs* that not only condemned the action but also made it clear that her opposition to the Sandinistas did not constitute approval of Reagan's policies. Again she called for a national dialogue to return Nicaragua to normalcy. The paper was later reopened as defiant as ever—Chamorro's remained one of the principal voices against Sandinista rule. Her editorials were continually censored, and Sandinista mobs vandalized her home. In 1988 the Sandinistas began a propaganda campaign against her and *La Prensa*.

They attempted to tie Chamorro to the U.S.-sponsored contras. The tactic did not work, and diverse anti-Sandinista groups came together under the Unión Nacional Opositora (UNO) party to name Violeta to unseat Ortega after his February 1989 announcement that the elections would be moved up to November 1989. Ortega did this in exchange for the demobilization of the contras. These events were prompted by Costa Rican president Oscar Arias's leadership in formulating a peace accord among Central American countries. The goal was regional stability.

Chamorro claimed that she did not want the position of president, but the "people asked me to accept, and I did so gladly because the need in this country is so great." She centered her campaign on peace and reconciliation. Chamorro was compared to Aquino in the Philippines—she was considered brave, honest, and reliable. Her strong Catholic ties, like Aquino's, were apparent in her public speeches. In fact, once when asked to speak, she recited the Lord's Prayer. She also commanded the respect of those who held her husband in great esteem.

Foreign representatives from the Organization of American States (OAS), the United Nations (UN), and former U.S. President Jimmy Carter observed the elections. The assumption by Ortega was that the FSLN would win in a fair contest. However, much to his surprise, Violeta Chamorro won with 54.7 percent of the vote. Many did not think she would win because of her lack of political experience. However, in her political naïveté, there was a refreshing feeling of honesty.

Winning the election was one thing; effectively leading a war-torn country was another. Nicaragua and most of Central America were described by the International Commission for the Recovery and Development of Central America (the Sanford Commission) as trapped in a cycle of violence that impeded development. The resulting poverty, in turn, intensified the violence. The report outlined recommendations that included increasing social justice, democratic participation, and international development aid. Chamorro would have to achieve peace, stabilize the Nicaraguan economy, and institute democracy, while struggling to define her power base and fight for her political legitimacy.

Chamorro took power on 25 April 1990 before several heads of state and both FSLN and UNO supporters. In her inaugural speech, President Chamorro said that one of her primary tasks was to "instill in all our actions the spirit of reconciliation." It was the first peaceful transition of power in Nicaraguan history. Although she named herself minister of defense, she retained Daniel Ortega's brother, General Humberto Ortega, as head of the army. This turned out to be a controversial move. Her strategy was to use Humberto to lessen Sandinista opposition to her new government. However, in protest, two of Chamorro's cabinet ministers resigned, and the contras threatened to resist the demobilization efforts. They did not understand that Chamorro was attempting to disarm the volatile political climate that bred the contra war by establishing a middle ground. In addition to the job of demobilizing the contra forces and downsizing the Sandinista army, she also faced a terrible economic crisis. Per capita income was at the same level as in 1950, and the inflation rate was 43 percent. The ten-year contra war had crippled the Nicaraguan economy, and the subsequent U.S. embargo had been devastating. U.S. President George Bush was pleased in the change of leadership in Nicaragua but threatened to hold back $300 million in aid if he could not approve of Chamorro's political appointments. Despite these problems, it seemed as though the spirit of reconciliation was holding back the resumption of the civil war. As Chamorro put it: "Reconciliation is more beautiful than victory."

As president, Chamorro has demonstrated a penchant for using powerful symbols. In addition to evoking her husband's image at every opportunity, on one occasion she arranged for 15,000 automatic rifles to be dumped into a pit and covered with concrete. It was a ceremonial "farewell to arms" signifying the end of the contra war. In her first 100 days in office, Chamorro survived two general strikes, made progress in demobilizing the contras, and worked toward cooperation with the Sandinistas. The strikes were organized by the Sandinistas in protest of her economic austerity measures, which included layoffs, wage cuts, and attempts to sell state-owned companies. The contras also presented problems for Chamorro, as they formed an alliance with right-wing members of the UNO. In response, Chamorro negotiated a settlement and allotted contras land in demilitarized zones.

In 1991 Chamorro was besieged by political forces on all sides, despite her being loved by most Nicaraguans. Political opponents had trouble adapting to a woman and mother figure in power. One opposition official said that it was hard to criticize her because she was a woman. Her disarming demeanor also caught some politicians off guard (i.e., calling advisers "my love"). Labor groups affiliated with the FSLN seized new freedoms and, according to the president, "invented new ways almost everyday to go on strike." She stressed that time was needed to heal the country. Chamorro did make some headway with her trip to the United States in April 1991. She was able to clear up a $360 million World Bank debt with President Bush's help. In spite of Sandinista-led strikes and contra land seizures, Chamorro seemed to have established some type of equilibrium in Nicaragua.

By 1992 Nicaragua was on the road to recovery but was little noticed by the world. Chamorro seemed to realize that increased trade would revive the Nicaraguan economy faster than foreign aid. Bowing to the Nicaraguan right-wing and the United States, Chamorro announced the return of Sandinista-confiscated property in September 1992. Heeding U.S. Secretary of State James Baker, who warned Chamorro of the importance of security for investors, she also fired several Sandinista police officials. This move was tied to the freeing up of $104 million in U.S. aid.

In November 1993 the Sandinistas pressured Chamorro to reform the economic decision-making powers of the president. In fact, there were charges that the Sandinistas were staging crises in order to paralyze Chamorro's government. Most economic decisions had been made secretly between the government and the International Monetary Fund (IMF). The Sandinistas wanted to reform the constitution to prohibit the reelection of the president, subordinate the army to even more civilian control, and provide for a less partisan judiciary. In retaliation, Chamorro threatened to resign if anything other than minor changes were made to the constitution.

In January 1994 Chamorro announced her intent to readdress the problems of the poor in Nicaragua. The economic measures under her tenure in office had not necessarily helped the poor. She promised that in 1994 the government would support the small farmers. These policies were part of a new grassroots effort to build a social agenda that would respond to the economic demands of the rural poor living in communities where the contras had been using banditry to win their allegiance. The trouble was that social reform at the grassroots level tended to jeopardize the loan deals worked out with the IMF and World Bank.

Overall, criticism of Chamorro has centered on her lack of political experience and reliance on her husband's image: "Violeta Chamorro's status in Nicaraguan society is largely ascriptive...yet she achieved the ultimate status that a woman can attain in Nicaraguan society by being the devout widow of a politically correct martyr." However, she has not necessarily been a model for feminists interested in getting more women into positions of political power. During her presidential campaign she asserted, "I'm not a feminist. ... I am a woman dedicated to my home, as Pedro has taught me." She has not favored increasing the participation of women in politics and has given few political appointments to women. In spite of that, at least one other woman in Central America has been inspired to run for presidential office—Margairita Penón de Arias, wife of former Costa Rican President Oscar Arias. Chamorro has been forced to walk a tortuous path between renewed civil war and economic ruin. Her term ended in 1996. Her time in office was testimony to her ability to weather severe crises. Whether the opposition forces will be able to resolve their differences through peaceful means remains to be seen.

Legacy

The political history of Nicaragua has been characterized by invasions, civil wars, and coups d'etat. Democratic traditions have not been able to take root due to the debilitating effects of colonization by the Spanish in the sixteenth century and military intervention by the United States since the nineteenth century. Consequently, Nicaraguan political culture has been tainted by authoritarianism and dominance by the military.

In the authoritarian tradition, the Somosa family ruled Nicaragua from 1937 to 1979. With the help of the United States, the Somosa dictatorships held a firm grip on Nicaragua and ignored basic human rights. In 1979 the Sandinista (Sandinista National Liberation Front, or FSLN) forces toppled the Somosas and promised a socialist restructuring of society. However, the Sandinistas, led by Daniel Ortega, could not completely consolidate their grip on the country before the old Somosa guard, under U.S. direction and with U.S. support, rose in armed opposition. These "contra" rebels began a bloody civil war that lasted until 1990, when Violeta Chamorro won the presidency and negotiated an end to the conflict. Chamorro came to power after one of the most free elections in Nicaraguan history. She set out to bring peace, prosperity, and reconciliation to a divided Nicaragua and had some early policy successes. She brought the runaway inflation under control, cut the military by 75 percent, and demobilized the opposition contra rebels. She also restored basic political freedoms and human rights. However, Chamorro's power base began eroding in 1990. The electoral coalition that brought her to power began to abandon her. The Sandinistas, despite their retaining control of the military, police, and intelligence service, turned against Chamorro as well. Few national leaders have had to face the dual challenges of economic development and healing a divided nation torn by civil war. Violeta Barrios de Chamorro not only faced these challenges as the newly elected president of Nicaragua in 1990 but also did so as a woman leader in a political system dominated by men and the culture of machismo. Her continuing struggle to bring peace and prosperity to Nicaragua through reconciliation has been a daunting task. Oddly enough, Chamorro's role as healer of her own family—where half were pro-Sandinista and half pro-contra—reflected in microcosm her role as healer of the nation.

ISABEL PERON
Life Before Politics

Isabel Perón was born on 4 February 1931, in La Rioja, a provincial capital in the impoverished mountainous region of northwestern Argentina. Her father, a local bank manager, died when she was still a young child. By the time of her father's death, the family had moved to Buenos Aires, where she studied piano, dance, and French, although she was not able to finish her formal education.

After leaving school Isabel became a dancer, performing in folk music groups, nightclubs, and finally the ballet corps of two leading theaters in Buenos Aires. She acquired the name Isabel on her confirmation in the Catholic Church and adopted the name when she became a dancer. She met Juan Perón in 1955 during his exile in Paraguay. Perón was attracted to her beauty and believed she could provide him with the female companionship he had been lacking since the death of his second wife, Evita.

Political Career

Perón brought Isabel with him when he moved to Spain in 1960. Authorities in the strongly Catholic nation did not approve of Perón's living arrangements with this young woman, so in 1961 the former president reluctantly got married for a third time.

As Perón began to return to an active role in Argentinian politics, Isabel would often be used as a go-between from Spain to South America. Perón was forbidden from returning to Argentina, so his new wife would travel in his stead and report back to him when she returned.

It was also around this time that Isabel met José López Rega, an occult philosopher and fortune teller. Isabel was quite interested in such matters, so the two became fast friends. Under pressure from Isabel, Perón appointed Rega as his personal secretary.

In 1973 Perón was persuaded to return to Argentina and run for president. He agreed and, in a surprisingly controversial move, chose Isabel as his running mate. Isabel had very little in the way of politicial experience or ambitions and she had a very different personality from Evita, who had been denied the post of vice president years earlier.

The December 1973 elections in Argentina placed Dr. Hector J. Campora, a Perónist, in power. In July 1973, Campora resigns in favor of Raul Lastiri, also a Peronist, who calls for new elections. In the October elections, Juan Perón regains power, with Isabel de Perón, his third wife, as vice president. Isabel Perón becomes the first woman to head national government in the Western hemisphere following her husband's death. Her administration suffered from economic deterioration, intraparty struggles, and terrorism. Isabel Perón was ousted by military coup and the subsequent military rule restored order, but at the cost of many lives and human rights violations.

Perón died on 1 July 1974, less than a year after being elected. Isabel assumed the presidency and became the world's first female *president*. By this time, José López Rega, who had been slowly consolidating his power over the years by controlling Isabel, emerged as the clear power behind the throne—a notion which greatly frightened the military. Isabel agreed to fire López, but the military concluded that with Argentina's prevailing climate of widespread strikes and political terrorism, a weak-willed and unexperienced woman would not be a suitable president.

On 24 March 1976, she was kidnapped and deposed in a bloodless coup. After remaining under house arrest for five years, she was sent into exile in 1981. She was not allowed to return to Argentina until the presidency of Raúl Alfonsín in 1983.

Legacy

Isabel Martínez had an extraordinary life. Never in modern world history did a nightclub cabaret dancer rise to become the president of a country only to be exiled. She is best known as the first woman head of state in the Americas.

MIREYA MOSCOSO

Life Before Politics

Mireya Elisa Moscoso Rodríguez de Arias, Panama's first woman president, was born to a poor rural family on 1 July 1940 in Pedasi, Panama. After graduating from high school, she worked as a secretary and in the early 1960s met Arnulfo Arias, a former president of Panama. She began working on his political campaigns, and in October 1968 he was reelected. Arias was deposed shortly after his reelection by General Omar Torrijos and Moscoso joined Arias in exile in Miami, Florida. She studied interior design at Miami-Dade Community College, and in 1969, she married Arias. After Arias's death in 1988, she returned to Panama and in the early 1990s held several minor governmental posts. In 1990 Moscoso created the Arnulfista Party, becoming the party president the following year. In 1994 she unsuccessfully ran for the presidency of Panama earning a respectable 29 percent of the vote.

Political Career

Moscoso ran again for president in 1999. Her primary opponent was Martín Torrijos (the son of former dictator Omar Torrijos who had deposed her late husband Arnulfo Arias). Torrijos represented the ruling Democratic Revolutionary Party. The political platforms of the Arnulfista and DRP parties were actually quite similar. Moscoso was portrayed as the more populist candidate, whereas Torrijos was seen as the pro-business candidate. Both promised to reduce poverty, improve education, and create jobs. Moscoso also emphasized her intention to slow the government's policy of privatization. On 2 May 1999,

Moscoso defeated Torrijos, winning with 45 percent of the vote to Torrijos's 38 percent.

In December 1999 Moscoso oversaw the U.S. handover of the Panama Canal. Although she either fired or forced the resignation of every major officeholder appointed by the previous administration, the Panama Canal Authority remained autonomous and fulfilled its mission to run the canal in an orderly manner. During her administration Moscoso faced frequent charges of nepotism in government appointments.

Moscoso began her term in office with widespread popularity and hope for change. However, throughout her five-year tenure in office, numerous corruption scandals were exposed by the media and none of her close allies were ever investigated. One of the most famous corruption scandals was the "Durodollar" scandal. Moscoso's executive secretary filed a complaint with the police accusing her gardener of stealing thousands of dollars from her freezer. The gardener was put in jail, but the police never asked why a secretary had thousands of dollars inside her freezer. Moscoso aroused suspicion when she gave all seventy-two Panamanian legislators expensive Cartier watches and earrings (worth an estimated $146,000) just before the vote on the government-proposed budget package. She claimed they were Christmas gifts and that she paid for them from her own money, not from public funds. No investigation was ever made.

Her approval rating at the end of her term in office was the lowest for any Panamanian president. She was succeeded on 1 September 2004 by Martín Torrijos. The Arnulfista Party (Moscoso's party) received only 16 percent of the votes, finishing in a distant third place. The blame for this humiliating loss was placed mainly on Moscoso. During the campaign, she openly attended rallies organized by her hand-picked candidate, overshadowing him. Days before Moscoso ended her term and retired to her home in Florida, she pardoned four Cuban exiles accused of plotting to assassinate Fidel Castro, causing Cuba to break off diplomatic relations with Panama. The relations were nevertheless reestablished under her successor, President Martín Torrijos.

With the new government, numerous mechanisms to investigate corruption cases were instituted. It is alleged that Taiwan's donations to the Panamanian government were put under private foundations that were controlled by Moscoso's cabinet and close friends.

Moscoso is now facing numerous corruption investigations in Panama. And while she blames Fidel Castro for initiating the corruption allegations, even Moscoso's close aides point to Panamanian political rivals as the source. On her way out of office, Mireya Moscoso pardoned most of the people around her who were or probably would be major figures in public corruption scandals. The ex-president herself will be a member of the Central American Parliament (PARLACEN), which confers immunity from prosecution or investigation on its members.

Legacy

The president of Panama pardoned four men accused of attempting to assassinate Cuba's Fidel Castro. Cuba warned it would cut diplomatic ties with Panama if Moscoso pardoned the men. The men—all Cuban emigres—were convicted and jailed initially for threatening public security and falsifying documents. They were not charged with attempted murder as there was said to be a lack of evidence.

The names of the four men accused of attempting to assassinate Castro—Luis Posada Carriles, Gaspar Jimenez, Guillermo Novo, and Pedro Remon—were on a list of presidential pardons announced by Moscoso less than a week before she left office. Reports said they had already been flown out of the country, possibly to Miami. Of the six men arrested, five were Cubans and one was a Panamanian.

President Mireya Moscoso ended her tenure in office regarded as the worst head of state in the past fifteen years in Panama. A clear majority of 59.1 percent gave her an unfavorable rating according to a poll published by *La Prensa*. The study showed 37 percent of the questioned people said Moscoso's mandate was bad, 22.1 percent, very bad, 32.2 percent, good, and only 5.7 percent, excellent. The people polled criticized Moscoso because she did not fight corruption head-on, and during her mandate, Panama's international relations got worse. Also, 77 percent of the questioned people want Moscoso to be investigated for corruption.

MICHELLE BACHELET

I am a socialist, but I wear many hats. I was not a minister of the socialists, I was a minister of all the Chileans. If I am president, I will be president for all the Chileans.

Life Before Politics

Verónica Michelle Bachelet Jeria was born on 29 September 1951 in Santiago, Chile, to anthropologist Ángela Jeria and Air Force General Alberto Bachelet. She graduated from high school in 1969 and then entered medical school at the University of Chile. Under the government of socialist President Salvador Allende, Bachelet's father was put in charge of the Food Distribution Office. Unfortunately, on the day of the 11 September 1973 coup by General Augusto Pinochet (assisted by the American CIA), Bachelet's father was arrested under charges of treason. Her father was tortured to death in March 1974. Bachelet's then-boyfriend, Jaime López, was also detained and tortured before he too disappeared. In January 1975, Bachelet and her mother were also detained, and tortured at Villa Grimaldi, a notorious detention center in Santiago, for twenty-one days. Luckily both mother and daughter were exiled to Australia, where Bachelet's older brother Alberto lived. Bachelet and her mother then settled in East Germany where Bachelet learned German and continued with her medical studies at Humboldt University of Berlin.

Bachelet returned to Chile in 1979, where she concluded her studies and graduated three years later from medical school as a surgeon at the University of Chile. Between 1983 and 1986 she specialized in pediatrics and public health at a children's hospital. During this time, she returned to politics, to fight for the reestablishment of democracy.

Political Career

Between 1985 and 1987 she was associated with an armed group which, among other activities, attempted to assassinate Pinochet in 1986. She aided nongovernmental organizations (NGOs), helping children of the tortured and the families of those who had disappeared in Chile. Following the return of democracy in 1990, Bachelet worked for the Ministry of Health and was a consultant for the Pan-American Health Organization, and the World Health Organization.

Between 1994 and July 1997, Bachelet worked as adviser for the Health Undersecretary. Later, driven by an interest in civil-military relations, she began to study military strategy at the National Academy of Political and Strategic Studies in Chile. She continued her studies in the United States at the Inter-American Defense College in Washington, DC, under a presidential scholarship. In 1998 she returned to Chile to work for the Defense Ministry as minister adviser and graduated from a Masters program in military science at the Chilean Army's War Academy.

As a university student, Bachelet was a member of the Socialist Youth. She joined the Socialist Party of Chile in the 1970s. In 1995 she became a part of the party's Central Committee, and from 1998 until 2000 she was an active member of the Political Commission. In 1996, she ran for mayor of Las Condes and lost. Bachelet was named minister of health by President Ricardo Lagos on 11 March 2000, and on 7 January 2002 she was appointed defense minister, becoming the first woman to hold this post in a Latin American country.

In late 2004, following a rise in her popularity in opinion polls, Bachelet was asked to become the Socialist candidate for president. In series of maneuvers, a liberal-centrist coalition was formed and Bachelet emerged as the nominee. In the 2005 election, Bachelet faced candidates from the center-right Sebastián Piñera (RN), the right-wing Joaquín Lavín (UDI), and the far-left Tomás Hirsch (JPM). She gained 46 percent of the vote, to Piñera's 25 percent, Lavín's 23 percent and Hirsch's 5 percent. In the resulting run-off election on 15 January 2006, Bachelet faced Piñera, and won the presidency with 53 percent of the vote, thus becoming her country's first female elected president, and the second in South America after Guyana's Janet Jagan and the fourth in Latin America after Jagan, Nicaragua's Violeta Chamorro, and Panama's Mireya Moscoso.

Michelle Bachelet has broken many political traditions. Not only is she a woman, but she is also a socialist, an agnostic, and she is a single parent with a 12-year-old daughter and two other grown children.

Chilean society is often portrayed as ultraconservative, dominated by men and the Roman Catholic Church. Only 4 percent of Chilean senators are women and divorce was only introduced in 2004. Bachelet believes this is only part of the picture and Chile is changing—as reflected by her rise to political power.

Bachelet became the sole candidate for the ruling center-left coalition after another woman, Soledad Alvear, dropped out of the contest in late May 2005. The coalition, known as *Concertacion,* has held power since the return of democracy in 1990 and Bachelet says she will carry on the tradition of maintaining strong economic growth. "We should continue growing economically, that is very important, but we have to make sure that everybody in this country will have the benefits of this growth." Chile is often described as the economic miracle of Latin America and the economy is believed to have expanded by more than 5 percent this year.

Bachelet becomes very serious when she discusses 90-year-old General Pinochet. He is under house arrest, and has been fighting legal battles for years. Pinochet has lost his immunity from prosecution and faces charges of tax fraud and other crimes related to secret multimillion dollar bank accounts, many of them with the Washington-based Riggs Bank. Bachelet says the general is now irrelevant as a political actor. However, under Chilean protocol he would be entitled to a state funeral as a former president. There is a big chance he could die while she is running the country. The election of a socialist doctor and former political prisoner may be part of Latin America's increasingly leftward movement.

Legacy

Ordinary Chileans have warmed to the hardworking, bespectacled Bachelet. Most connect easily with her plain manner and down-to-earth personality, and her reform agenda has won much support, making up for her mostly uneventful term as a cabinet minister. While benefiting from the boom in what is generally regarded as Latin America's showcase economy, she's also pledged to lower the nation's unemployment rate, which peaked at 10 percent this year, and reduce income disparities—among the ten worst in the world. Bachelet has also proposed a social-welfare program that would ensure full access to education, health care, and proper nutrition for all underprivileged children under the age of 10.

Bachelet also intends to boost the political profile of women in Chile. Half of all portfolios in her cabinet will be reserved for women, and as president she will push for legislation requiring political parties to fill an established quota of female candidates for elected office. The first woman to become president of Chile is unlikely to be the last, if she has any say in the matter. "We are going to set a standard for Latin America," she said. She is a very well-educated woman with incredible political experience, and great charisma. She speaks Spanish, English, German, Portuguese, French, and some Russian. We believe she will be a force in international politics for years to come.

7

Conclusion

I'm not some Tammy Wynette standing by my man.
                                    U.S. Senator Hillary Rodham Clinton

The problem here is that there will always be some uncertainty about
how quickly Saddam can acquire nuclear weapons. But we don't
want the smoking gun to be a mushroom cloud.
                                    U.S. Secretary of State Condoleezza Rice

Gender theories attempt to both explain as well as value something about
gender politics. An attempt is made to explain why, or why not, a
nondominant group (primarily women) come to power, particularly as
world leaders. At the same time we are offered reasons as to why this
would be beneficial or not. It is beneficial perhaps because it is a sign of
gender equity—that there ought to be equality between men and women
and that one sex should not be favored over the other. It is beneficial
perhaps because women have something very particular to offer the
political world, whether it be a sense of caring that has so far been grossly
lacking in world politics, or at the very least shades of new perspectives
upon the global dilemmas that face us. And, it could also be that by
electing more women, different styles of leadership may emerge that
would include both men and women as leaders (transformational leadership based on social justice and peaceful security).[1] Frankly, it is very
difficult to really say whether women can and do bring something new
and different to the table. This is clear when we examine the range on the
political spectrum that these women represent.

PARTY AFFILIATION

As the gender theories in Chapter 2 demonstrated, we have the tendency to make a great deal of generalizations about gender, and women in particular. From a liberal feminist point of view, a woman's leadership probably would not deviate greatly from that of a man, so long as she had equal rights and access to resources as he. A radical feminist perspective may find women working to break down patriarchy, whereas the Marxist feminist leader would have a clear class-based agenda in her politics. The difference feminism approach emphasizes features of womanhood that are distinct to leadership, such as caring and mother-hood (or image of mother). A postmodern approach might best merge with the multicultural/non-Western approach whereby a multiplicity of standpoints or positions may inform this style of leadership. These are all, of course, simplistic reductions of what these various gender perspectives have to offer, and of course, gender theories are not limited to just these perspectives either. We can apply such theoretical tools to men as well as women, either naturalizing men to be brutes of war bent solely upon power, or instead men who, just like women, function within this system of patriarchy but from a position of greater privilege than do women.

What our overview of twenty-two women has shown, we think, is that the variety of gender perspectives is in fact important. No one view can illuminate the full complexity of what it means to be a woman in a leader-ship position, but they do all contribute to our understanding of how we perceive women differently, what sort of structural impediments they face, how some women have managed to overcome these impediments (and in different ways and forms, as suggested by their different global backgrounds) and what the combination of these struggles might mean for their respective leaderships. Another way of simply picturing this diversity can also be through the party affiliations these women have represented. Again, no plain generalizations can be made.

An initial, overarching question we had while learning and writing about these many women is whether or not a conservative party affilia-tion was at all central to the success of woman leadership? Margaret Thatcher, Kim Campbell, and Angela Merkel are all women with conservative tags. What is the attraction of the conservative platform to these women? Is this the "safe" party route, in that voters might have confidence in voting for a woman in these parties because they feel secure that the party platform will not let them stray too far or get too "womanly?" Are these the women who do the job just like men? Does this trend continue, or are women spread relatively evenly over the political spectrum? On the other hand, is it possible that despite these conservative "oddities" that most women fall into a more social-oriented camp, reflecting their social caring?

We must first define what we mean by these terms. We are not referring to the names of the political parties these women do or have represented, but rather make a judgment about the political position these parties reflect. This is not an easy exercise—what is conservative in one country might be fairly liberal in another (e.g., many conservatives in Canada may not be as conservative as those in the United States; and the difference may even be greater between conservatives in Norway and those in the United States). However, we use the following as broad and rough definitions to try to get an idea of what party affiliations these women world leaders have represented.

By conservative we are here meaning a relatively narrow social platform (usually more "traditional," claiming "family values" sometimes manifesting itself in restricted reproductive rights such as abortion or access to birth control, sometimes linked to a religious set of moral values) with a wider economic agenda allowing for an open competition in the free market (to a point—state interests might reign this in somewhat). Social support programs would be limited as people are encouraged to become competitive and self-sustaining (and if they need help, the family, church, community, are the first stops for assistance, not the state).

A liberal affiliation would mean social programming, or state support that provides for the "have-nots" within the state (those who do not have access to resources to enable them to sustain themselves). The state allows for greater social freedom as compared with a conservative one (greater reproductive rights, including access to abortion and divorce, for example) but interferes more with the economy to protect the vulnerable and regulate against market failures.

These broad and rough distinctions manifest themselves in fairly varied ways of course. To make the distinctions less polarized we also include what we refer to as a "centrist" position—in a sense a more pragmatist position that tries to balance between a strictly conservative and a strictly liberal position. This position might find itself bending toward either a more conservative or a more liberal position (although not strictly so) depending on the mood of the times. In some respects we see a blend between a more open market, reduced social program approach combined with a more open social stance (not restricting social freedoms and access to divorce, abortion).

We also include in our evaluation the terms socialist and communist, which advocate increasing state intervention and planned economies respectively, theoretically treating all persons as equals, providing access to all basic resources and limiting the extent to which individuals can try to gain power or resources over others. A socialist agenda may still interact somewhat with market economies albeit in a restrictive sense, where the state intervenes in foreign access to the domestic market and in domestic access to foreign markets. Communism suggests a near to completely closed system highly regulated by the state for the benefit of the people within. All are cared for, all have a role in society to contribute to the communal good, and no one is encouraged to excel over the other. These are all rather vague and somewhat "idealistic" categories. But hopefully they provide a general sense of how we evaluate the party affiliations of the various woman world leaders.

Of the twenty-two women highlighted in this book the split between conservative and liberal is even (seven which we have identified as conservative and seven as liberal). We also refer to a centrist-conservative leaning, or a centrist-liberal leaning (see Table 7.1).

With centrist qualifications, we still have an even split between conservative and liberal (eight on each side). The centrists can be thought of as a neutral balance between the two, responding to trends in their societies that may waver between liberal and conservative tendencies without really committing to one direction or another. Otherwise we have the two socialist leaders, which puts a slightly left-leaning tendency on our group overall. But this is not such a significant difference, making the relatively even split between party affiliations rather interesting. Our sample was not chosen on the basis of party affiliation—in fact this analysis (see Table 7.2) is one which we have literally carried out at the end of this process (largely borne out of our own curiosity). Does this sample represent the entire world of women leaders? Since we chose women from different regions as representative of that region of the world, we think it might. But let us look at the regions with respect to the women we have chosen for this study (Table 7.2).

Africa and the Middle East tend to be the most conservative region for those women who have come to power, with Golda Meir as the socialist exception (as there was not much choice, we have covered all the women world leaders in this area). We could not present biographies of all the women leaders in Europe and Asia, but amongst those that we chose, there is a stronger liberal tendency than conservative (more strongly in Asia than in Europe in our sample). The Americas are interesting—mainly conservative/centrist, but then some significant socialist

Table 7.1
Party Affiliations of the 22 Women Featured

Conservative	7
Centrist-Conservative	1
Centrist	3
No Party	1
Centrist-Liberal	1
Liberal	7
Socialist	2

Table 7.2
Regions and Political Affiliations

Africa/Middle East
2 Conservative
1 Centrist-Conservative
1 Centrist
1 Socialist
Europe
2 Conservatives
4 Liberals
1 No Party
The Americas
2 Conservatives
1 Centrist
2 Socialist
Asia
1 Centrist
1 Liberal-Centrist
2 Liberal
1 Socialist

Table 7.3
Current Women World Leader
Party Affiliation (12)

2 Socialist
2 Liberal
2 Liberal-Centrist
1 No party affiliation
2 Centrist
3 Conservative

Table 7.4
All Women Elected as President
or Prime Minister (58)

2 Communist
7 Socialist
15 Liberal
3 Liberal-Centrist
8 Centrist
7 No Party Affiliation
1 Conservative-Centrist
16 Conservative

tendencies, particularly most recently. Of course, the socialist trend is not happening in the northern part of the Americas, and does not seem likely to arise there in the near future either. But let us look at the most recent leaders to see if there are any trends emerging (see Tables 7.3 and 7.4).

Amongst current women world leaders it appears that they represent liberal-based parties more than conservative. Amongst all the women elected president or prime minister (again note that we have not included those with the title of premier or captain regent on our list as mentioned in the introduction) there is a stronger tendency toward the liberal side of the spectrum, although the spread goes well beyond a liberal party position, including both socialist as well as communist leaders. However the conservatives are not completely out, and a substantial number of women have led conservative parties (almost 30 percent of women world leaders have been conservative).

If this tells us anything, it is that we cannot take women's leadership for granted, nor can we conclude that women are more one thing or another politically. Women may join a party for both principled as well as strategic reasons (increased chances of getting elected through one party platform versus another, for example). The tendency toward "motherliness" (or not) is not necessarily linked toward their political party connections, either.

What are some of the trends we are seeing then, and can we make any tentative conclusions? We suggest the following:

1. women appear to be coming to power more and more in the developing or conflict ridden areas of the world,

2. these women leaders from the developing world have a different view of feminism and leadership than do women of the Western world,

3. most key positions in defense (both public and private sector) and the energy industry are still out of the reach of most women,

4. women appear to have access to a wide range of political parties, including conservative,

5. religious fundamentalism seeks to push back gains made for women in terms of equality (in both the Western part of the world such as the United States, as well as in places such as Afghanistan),

6. women are still woefully underrepresented in the most powerful nations, most noticeably in the United States,

7. women often have different reasons for coming to power than men do, but there are also differences in reasons between the women themselves,

8. both male and female leaders can and do benefit from family connections to political power—leadership is often a manifestation of privilege for both sexes,

9. the power of nationalism can not be underestimated in terms of choosing leaders (whether male or female),

10. women's issue organizations have little funding to support women candidates to office, whereas defense contractors and energy corporations have plenty of money and give it readily to male candidates,

11. global feminism, wherein women's experiences are dependent on different standpoints, race, class, ethnicity, and other differences across the globe, appears to be on the rise,

12. gender studies has come to be known as women's studies,

13. the language of power is still male.

Women seem to be coming to power more and more in the developing or conflict ridden areas of the world. Currently, of the twelve women who have been elected as heads of state or government in their respective countries, more than half are from developing, conflict, or post-conflict regions of the world (in fact seven). These too are loose categories, largely meaning that they are not a part of the affluent, post-industrial group of countries in North America and (largely Western) Europe. They range from Chile to Serbia, Sri Lanka to Sao Tome and Principe. These "non-Western" regions of the world are reaching out to their women to lead even though most people assume that women are coming to power more quickly in the post-industrialized world. Women leaders might be perceived as being less corruptible, mother figures, and often tap into the power of martyred husbands and fathers. Liberia's new president and the first woman elected president in the whole of Africa, Ellen Johnson-Sirleaf, is referred to as "Ma Ellen" by many, and she has herself proclaimed that she does not shun the stereotypical image of mother or other feminine roles if it is appealing to the electorate. She is also, however, referred to as the Iron Lady, reminiscent of Thatcher, due to Sirleaf's experience with the bloody war that has raged around her for the past fourteen years. The title also reflects her ability to maintain her position in such a male dominated world. Ironically, some of these same societies that elect women to positions of power do not afford basic rights to ordinary women. The United States, as the sole remaining superpower, does not seem ripe for women's leadership.[2]

Women leaders from the developing world have a different view of feminism and leadership than do women of the Western world. Some of the leaders we have profiled consider themselves mothers, not feminists. These leaders capitalize on the universal image of the mother to secure their positions of power. Yet, they do not all seek power the same way men do. Many of these women felt a calling to help their countries. It was power by invitation. They have also relied on family connections and martyrdom of a male family member.

In general, most key positions such as defense (both public and private sector) are still out of the reach of most women. Whether greater access to these positions by women will in fact change anything has yet to be seen. Even with the few who have sat in these positions (such as Kim Campbell of Canada), it appears that little will change in the world in terms of militarization and war in the near future at least. Although she never held the position of minister of defense per se, Thatcher was one woman world leader who appeared to have some influence on the military, albeit in fairly traditional terms (case in point, the Falklands war). Socialist Golda Meir also tried her hand at war. There is no guarantee that women always make a positive difference in terms of limiting military options, reducing arms, and promoting peaceful solutions to seemingly intractable world problems and sources of regional conflict.

It appears at least as easy for women to gain leadership positions if they come from their country's conservative party as for any other political party. Thatcher is the only women to have come to power in Great Britain. The British parliament has only 19.7 percent women and ranks 51st in the world.[3] Her coming from the conservative party and not being connected to any specific women's issues made her safe for established business and defense interests. They could rest assured that she would not deviate from mainstream policies of the party and pursue a progressive feminist agenda. The same could probably be said for Kim Campbell, who comes from Canada's conservative party. The latest addition would be Angela Merkel who comes from the CDU, the conservative party in Germany.

Although many of the world's religions revere women and the role of women in society, radical religious fundamentalism (especially in the United States and in some Muslim countries) seeks to push back gains made for women in terms of equality. This is closely related to violence versus women. Honor killings are on the rise from the Middle East to Sweden, and in the United States, the right to an abortion is under attack as the pro-life movement pressures the U.S. Congress to appoint Supreme Court justices that would overturn *Roe v. Wade* (1973).[4] Conservative Christians have flocked to the Republican Party in the United States—a party that protects corporate interests and promotes an aggressive foreign-policy agenda. Former U.S. President Jimmy Carter holds that religious fundamentalists (Christian or otherwise) believe that only their own concept of God is the proper one. And since they feel that they have the proper concept of God, they are particularly blessed and singled out for special consideration above and beyond those who disagree with them. Second, anyone who does disagree with them must be wrong, since God is on their side. The next step is to feel that the person who does not believe the way you do, is by definition, inferior to you. And then the ultimate progression of that is that you're not only different and wrong and inferior but in some ways you are subhuman. So there's a loss of concern, even about the deaths of those who disagree. And this takes fundamentalism to the extreme. Religious fundamentalism is dominated by men who use it to gain power in society and over women. They thereby hold to the proposition that women are inherently inferior.[5]

The impact of women leaders goes relatively unnoticed because women are still dramatically underrepresented in the most powerful nations, most noticeably in the United States. Many people in the United States believe that the 2008 election may see at least one woman candidate (Hillary Clinton more than likely).

Many people have criticized women who gain political opportunities based on family connections. What such criticisms ignore is that men have used such connections for years and no one has complained or made an issue of this.[6] The story of Sonia Gandhi and her failure to take a position of power in India perfectly illustrates many of the issues this book has addressed including family ties to leadership, the will to power, the power of nationalism and xenophobia, and women leaders in developing regions.

In the United States especially, it takes a lot of money to get elected. In 2004, it cost an average of $8 million to run a successful campaign for the U.S. Senate.[7] The fact is that women's issue organizations have little funding to support women candidates to office, whereas defense contractors and energy conglomerates have plenty of money and give it readily to male candidates, and thus women will continue to be underrepresented in national positions of power. The lack of a multiparty system is partly to blame as well as the campaign finance reform's failure to remedy the problem.[8]

Another problem that women face is that in terms of academic research, gender studies is code for women's studies. The ultra conservatives in the United States have been at war against feminists since the 1980s. Conservatives have a tendency to broad-brush all academics as left-wing radicals (just tune in to the U.S. cable network Fox News any given night). By narrowly focusing on women when studying gender, the point of equality is missed. Conservative talk shows on U.S. radio call feminists, "feminazis." A more inclusive study of gender would disarm these rightwing critics. The study of gender is the study of men and women. Polarizing debates never accomplishes much good. Unfortunately, some academics play right into the hands of the conservative radicals. When anyone needs to hire someone to deal with gender issues, it is assumed that only a woman can handle the job. This only serves to propagate stereotypes and relegate woman to certain well-defined, gender specific roles. We must realize that there are two genders and both are capable of studying gender issues.[9]

It is clear that the language of power is still male. Men dominate the areas of defense and energy industries. Only a few women representatives are allowed in, but are never in charge. The United States seems unwilling to allow women to become secretary of defense, vice president or president or CEO of any major defense contractor or oil company. It is assumed that this is a male domain. Strength is considered a male quality.

In a book named *The Myth of Male Power*, the author Will Farrell calls for a gender transition movement not specifically limited to men or feminists.

He shows how men's workshops and feminist organizations promulgate sexism and support limited goals while not fully addressing the issues and responsibilities involved in fully empowering both sexes. He claims that men still do the most dangerous jobs (including combat infantry) and die earlier than women do. As the subtitle of the book suggests, "The weakness of men is the facade of strength: the strength of women is the facade of weakness."

Although women make up almost half of America's labor force, only two Fortune 500 companies have women CEOs or presidents, and 90 of those 500 companies don't have any women corporate officers. Catalyst, the nonprofit New York-based women's research organization, points out, however, that its data shows a change over the past five years. A recent survey revealed that 10 percent of the Fortune 500 companies have women holding at least one-quarter of their corporate officer positions. This percentage rose from only 5 percent in 1995. Some political theorists believe in the "shrinking institutions theory," which holds that women are being elected to public office because real power is being shifted to the private sector, where men still dominate. Many other theorists discount this theory.[10] Often times in research, political considerations influence the outcome. Pointing out that corporate power has become more important than elected government itself tends to make those in power angry and likely do all that they can to stifle, discredit, and derail such conclusions.

GERALDINE FERRARO: THE TRAIL-BLAZER

In her acceptance speech in 1984, Geraldine Ferraro spoke of the realization of the American dream: "Tonight, the daughter of an immigrant from Italy has been chosen to run for vice president in the new land my father came to love." She is best known as the first and, so far, only woman to be a candidate for vice president of the United States on a major party ticket (although women on third-party tickets have and continue to run for the position). Geraldine Anne Ferraro was born on 26 August 1935 in Newburgh, New York.

Her father was an Italian immigrant who died when Ferraro was only 8 years old. She earned a J.D. degree from Fordham University School of Law, going to classes at night while working as a second-grade teacher in public schools during the day. She was one of only two women in her graduating class. She married John Zaccaro, a real estate manager, and raised three children. Her career began in the Queens County district attorney's office. Ferraro was then elected to Congress (New York's Ninth Congressional District in Queens) in 1978 and served three terms in the House of Representatives. During her six years in Congress, she had a liberal voting record, but stayed in close contact with conservative voters in her district. In Congress, Ferraro led efforts to pass the Equal Rights Amendment. As a Catholic, Ferraro was often criticized by the Roman Catholic Church for being pro-choice.

In 1984 Ferraro was chosen by Walter Mondale as the Democratic vice presidential nominee. The Mondale-Ferraro ticket was defeated in a massive landslide by President Ronald Reagan and Vice President George H.W. Bush in the 1984 election. During the vice presidential debate on 11 October 1984 in Philadelphia, Ferraro laid out the Mondale-Ferraro liberal vision for America:

> I hope somebody wants to applaud. Being the candidate for vice-president of my party is the greatest honor I have ever had. But it's not only a personal achievement for Geraldine Ferraro—and certainly not only the bond that I feel as I go across this country with women throughout the country. I wouldn't be standing here if Fritz Mondale didn't have the courage and my party didn't stand for the values that it does—the values of fairness and equal opportunity. Those values make our country strong and the future of this country and how strong it will be is what this election is all about. Over the last two months I've been traveling all over the country talking to the people about the future. I was in Kentucky and I spoke to the Dyhouse family. He works for a car dealer and he's worried about the deficits and how high interest rates are going to affect his job. Every place I go I see young parents with their children and they say to me what are we going to do to stop this nuclear arms race. I was in Dayton, Ohio, a week and a half ago and I sat with the Allen family who live next door to a toxic dump and they're very, very concerned about the fact that those toxics are seeping into the water that they and their neighbors drink. Now those people love this country and they're patriotic. But it's not the patriotism that you're seeing in the commercials as you watch television these days. Their patriotism is not only a pride in the country as it is, but a pride in this country that is strong enough to meet the challenges of the future. Do you know when we find jobs for the eight and a half million people who are unemployed in this country, you know we'll make our economy stronger and that will be a patriotic act. When we reduce the deficits and we cut interest rates, and I know the president doesn't believe that, but it's so—we cut those interest rates young people can buy houses, that's pro-family and that will be a patriotic act. When we educate our children—good Lord, they're going to be able to compete in a world economy and that makes us stronger and that's a patriotic act. When we stop the arms race, we make this a safer, saner world, and that's a patriotic act, and when we keep the peace young men don't die, and that's a patriotic act. Those are the keys to the future and who can be the leader for the future? When Walter Mondale was attorney general of Minnesota, he led the fight for a man who could not afford to get justice because he couldn't afford a lawyer; when he was in the Senate he fought for child nutrition programs, he wrote the Fair Housing Act, he even investigated the concerns and the abuses of migrant workers. And why did he do that? Those weren't popular causes. You know, no one had ever heard of

Clarence Gideon, the man without a lawyer. Children don't vote and migrant workers exactly a powerful lobby in this country, but he did it because it was right. Fritz Mondale has said that he would rather lose a battle for decency than win one over self-interest. Now I agree with him. This campaign is not over. For our country, for our future, for the principles we believe in Walter Mondale and I have just begun to fight.[11]

The Mondale-Ferraro ticket gained only one state, Mondale's home state of Minnesota. Reagan had galvanized his base and picked up defecting conservative Democrats (known as Reagan Democrats) who shied away from Mondale's liberal vision for America. Honesty about raising taxes backfired on Mondale. The Conservative Revolution was in full swing as the liberal policies dating back to FDR had run their course and did not play well with the electorate in the post-Vietnam War political culture. Although Mondale and Ferraro lost, Ferraro's candidacy changed the American perception of women in politics. She published an autobiography, *Ferraro: My Story*, in 1985, and in 1992 ran unsuccessfully for the U.S. Senate. From 1996–1998 she was cohost on *Crossfire* on CNN. In addition to being on the faculty at Georgetown University, Ferraro serves as president of G&L Strategies, a management consulting firm.

In 1993 Ferraro was appointed by President Clinton to lead the United States delegation to the United Nations Human Rights Commission. She was also the alternate United States delegate to the World Conference on Human Rights held in Vienna in June 1993. She is an active participant in the U.S. foreign policy debate, and serves as a board member of the National Democratic Institute of International Affairs and is a member of the Council on Foreign Relations. In addition to numerous articles, Ferraro has written two books: *Ferraro: My Story*, which recounts the 1984 campaign, and *Geraldine Ferraro: Changing History*.

WHEN WILL ANOTHER WOMAN BE NOMINATED?

Ever since Geraldine Ferraro's historic nomination as the Democratic vice presidential nominee in 1984, political observers have debated about when another woman would be nominated on a major party ticket in a presidential race. In her book, *My Story*, Ferraro recalled the historic 1984 presidential campaign as both "incredible" and a "personal agony." Upon her nomination there was euphoria and support among women's groups across the nation that an important political barrier had been broken, while after the nomination the grueling campaign schedule and public interrogations that Ferraro and her family had to undergo, mostly her husband's business dealings, took its toll emotionally. Yet Ferraro feels a sense of great accomplishment and optimism about future female candidates for national office. She said that her candidacy "was like a giant light bulb going on . . . A new political consciousness was born that no longer asked 'why' a woman candidate, but 'why not?' . . . The real test of my candidacy will come when the next woman runs for national office."[12]

Why neither the Democratic nor the Republican party had nominated a women as a vice presidential candidate since 1984, or why the excitement over Elizabeth Dole's brief jump into the 2000 Republican primaries was so short lived, are complex questions involving an elaborate analysis of electoral and party politics, voting behaviors, campaign finance, and the political environment at various levels of government. Our question is simpler: will the Republican and/or the Democratic party nominate a woman in the 2008 presidential race?

In general, we must look at characteristics of successful candidates. The constitutional requirements for the office of the presidency are rather simple—being at least 35 years old, a fourteen-year U.S. resident, and a natural born citizen—no other formal criteria exist for presidential candidates. That being said, other factors such as religion, race, and gender have tended to make the pool of candidates for both president and vice president almost exclusively Protestant, white, and male. John F. Kennedy, a Catholic, was the only non-Protestant to hold the office of the presidency. The health and age of the candidate, as well as family ties and personal relationships (particularly marital status and fidelity) are also important characteristics for both presidential and vice presidential candidates in the public's mind.

The character, personality, and style of presidential candidates have become extremely important during both the primaries and the general election. The main characteristics that Americans look for in a candidate include honesty, integrity, intelligence, strong communication skills, flexibility, compassion, open-mindedness, and a commitment to the democratic process. The pool of potential nominees has traditionally consisted of governors, prominent U.S. senators, a few members of the House of Representatives, and a handful of ex-governors or vice presidents who have managed to keep themselves in the news media.

A potential president must create a strong image of leadership in the minds of American voters. Appearing presidential, both during the campaign and once in office, is an essential ingredient for political success (Reagan is a good example of a candidate who acted presidential long before it was clear he was a serious candidate). Presidential candidates must exhibit both the knowledge and skills necessary for the job, and should appear to be strong, assertive, and dominant (important presidential skills in times of crisis).

When considering the current political environment for presidential candidates, as well as the leadership challenges that a president faces while in office, how would a woman perform under these conditions? Given the necessary traits it takes to run for president, as well as the skills necessary to be a successful leader in the White House, it is important to know how women have fared as candidates for Congress or statewide offices. Women have made gains in the past decade in holding more elected positions at both the state and federal level, but barriers still exist for women seeking elected government positions. These barriers, that can either deter women from running for office or keep them from winning if they do run, include:

1. stereotypes (politics interferes with the traditional female role in society);
2. career choice and preparation (women are underrepresented in traditional work fields for politicians such as law and business);
3. family demands (women are still the primary care-givers);
4. sex discrimination (lack of party support for women candidates); and
5. the political system (money, campaign finance laws, party organization, winner-take-all electoral systems, and incumbency).

In many campaigns, news media coverage has perpetuated negative stereotyping of women candidates. The news media pays more attention to style than substance when covering female candidates. Since many voters may doubt the policy qualifications of women candidates, news coverage that downplays issues and highlights personal traits develops less favorable images for female candidates. Also, traditionally "male" issues (the economy, defense, foreign policy) are highlighted during U.S. Senate campaigns, while traditionally "female" issues (education, health care) are emphasized in gubernatorial races. Women candidates also need to stress typically "male" traits, such as competence and leadership, during their campaigns.

Studies also suggest that women continue to face barriers once they hold an elected office. In both Congress and state legislatures, positions of power and leadership are based on seniority within the institution. Since many women become elected officials later in life than men, due mostly to family responsibilities, they are at an immediate disadvantage in moving up within the leadership ranks. Many women legislators at both the state and federal levels have reported attempts by their male colleagues to keep them out of leadership positions. Similarly, women have difficulty in obtaining the position of committee chair since they often lack the necessary seniority. Women are also routinely appointed to committees dealing with traditional women's issues, such as education and health, and are often denied appointments to the more powerful and prestigious committees dealing with economic policy (or defense and/or foreign policy in Congress).

Studies that have looked at gendered differences in leadership show that in some areas, particularly politics and business, women often bring "a more open, democratic, and people-centered approach to their leadership positions." However, it has also been suggested that a more inclusive and participatory approach to leadership is not exclusive to women, and that since women have yet to reach parity with men in leadership positions, not enough evidence yet exists to categorize leadership styles based on gender alone.[13]

Based on the foregoing, we will look at two likely presidential candidates for 2008: Hillary Rodham Clinton and Condoleezza Rice.

THE 2008 ELECTION: A SHOWDOWN OF COMPETING FEMINISMS?

It took 200 years for the first woman to be elected to the U.S. Senate in her own right. In 1978, Nancy Kassebaum of Kansas was voted into office.[14] In 1992, there were two women senators and by 2001, the number had grown to thirteen. Today, a record fourteen women hold this prestigious office. These women are transforming the Senate in spite of their being outnumbered by male senators. The fact that the United States did not ratify *the Convention on the Elimination of All Forms of Discrimination against Women (CEDAW)* is both disturbing and perhaps partially an explanation for the lack of women leaders in the United States.[15] Americans have great difficulty dealing with international law and its effect on U.S. law and policies. Some have called this rugged individualism. By accepting international laws that could potentially set a precedence for influencing policies in the United States, this would provide a significant threat to the domination of the defense and oil industries in America today.[16]

In terms of a woman ascending to the highest office, that of U.S. president, we can only imagine when that will happen. Occupying polar opposite political ideological perspectives, it could be useful to imagine a hypothetical confrontation between Hillary Rodham Clinton and Condoleezza Rice in the U.S. presidential election in 2008. This hypothetical examination may bring to light why a woman has not come to power yet in the United States and what such a rise to power would entail.

The current Bush administration foreign policy of preemption[17] would most likely continue if Secretary of State Rice became president. But what would Hillary do if she were elected president? If this political contest actually took place, the most powerful nation on earth would have come to quite a crossroads. The choice in this hypothetical 2008 election would be between secular democratic liberalism[18] and fundamentalist neoconservatism.[19]

We must assume that the only way a woman will win the U.S. presidency is if she is a martyr, a mother figure, or conservative enough to not pose a threat to the establishment (just like in Asia). We have seen that Hillary Clinton continues to move right politically in the run up to the next presidential election cycle. Her handlers have discovered that the more conservative she becomes, the more voters she attracts. In terms of the Iraq War, she is not siding with antiwar activists, in fact, she is closer to the administration policies in that regard. Also, you do not hear Clinton talking about health care other than electronic health records reform (even going as far as to team up with the conservative former Republican Speaker of the house, Newt Gingrich). It is important not to forget that Hillary was a Goldwater Republican early in her life. She has very conservative roots.

By focusing on Hillary Clinton and her chances in the next election one can see what is wrong with the U.S. electoral system. By 1975 the Vietnam War had destroyed the New Deal coalition that had allowed the Democrats to dominate since Roosevelt's four consecutive terms. The election of Jimmy Carter in 1976 was a rejection of the political system entirely, since Carter had no Washington connections. His was a transitional tenure. The real change came with the election of Ronald Reagan. Reagan ushered in the Conservative Revolution that basically dismantled the New Deal, piece by piece. The notion of the federal government as the protector of the common man changed. The federal government's role became one of promoting corporatization and the destruction of labor unions. The strides that had been made in terms of women's rights and civil rights in general reached their zenith in the mid-1970s shortly after the *Roe v. Wade* decision. The coalition that formed around Reagan included big business, defense industry, and fundamentalist Christian groups. In other words, Americans had a better chance of getting a woman president prior to 1980 than they do now.

HILLARY RODHAM CLINTON
Life Before Politics

Hillary Diane Rodham was born in Chicago, Illinois, on 26 October 1947. She has two younger brothers, Hugh and Tony. Hillary spent her childhood in Park Ridge, Illinois, where she enjoyed sports and her church, and was a member of the National Honor Society, and a student leader. She pursued her undergraduate education at Wellesley College. Hillary supported the candidacy of Barry Goldwater in the 1964 presidential election. At Yale Law School in 1969, Hillary served on the board of editors of the *Yale Law Review* and *Social Action*, interned with children's advocate Marian Wright Edelman, and met Bill Clinton.

After graduation, Hillary advised the Children's Defense Fund in Cambridge and joined the impeachment inquiry staff advising the Judiciary Committee of the House of Representatives. After completing those responsibilities, she moved to Arkansas where Bill had begun his political career.

Bill and Hillary married in 1975. She joined the faculty of the University of Arkansas Law School in 1975 and the Rose Law Firm in 1976. In 1978, President Jimmy Carter appointed her to the board of the Legal Services Corporation, and Bill Clinton became governor of Arkansas. Their daughter, Chelsea, was born in 1980.

Political Career

Hillary served as Arkansas's First Lady for twelve years, balancing family, law, and public service. As the nation's First Lady, Hillary continued to balance public service with private life. Her active role began in 1993 when the president asked her to chair the Task Force on National Health Care Reform. She continued to be a leading advocate for expanding health insurance coverage, ensuring children are properly immunized, and raising public awareness of health issues. She wrote a weekly newspaper column entitled "Talking It Over," which focused on her experiences as First Lady and her observations of women, children, and families she has met around the world. Her 1996 book *It Takes a Village and Other Lessons Children Teach Us* was a best seller.

As First Lady, her public involvement with many activities sometimes led to controversy. Undeterred by critics, Hillary won many admirers for her staunch support for women around the world and her commitment to children's issues. Bill Clinton was the first *Baby Boomer* elected to the White House, a cultural shift that generated controversy, and his wife Hillary quickly became the most politically active First Lady in American history. In 1993 the president asked her to chair the Task Force on National Health Care Reform, dedicated to reforming the American health care system, commonly known as the complex Clinton health care plan, which, despite Clinton's campaign promises to the country, made no progress in Congress and was abandoned in September 1994. Opponents seized on Hillary Clinton's role in drafting the plan, dubbing it "Hillarycare." Both Clintons were criticized that it was inappropriate for a First Lady to play a role in matters of public policy.

When long-time New York Senator Daniel Patrick Moynihan announced his intent to retire, intense speculation began over the possibility of Hillary Clinton moving to New York to run for Senate in the election. Leading New York Democrats, including Moynihan himself, urged her to run. Initially, she forcefully insisted she would not do so, but eventually changed her mind, and in a blaze of international publicity, made a run for the seat, thus becoming the first sitting First Lady to be a candidate for elected office. She was elected U.S. Senator from New York on 7 November 2000.

Senator Clinton serves on the Senate Committees for Environment and Public Works; Health, Education, Labor, and Pensions; and is the first New York Senator to serve on the Senate Armed Services Committee. During the 108th Congress, Senator Clinton made homeland security, economic security, and national security her top priorities. Senator Clinton's latest book, *Living History*, was released in June of 2003. *Living History* was an immediate best seller, selling more than 1.5 million copies in the United States and another 1.5 million copies abroad.

Legacies: Possible Run for the White House?

Senator Clinton has a well-established national image that makes her future political aspirations a popular and highly controversial topic among media pundits, bloggers, and the public at large. In particular, she has been frequently discussed as a possible presidential candidate in 2008. After months of speculation, Clinton herself announced in November 2004 that she would run for a second term in the Senate in 2006. Confirming this in an article in the *New York Times*, her advisors and congressional allies admit that this will further complicate an already contentious situation. One congressional ally remarked that if Senator Clinton were perceived as a viable candidate for the 2008 nomination, "the whole Republican apparatus" would focus its attention on knocking her out of the Senate race in 2006.

There is little room in the political calendar between the bid for the 2006 Senate race and the start of the 2008 campaign schedule: the Iowa caucuses will be held just fourteen months after the Senate election. If Clinton followed recent tradition, she would be sending out feelers for the presidential bid within weeks after her Senate race was completed. Senator John Kerry was in a similar position in 2002 (though his seat in the Senate was broadly considered safely Democratic). Kerry was reelected that November, and soon after, began his campaign for the presidency. Ari Fleischer, a former aide to President Bush, says the 2008 Democratic nomination for president is all Hillary Rodham Clinton's if she wants it.

Polls have shown Clinton leading the field for the Democratic presidential nomination. Nonetheless, the former first lady and her top aides maintain her focus is on winning a second Senate term in 2006, and they have stopped talking publicly about the White House and the next presidential election. Even so, veteran Republican operative Arthur Finkelstein has launched a campaign called "Stop Her Now," featuring telephone calls aimed at "spreading the truth about Hillary Clinton and her dangerous plans for our country."

Table 7.5
Senator Hillary Rodham Clinton Approval Ratings

	Feb 2002	Feb 2005
Overall	58 percent	69 percent
Republicans	37 percent	49 percent

Another measure of how far Senator Clinton has come was when Senator John McCain, Republican from Arizona, said on "Meet the Press" that he thought Clinton, a Democrat, would make a good president, although he said that he would support his party's nominee. She returned the compliment, saying when asked by the program's host, Tim Russert, that Senator McCain would also be a good president.

Senator Clinton has strong bipartisan support in New York. Her approval ratings are shown in Table 7.5.

In October 2005, Clinton held a 65 percent favorable rating, one of the highest in the Senate. She continues to have the support of Republicans as well as Democrats.[20]

The changing view of Senator Clinton coincides with a period following the November election in which she offered a series of speeches filled with references to faith and prayer, while putting less emphasis on polarizing social issues such as gay marriage and abortion. The result of these comments has been an emerging image of Senator Clinton that is far different from the caricature that Republicans have painted of her: that of a secular liberal whose stances are largely at odds with a public that they say is concerned about the nation's moral direction.

The new attitudes toward Clinton may be forcing Republicans to reconsider how to deal with an opponent they had until now viewed as an enticing target because of the depth of negative feelings she inspires among large numbers of New York voters. Clinton could run as a Lieberman Democrat (Senator Joe Lieberman being a conservative Democratic senator from Connecticut). With her charisma and by stressing her social conservatism on some issues, she could generate the momentum which Lieberman himself lacked in his presidential bid in 2004.

To be sure, Clinton has cast many roll-call votes that make conservatives cringe: for example, she voted against the bill banning the procedure known as partial-birth abortion. But on other issues she seems to be shifting right. In March 2005 Senator Clinton joined conservative Senator Rick Santorum from Pennsylvania to sound an alarm on electronic media effects on children

Senators Clinton, Santorum, and Lieberman of Connecticut requested $90 million in federal funds for research on how the Internet, i-Pods, and other electronic media affect children's emotional and behavioral development. The senators pointed to research by the Kaiser Family

Foundation reporting that on average American children spend 6.5 hours a day watching television, staring at Web sites, or using other electronic media. "We are exposing children to so much media that it is becoming the dominant force in so many children's lives," Clinton told reporters. Some see this and her 25 January 2005 speech on teenage sexual abstinence as a shift to a more conservative stance. But Clinton also talked about abstinence in her speech to the abortion rights group NARAL six years ago, even if she didn't make it her primary focus. Clinton seems to be pushing the idea that she is not a doctrinaire cultural liberal and that she has consistently favored working toward conservative goals (preservation of the family, protection of children) by using activist government means.

Republicans and Democrats who believe that Hillary Clinton could never be elected president may be wrong. A Fox News poll taken in January 2005 showed that, Americans felt Hillary Clinton was "qualified to be president of the United States" by 59–34 percent. Clinton showed strength among all traditional Democratic voters, winning the approval of John Kerry supporters by 80–13, blacks by 80–8, all women by 64–29 and unmarried women by 69–24, and people under 30 by 73–20.

But she also did well among more traditionally Republican constituencies. Men said she was qualified by 53–40. Southerners agreed by 55–36, as did those earning more than $75,000 per year, who felt she was qualified by 58–39. While 80 percent of liberals felt she was qualified, so did 59 percent of moderates and 43 percent of self-described conservatives. Incredibly, so did 33 percent of Republicans and 37 percent of Bush voters. Whether or not these people polled would actually vote for Clinton is another matter, but she is a serious candidate, and a serious threat to the Republican hold on power.

The Fox News poll tested Hillary against several possible 2008 GOP contenders and found that she ran ahead of Florida Governor Jeb Bush by 46–35, ahead of New York Governor George Pataki by 41–35 and ahead of Senate Majority Leader Bill Frist by 40–33. There does not seem to be any basis for believing that a Hillary Clinton candidacy would trigger

Table 7.6
Clinton Polling Data for 2008

Giuliani	50 percent
Clinton	43 percent
McCain	50 percent
Clinton	41 percent
Clinton	50 percent
Rice	41 percent

Source: http://www.pollingreport.com/2008.htm

a backlash among men, conservatives, and Republicans. The strongest candidates against Hillary are former New York Mayor Rudy Giuliani, Senator John McCain of Arizona, and Secretary of State Condoleezza Rice. But each of those Republican challengers would have to be nominated by his or her party first. With Giuliani you have to ask: can a pro-abortion-rights, pro-affirmative-action, pro-gay-rights, pro-gun-control, pro-immigration moderate win Republican primaries?

In a WNBC/Marist Poll taken in October 2005, Clinton fared as shown in Table 7.6 against opponents in the 2008 presidential election.

Unlike Giuliani, McCain and Rice could probably both win the Republican nomination. A social conservative who will elaborate her largely traditional views on important values issues as an inevitable part of her service as secretary of state, Rice can win primaries. McCain has broad support and could also win primaries, and with his recent successful challenge to President Bush regarding use of torture in the War on Terror, he may have gathered international support as well.

Hillary Clinton is the strongest democratic contender since her husband ran. Like Bill, she will tack to the center and take a traditional line on controversial social issues such as gay marriage. It has been said that Bill was a moderate who became a liberal when he had to and that Hillary is a liberal who pretends moderation when she has to.

Ronald Reagan used to be a New Deal Democrat. He was fond of saying that he did not leave the Democratic Party, the party left him. Hillary could be using her conservative roots, having been a Barry Goldwater supporter, to gain conservative supporters. Reagan Democrats were comforted by the fact that he used to be a Democrat, Clinton Republicans may feel comforted by the fact that she used to be a Republican, and a very conservative one at that. But political operatives in the Democratic Party think that she is a loser. This is similar to the Republicans who felt that Reagan was too conservative, too old, and just a movie actor who could never be elected president. Democratic operatives have said that Clinton is too liberal, too feminist, and too connected to Bill Clinton. But the poll numbers do not support these generalizations. She has broad support. Clinton, like Reagan in 1980, has much more charisma than her party opponents. Clinton, according to a recent Gallup poll, is considered a moderate by 30 percent of those polled, and 9 percent even think she is conservative. The National Journal rates each of the U.S. senators for liberalism based on votes concerning economic issues, social issues, and foreign policy issues. Clinton got a score of 71 percent which placed her right in the middle of other democrats (John Kerry had the highest liberal score by the way).

Americans may be ready to elect a woman president: 74 percent told Gallup that they'd be either "somewhat" or "very" likely to vote for a woman in 2008. In 1999, 56 women sat in the House of Representatives, and 9 in the Senate and only 3 women were governors. Six years later, there are 14 women in the Senate, 66 in the House, and 8 women governors.

To win, Clinton has to play electoral college politics. She needs Florida, Iowa, New Mexico, and Ohio. Whoever wins in 2008 will be a candidate (1) with charisma, money, and a broad following in his or her party; and (2) with a ticket that espouses the values and policies that folks in the heartland of middle America agree with. That just might be Senator Hillary Clinton.

McCain may be the most serious threat to Clinton in 2008. But the Republican conservative base remains leery of him. To edge out McCain, Clinton will need the equivalent of Karl Rove. Someone who is a winner and understands the political undercurrents and is ruthless if need be. Hillary has Bill, McCain does not have someone of that skill level in his camp.

CONDOLEEZZA RICE

Life Before Politics

Condoleezza Rice was born on 14 November 1954 in Birmingham, Alabama under the specter of racial segregation. Rice said that to get ahead she had to be "twice as good" as others. Growing up under segregation galvanized her strong determination and sense of self-respect. Taught by her parents that education provided armor against segregation and prejudice, Rice worked her way to college by the age of 15. She earned her bachelor's degree in political science from the University of Denver in 1974. She went on to earn her master's from the University of Notre Dame in 1975, and her Ph.D. from the Graduate School of International Studies at the University of Denver in 1981.

Political Career

In June 1999, she completed a six-year tenure as Stanford University's Provost, during which she was the institution's chief budget and academic officer. As Provost she was responsible for a $1.5 billion annual budget and an academic program involving 1,400 faculty members and 14,000 students.

As professor of political science, Dr. Rice has been on the Stanford faculty since 1981 and has won two of the highest teaching honors— the 1984 Walter J. Gores Award for Excellence in Teaching and the 1993 School of Humanities and Sciences Dean's Award for Distinguished Teaching.

At Stanford, she has been a member of the Center for International Security and Arms Control, a Senior Fellow of the Institute for

International Studies, and a Fellow (by courtesy) of the Hoover Institution. Her books include *Germany Unified and Europe Transformed* (1995) with Philip Zelikow, *The Gorbachev Era* (1986) with Alexander Dallin, and *Uncertain Allegiance: The Soviet Union and the Czechoslovak Army* (1984). She has also written numerous articles on Soviet and East European foreign and defense policy, and has addressed audiences in settings ranging from the U.S. Ambassador's residence in Moscow to the Commonwealth Club to the 1992 and 2000 Republican National Conventions.

From 1989 through March 1991, the period of German reunification and the final days of the Soviet Union, she served in the Bush administration as director, and then senior director, of Soviet and East European Affairs in the National Security Council, and a special assistant to the president for National Security Affairs. In 1986, while an international affairs fellow of the Council on Foreign Relations, she served as special assistant to the director of the Joint Chiefs of Staff. In 1997, she served on the Federal Advisory Committee on Gender—Integrated Training in the Military.

She was a member of the boards of directors for the Chevron Corporation, the Charles Schwab Corporation, the William and Flora Hewlett Foundation, the University of Notre Dame, the International Advisory Council of J.P. Morgan, and the San Francisco Symphony Board of Governors.

It is difficult to make generalizations about Condoleezza Rice. She is an African-American woman serving as secretary of state, but for a Republican administration that won just 10 percent of the black vote. Some profiles of Rice describe her as precise and prissy. Rice's belief in education and self-improvement seem to be the key to understanding her.

Dr. Condoleezza Rice became secretary of state on 26 January 2005. Prior to this, she was the assistant to the president for National Security Affairs, commonly referred to as the national security advisor, since January 2001.

Condoleezza Rice is the first woman to occupy the key post of national security adviser. She is the most academic member of the Bush foreign affairs team and, because of her gender, background and youth, one of the most distinctive. She is personally close to President Bush, barely leaving his side during the 2000 presidential election. And, as a well-liked and trusted policy adviser, she has proved a useful ally for a president with little experience of foreign affairs.

Rice's influence over the new administration's early foreign policy strategy has been considerable. She led the tricky negotiations with Russia (her academic specialization) over missile defense, and is thought to have spearheaded the unilateralist tone of the first months of the Bush presidency.

Her uncompromising positions on missile defense, Russia, and the environment won respect, and helped build the European picture of the new president as a swaggering cowboy. She has since admitted that the Kyoto decision could have been handled better.

However, Rice, like many in the administration, thinks of U.S. foreign policy largely in terms of U.S. national and strategic interest, and she is no fan of the United States acting as a nation-builder.

Legacies: A Run for the White House?

Condoleezza Rice described her ideology best in a speech she made recently in Brazil:

> Our world is moving toward greater freedom and democracy. And President Bush has outlined the charge of our times: Those of us who are on the right side of freedom's divide have an obligation to those who are still on the wrong side of that divide...Our challenge now is to use the power of our democratic partnership for two great purposes: to deliver the benefits of democracy to all of our citizens...and to support all peoples who desire democratic change—wherever they may live on this globe...Education gives people the power to rise as high as their natural talents will take them. Social mobility, fueled by merit and encumbered by nothing, must be the goal of every democracy...Those on the margins of society must know that, even if their lives are not what they had hoped, their children will have a bright future and limitless horizons.[21]

Based on the fact that her interests, ideology, and career pattern seeks to reinforce the established male dominant culture of war and worldwide energy monopolization, she will be seen as a safe choice for the highest office in the United States. Neoconservatism has joined with Reaga-nomics[22] to form the nucleus of the Republican stranglehold on power in the United States. Condoleezza is at the center of this dynamic power structure. In a hypothetical race between Rice and Clinton, polls show that Clinton would win. The only way Rice could beat Clinton would be if she could push Hillary to the left out of the conservative center comfort zone that she is creating for herself. A McCain/Rice ticket would be extremely tough for Hillary to beat.

Appendix: Women in Power

NAME	COUNTRY	IN OFFICE		TITLE	US GNP	REGION	VOTE	PARTY
Aquino, Corazon	Philippines	1986–1992	X	President	5000	A	1937	Centrist
Arteaga, Rosalia	Ecuador	1997		President	3700	LA	1967	Liberal-Centrist
Bachelet, Michelle	Chile	2006–	X C	President	10700	LA	1949	Liberal-Centrist
Bandaranaike, Sirimavo	Sri Lanka	1960–1965, 1970–1977, 1994–2000	X	Prime Minister	4000	A	1931	Liberal
Barbara, Agatha	Malta	1982–1987		President	18200	E	1947	Liberal
Bergman-Pohl, Sabine	German Democratic Republic	1990		President	n/a	E	1918	Communist
Bhutto, Benazir	Pakistan	1988–1990, 1993–1996	X	Prime Minister	470	A	1947	Liberal
Boye, Madior	Senegal	2001–2002		Prime Minister	500	AF	1945	Liberal
Brundtland, Gro Harlem	Norway	1981, 1986–1996	X	Prime Minister	40000	E	1913	Liberal
Busigani, Patricia	San Marino	1993		Captain Regent	34600	E	1959	
Campbell, Kim	Canada	1993	X	Prime Minister	20140	NA	1918	Conservative
Ceccoli, Edda	San Marino	1991–1992		Captain Regent	34600	E	1959	
Chammoro, Violeta de	Nicaragua	1990–1996	X	President	410	LA	1955	Centrist
Charles, Eugenia	Dominica	1980–1995		Prime Minister	5500	CAR	1951	Conservative
Çiller, Tansu	Turkey	1993–1996	X	Prime Minister	2900	ME	1930	Conservative
Clark, Helen	New Zealand	1999–	C	President	23200	AP	1893	Liberal-Centrist
Costa Gomez-Mattheeuws, Lucinda da	Netherlands Antilles	1977		Prime Minister	11400	CAR		Conservative
Cresson, Edith	France	1991–1992	X	Prime Minister	24170	E	1944	Liberal
das Neves, Maria	Sao Tome and Principe	2002–	C	Prime Minister	1200	AF	1975	Socialist
Degutiene, Irena	Lithuania	1999		Prime Minister	12500	E	1921	Conservative
Domitien, Elizabeth	Central African Republic	1975–1976		Prime Minister	1100	AF	1986	Centrist
Dreifuss, Ruth	Switzerland	1998–1999		President	33800	E	1971	Liberal

NAME	COUNTRY	IN OFFICE			TITLE	US GNP	REGION	VOTE	PARTY
Finnbogadottir, Vigdis	Iceland	1980–1996	X		President	25000	E	1915	NP
Gandhi, Indira	India	1966–1977, 1980–1984	X		Prime Minister	3100	A	1949	Socialist
Godett, Mirna Louisa	Netherlands Antilles	2003–2004			Prime Minister	11400	CAR		Socialist
Gordon, Pamela	Bermuda	1997–1998			Premier	36000	CAR	1944	
Gueilier, Lidia	Bolivia	1979–1980			President	2600	LA	1938	Socialist
Halonen, Tarja K.	Finland	2000–	X	C	President	29000	E	1906	Liberal
Indzhova, Renata	Bulgaria	1994–1995			Prime Minister	8200	E	1947	NP
Jaatteenmaaki, Annelli	Finland	2003			Prime Minister	29000	E	1906	Centrist
Jagan, Janet	Guyana	1997–1999			Prime Minister	3800	LA	1945	Socialist
Johnson-Sirleaf, Ellen	Liberia	2005–	X	C	President	900	AF	1946	Centrist
Kinigi, Silvie	Burundi	1993–1994	X		President	600	AF	1961	Conservative
Kumaratunga, Chandrika	Sri Lanka	1994–		C	President	4000	A	1931	Liberal
Macapagal-Arroyo, Gloria	Philippines	2001–		C	President	5000	A	1937	Centrist
McAleese, Mary	Ireland	1997–		C	President	31900	E	1945	Conservative
Meir, Golda	Israel	1969–1974	X		Prime Minister	20800	ME	1948	Liberal
Merino-Lucero, Beatriz	Peru	2003			Prime Minister	5600	LA	1955	NP
Merkel, Angela	Germany	2005–	X	C	Chancellor	28700	E	1918	Conservative
Michelotti, Maria Domenica	San Marino	2000			Captain Regent	34600	E	1959	
Micic, Natasa	Serbia	2002			President	2370	E		Liberal
Moscoso Rodrguez, Mireya Elisa	Panama	1999–2004	X		President	6900	LA	1941	Conservative
Pascal-Trouillot, Ertha	Haiti	1990–1991			President	1500	CAR	1950	NP
Pedini-Angelini, Maria	San Marino	1981			Captain Regent	34600	E	1959	
Peron, Isabel	Argentina	1974–1976	X		President	12400	LA	1947	Conservative
Perry, Ruth	Liberia	1996–1997			Chairman State Council	900	AF	1946	Conservative

Peters, Maria Liberia	Netherlands Antilles			1984-1986, 1988-1994	Prime Minister	11400	CAR		Conservative
Petersen, Marita	Faroe Islands			1993-1994	Prime Minister	22000	E		Liberal
Pintassilgo, Maria de Lourdes	Portugal			1979-1980	Prime Minister	17900	E	1934	NP
Planinc, Milka	Yugoslavia			1982-1986	Prime Minister	n/a	E		Communist
Plavsic, Biljana	Bosnia-Hercegovina			1996-1998	President	6500	E	1949	Centrist
Prunskiene, Kazimiera	Lithuania			1990-1991	President	12500	E	1921	Centrist
Rannocchini, Gloriana	San Marino			1984, 1989-1990	Captain Regent	34600	E	1959	Liberal
Robinson, Mary	Ireland	X		1990-1997	President	31900	E	1945	Conservative
Romer, Suzanne	Netherlands Antilles			1993, 1998-1999	Prime Minister	11400	CAR		NP
Sang, Chang	South Korea			2002	Prime Minister	8490	A	1946	Conservative
Shipley, Jenny	New Zealand			1997-1999	Prime Minister	23200	AP	1893	Liberal
Smith, Jennifer	Bermuda			1998-2003	Premier	36000	CAR	1944	Liberal-Centrist
Suchocka, Hanna	Poland			1992-1993	Prime Minister	12000	E	1918	Conservative
Sukarnoputri, Megawati	Indonesia	X	C	2001-	President	600	A	1945	
Thatcher, Margaret	England	X		1979-1990	Prime Minister	23590	E	1918	Conservative
Tuyaa, Nyam-Osoriyn	Mongolia			1999	Prime Minister	1900	A	1924	Conservative-Centrist
Uwilingiyimana, Agathe	Rwanda	X		1993	Prime Minister	250	AF	1961	NP
Vike-Freiberga, Vaira	Latvia		C	1999-	President	11500	E	1918	Liberal
Wajed, Sheikh Hasina	Bangladesh			1996-2001	Prime Minister	2000	A	1972	Liberal
Werleigh, Claudette	Haiti			1995-1996	Prime Minister	1500	CAR	1950	
Zafferani, Rosa	San Marino			1999	Captain Regent	34600	E	1959	
Zia, Khaleda	Bangladesh		C	1991-1996, 2001-	Prime Minister	2000	A	1972	Conservative

X=Biography included in this book; C=Current leader; D=Developed; N=Newly developed; L=Less developed; NA=North America; E=Europe; CAR=Caribbean; AF=Africa; LA=Latin America; A=Asia; AP=Asia/Pacific; ME=Middle East.

Notes

CHAPTER 1: INTRODUCTION

1. Edward Gibbon, *The History of the Decline and Fall of the Roman Empire*, ed. J.B. Bury, 7 vols, vol. I (1896), 149. Obtained from Antonia Fraser, *The Warrior Queens: The Legends and the Lives of the Women who have Led Their Nations in War*. Markam, Ontario: Penguin Books Canada, 1990, 9.

2. Statistics from the Inter-Parliamentary Union, April 2000.

3. Ibid.

4. Note that this claim is based on the information we have available to us in 2005—this situation can change in any of these countries with one election.

CHAPTER 2: WOMEN IN THEORY AND PRACTICE

1. Here we use the term gender and sex interchangeably. There is a debate as to whether this is an accurate or effective use of these terms, but for the purposes of this book which is meant to provide an overview of the debates rather than engage in more detailed, substantial, and/or academic issues, it suffices to equate these terms.

2. Sarler, Carol, 29 December 2005, "We've Gone from Being Amazons to Can't Cope, Won't Cope Wusses," *Times Online*. Internet. Available at: http://www.timesonline.co.uk/article/0,,1072-1961661,00.html accessed on 21 April 2006.

3. See the discussion in Chapter 1 on employment equity and affirmative action.

4. Sarler, Carol, 29 December 2005, "We've Gone from Being Amazons to Can't Cope, Won't Cope Wusses," *Times Online*. Internet. Available at http://www.timesonline.co.uk/article/0,,1072-1961661,00.html accessed on 21 April 2006.

5. Sarler.

6. In other words, these differences were not rooted in biology, but in masculinist structures that were designed to oppress women.

7. Hollander, 2002: 490.

8. Drude Dahlerup, available at: http://www.nikk.uio.no/publikasjoner/nikkmagasin/news/news992.pdf accessed on 21 April 2006.

CHAPTER 3: AFRICA AND THE MIDDLE EAST

1. Development Bank of South Africa, *Development Report 2003: Statistics*. Available at: http://www.dbsa.org/document/pDevelopmentReport/devreport2003/StatSocial.pdf accessed on 12 December 2005.

2. Ibid.

3. Ibid.

4. Robert F.Worth, "The Reach of War; Government; In Jeans or Veils, Iraqi Women are Spilt on New Political Power." *New York Times*, 13 April 2005.

5. Ibid.

6. Arab Human Development Report, 2004: I.

CHAPTER 5: EUROPE

1. Information accessed at: http://europa.eu.int/comm/employment_social/gender_equality/index_en.html. Accessed website on 21 April 2006.

2. Technically, the term "Norden" refers to all five Nordic countries: Norway, Iceland, Sweden, Denmark, and Finland. Scandinavia usually refers only to Norway, Sweden, and Denmark. For the purposes of this book, I use the more common term "Scandinavia" to mean all five Nordic countries.

3. Haavio-Mannila and Skard, 1985: 2.

4. Mim Kelber, ed., *Women and Government: New Ways to Political Power*. Westport, CT: Praeger, 1994, 61–62; Marit Tovsen, "Women in Politics in Norway." Seminar paper for Women from Eastern Europe, Denmark, 19 August 1992, mimeograph, 3; Erna Solberg, member of Parliament, Bergen, Norway. Interviews conducted between 8th and 10th March 1995 in Seattle, Washington.

5. Norwegian Equal Status Council, "Women in Politics: Equality and Empowerment." Oslo, Norway, 1994, 1–9.

6. For ODA as percentage of GNP data, please see: http://www.oecd.org; Tovsen, 1992: 4; Solberg interview.

CHAPTER 6: THE AMERICAS

1. John Tierney, "Male Pride and Female Prejudice." *New York Times*. 3 January 2006. Internet. Accessed at: http://select.nytimes.com/2006/01/03/opinion/03tierney.html?tsType=try&oid=82&oids=81 I 82&incamp=ts:chall_article_trial&headline=Male+Pride+and+Female+Prejudice& on 3 January 2006.

2. The telephone poll of 1,125 registered voters was conducted between 10th and 17th February and has a sampling error margin of plus or minus 3 percentage points. The results were first reported in the *Times Union* of Albany.

3. A more in-depth discussion of these leadership hopefuls is presented in the concluding chapter.

4. Edward Keenan, "Daylight upon Magic: The Essential Truth of the Martin Coronation Metaphor." *Eye Weekly*. 20 November 2003. Internet. Accessed at: http://www.eye.net/eye/issue/issue_11.20.03/city/liberals-web.html on 1 January 2006.

CHAPTER 7: CONCLUSION

1. See Bruce O. Solheim, *On Top of the World: Political Leadership in Scandinavia and Beyond*. Westport, CT: Greenwood, 2000, 6–7.

2. Preservation of empire, both commercial and military, and securing ever diminishing stores of petroleum does not seem to be a job that Americans want to assign to a woman. For instance, energy industry companies contributed 75 percent of their political campaign finance money to mostly male Republican candidates in 2004. There is a clear connection between energy interests and the defense industry. It is no secret to people in the Middle East and around the world that the United States had designs on Iraq's oil prior to the invasion. Controlling oil fields was all part of the plan, not securing democracy for the Iraqi people as it is now claimed, or to destroy Hussein's weapons of mass destruction (WMD) as was claimed at the outset of the war. That is why insurgents are blowing up oil fields, to keep the oil and the money from the oil out of the hands of Shell and Chevron billionaires. See *Secret US Plans for Iraq's Oil* by Greg Palast, accessed at: http://news.bbc.co.uk/1/hi/programmes/newsnight/4354269.stm on 21 April 2006.

3. Information accessed at: http://www.ipu.org/wmn-e/classif.htm on 21 April 2006.

4. Thousands of girls and women across the globe (although mostly centered in the Middle East) are murdered by male family members each year in the name of family honor. Honor killings are executed for instances of rape, infidelity, flirting, or any other instance perceived as disgracing the family's honor, and the woman is then killed by a male relative to restore the family's name in the community. Many women are killed based on suspicions of a family member and are not given the chance to defend themselves. The allegation alone is enough to defile a man's or family's honor and is therefore enough to justify the killing of the woman. The men who commit the murder typically go unpunished or receive reduced sentences.

Honor killings have been reported in Bangladesh, Brazil, Ecuador, Egypt, India, Israel, Italy, Jordan, Morocco, Pakistan, Sweden, Turkey, Uganda, and the United Kingdom. Honor killings tend to be prevalent in countries with a majority Muslim population, but many Islamic leaders and scholars condemn the practice and deny that it is based on religious doctrine. Honor killing is actually a pre-Islamic, tribal custom stemming from the patriarchal and patrilineal society's interest in keeping strict control over familial power structures.

5. Information accessed at: http://www.prospect.org/web/page.ww?section= root&name=ViewWeb&articleId=7572 on 21 April 2006.

6. One need go no further than the United States to see how family connections help politicians (i.e., George H.W. Bush and George W. Bush).

7. Information accessed at: http://www.campaignaudit.org/articles/0012. shtml on 21 April 2006.

8. For example, in a 2004 U.S. congressional district race in southern California, Republican incumbent David Dreier had over $2 million in his campaign war chest whereas his Democratic challenger, a woman named Cynthia Mathews, had approximately $40,000. Full disclosure of where campaign money comes from for each candidate is available at www.opensecrets.org

9. I am reminded of a teaching job I had ten years ago. The college I was working at wanted someone to teach women's history. I volunteered since I was conducting research on women leaders that eventually became my first book on the subject. I was told by the Dean that men cannot teach women's history.

10. The structurally conditioned and veiled aspects of the oppression of women today may be illustrated by what I call women's integration into superfluous or shrinking institutions. Women, as it were, inherit from men positions that have become insignificant or less important as departure points for power and influence. Hege Skjeie, "The Feminization of Power: Norway's Political Experiment (1986–)," Oslo: Instittut for Samfunsforskning Rapport 88/8, August 1988, 4; Bruce O. Solheim, *On Top of the World: Women's Political Leadership in Scandinavia and Beyond*. Westport, CT: Greenwood, 2000, 43–45, 53, 56.

11. Information accessed at: http://www.debates.org/pages/trans84.html accessed on 23 May 2006.

12. Geraldine A. Ferraro with Linda Bird Francke, *Ferraro: My Story*. New York: Bantam Books, 1985, 319.

13. Lori Cox Han, accessed at http://www.findarticles.com/p/articles/ mi_m0KVD/is_3_1/ai_82476769 accessed on 23 May 2006.

14. Kassebaum was voted in without having previously filled an unexpired congressional term. Rebecca Latimer Felton of Georgia, the first woman to serve in the U.S. Senate, took the oath of office on 21 November 1922. Having been appointed to fill a vacancy, Felton served for just twenty-four hours. The 87-year-old Felton's largely symbolic Senate service capped a long career in Georgia politics and journalism. The first woman *elected* to the Senate was Hattie Wyatt Caraway of Arkansas who was appointed to fill the vacancy caused by the death of her husband, U.S. Senator Thaddeus Caraway. To date, thirty-three women have served in the United States Senate. The fourteen current U.S. senators are listed below:

Barbara Mikulski (D-Maryland), 1987–
Dianne Feinstein (D-California), 1993–
Barbara Boxer (D-California), 1993–
Patty Murray (D-Washington), 1993–
Kay Bailey Hutchison (R-Texas), 1993–
Olympia Jean Snowe (R-Maine), 1995–

Mary Landrieu (D-Louisiana), 1997–
Susan Collins (R-Maine), 1997–
Blanche Lincoln (D-Arkansas), 1999–
Hillary Rodham Clinton (D-New York), 2001–
Deborah Stabenow (D-Michigan), 2001–
Maria E. Cantwell (D-Washington), 2001–
Lisa Murkowski (R-Alaska), 2002–
Elizabeth Dole (R-North Carolina), 2003–

15. The Convention on the Elimination of All Forms of Discrimination against Women (CEDAW), adopted in 1979 by the UN General Assembly, is often described as an international bill of rights for women. Consisting of a preamble and thirty articles, it defines what constitutes discrimination against women and sets up an agenda for national action to end such discrimination.

16. U.S. Speaker of the House, Republican Tom DeLay of Texas, criticized U.S. Supreme Court Justice Kennedy because "[he] is writing decisions based upon international law, not the Constitution of the United States. That's just outrageous." See http://www.cnn.com/2005/POLITICS/04/20/delay.judges.ap/ accessed on 21 April 2006.

17. Preemption holds that the United States can launch attacks against states before their threat is fully formed if the United States feels that such a rogue nation would threaten the United States or her allies.

18. Secular democratic liberalism holds that: (1) The U.S. political and military strategy should be the preservation of international peace and law, (2) the United States will safeguard U.S. interests and values within the context of a global society and in consideration of the diversity of other cultures and societies, and (3) the United States will work with other nations on a multilateral basis if possible.

19. Neoconservativism holds that: (1) The number one objective of U.S. post-cold war political and military strategy should be preventing the emergence of a rival superpower, (2) U.S. objective should be to safeguard U.S. interests and promote American values, and (3) if necessary, the United States must be prepared and willing to take unilateral action.

20. Information accessed at: http://www.surveyusa.com/client/PollReport.aspx?g=8b411f97-2a04-4e78-8c20-118231870f84 accessed on 21 April 2006.

21. Remarks at the Memorial Museum of Juscelino Kubitschek by Secretary Condoleezza Rice in Brasilia, Brazil, on 27 April 2005, accessed at: http://www.state.gov/secretary/rm/2005/45276.htm accessed on 23 May 2006.

22. Reaganomics is the essence of the conservative revolution that began in 1980. It is defined by deregulation of business, lowering of taxes, decreasing social programs, increasing defense as necessary, and promoting nongovernmental responsibility for providing a social safety net.

Selected Bibliography

Abrahams, Naomi. "Negotiating Power, Identity, Family, and Community." *Gender & Society* 10/6 (December 1996): 768.

Ackelsberg, Martha and Irene Diamond. "Gender and Political Life: New Directions in Political Science," in Beth B. Hess and Myra M. Ferree, eds. *Analyzing Gender: A Handbook of Social Science Research*. Newbury Park, CA: Sage Publications, 1987, 504–525.

Adams, John D., ed. *Transforming Leadership: From Vision to Results*. Alexandria, VA: Miles River Press, 1986.

Aderinwale, Ayodele, ed. Empowering African Women for the 21st Century: The Challenges of Politics, Business, Development and Leadership—Summary Report of the 9th Annual Conference of the Africa Leadership Forum, Accra, Ghana, 27–29 January 1997.

Adler, David A. *Our Golda, The Story of Golda Meir*. New York, NY: Viking, 1984.

Adler, Nancy J. and Dafna N. Izraeli, eds. *Competitive Frontiers: Women Managers in a Global Economy*. London: Blackwell Publishers, 1994.

African Women's Development and Communication Network. "African Women Participation in Politics and Decision-making in a Globalizing World." CSW 2002, Nairobi.

Agathe Uwilingiyimana: Biography, Forum for African Women Educationalists, February 2000. Accessed at: http://www.fawe.org/publications/Rolepercent20Models/Agathein.pdf accessed on 23 May 2006.

Alastain. *Sonia Gandhi: Heir to a Dynasty*. BBC News, 19 April 1999 (bbc.co.uk).

Alexander, Deborah and Kristi Andersen. "Gender as a Factor in the Attribution of Leadership Traits." *Political Research Quarterly* 46 (September 1993): 527–545.

Alvarez, Sonia E. *Engendering Democracy in Brazil*. Princeton, NJ: Princeton University Press. 1990.

Anderson, Nancy Fix. "Benazir Bhutto and Dynastic Politics: Her Father's Daughter, Her People's Sister." in Michael A. Genovese, ed., *Women as National Leaders*. Newbury Park, 1993, 41–69.

Aquino, Belinda A. "Democracy in the Philippines." *Current History* 88 (April 1989): 181–202.

Arab Women Connect. Accessed at: http://www.arabwomenconnect.org accessed on 23 May 2006.

Asia Foundation. Accessed at: http://www.asiafoundation.org accessed on 23 May 2006.

Asia's Women Leaders on the Outs, Global Beat Issue Brief No. 34, May 6, 1998 By Richard Halloran.

Association for Women's Rights in Development. Accessed at: http://www.awid.org/ on 2 April 2006.

Astin, Helen S. and Carole Leland. *Women of Influence, Women of Vision: A Cross-Generational Study of Leaders and Social Change*. San Francisco, CA: Jossey-Bass Publishers, 1991.

Banducci S. and Karp, J.A. "Gender, Leadership and Choice in Multiparty Systems." *Political Research Quarterly*. Amsterdam, The Netherlands: Amsterdam School of Communications Research (ASCoR), December 2000, Rev. ed., April, 2000.

Barker, Gary and Felicia Knaul. *Urban Girls: Empowerment in Especially Difficult Circumstances*. Updated by Neide Cassaniga with Anita Schrader. London: Intermediate Technology Publications, 2000.

Bartholomeusz, Tessa. "Mothers of Buddhas, Mothers of Nations: Kumaratunga and her Meteoric Rise to Power in Sri Lanka." in *Feminist Studies*, Spring 1999 (findarticles.com).

Bass, Bernard M. *Leadership and Performance Beyond Expectations*. New York: The Free Press, 1985.

BBC World News, "Italian-born Sonia Gandhi has thrown Indian politics into turmoil with her announcement that she does not intend to become the country's next prime minister." 18 May 2004. Accessed at: *http://news.bbc.co.uk/2/hi/south_asia/3721863.stm* on 2 April 2006. Beckman, Peter R. and Francine D'Amico, eds. *Women, Gender, and World Politics: Perspectives, Policies, and Prospects*. Westport, CT: Bergin & Garvey, 1994.

Belenky, M. F., Clinchy, B. M., Goldberger, N. R., and Tarule, J. M. *Women's Ways of Knowing. The Development of Self, Voice, and Mind*. New York: Basic Books Publishers, 1986.

Bem, Sandra L. *The Lenses of Gender: Transforming the Debate on Sexual Inequality*. New Haven, CT: Yale University Press, 1993.

Benazir Bhutto biography. Accessed at: http://womenshistory.about.com/gi/dynamic/offsite.htm?site=http%3A%2F%2Fwww.wic.org%2Fbio%2Fbbhutto.htm accessed on 23 May 2006.

Bennis, Warren and Burt Nanus. *Leaders: The Strategies for Taking Charge*. New York: Harper & Row Publishers, 1985.

Berentsen, Kirsten K. "Drivkraften bak Gro." *Magasinet SAS Norge*, 4 (Summer 1995): 9–15.

Bergman, Solveig. "Nordic Cooperation in Women's Studies." *Womens Studies Quarterly* 20/3–4 (Fall/Winter 1992): 58–67.

Bhavnani, Kum-Kum, John Foran, and Priya A. Kurian. "An introduction to Women, Culture and Development." in Kum-Kum Bhavani, John Foran, and Priya A. Kurian, ed., *Feminist Futures: Re-imagining Women, Culture and Development*. London/New York: Zed Books, 2003, 3–21.

Bhutto, Benazir. *Daughter of the East*. London: Hamish Hamilton, 1988.

Bigombe, Betty. "Leadership Development in Africa." *Partnership*. Excerpts from presentation at the "Regional Seminar on Good Governance and Private Sector Development and Investment," Entebbe, Uganda, March 1997.

Biography of Margaret Thatcher. Accessed at: http://britishhistory.about.com/gi/dynamic/offsite.htm accessed on 23 May 2006.

Biography of Margaret Thatcher. Accessed at: http://www.britannia.com/gov/primes/prime56.html accessed on 23 May 2006.

Bjorklund, Tor. *Holdning til likestilling*. Arbeidersnotat 5/85. Oslo, Norway: Institutt for samfunnsforskning, 1985.

Blackman, A. *Seasons of Her Life. A Biography of Madeline Albright*. New York: Scribner, 1998.

Bolman, Lee G. and Terrence E. Deal. *Leading with Soul: An Uncommon Journey of Spirit*. San Francisco, CA: Jossey-Bass Publishers, 1995.

Boneparth, Ellen and Emily Stoper, eds. *Women, Power and Policy: Toward the Year 2000*. 2nd ed. New York: Pergamon Press, 1988.

Booth, John A. and Thomas W. Walker. *Understanding Central America*. Boulder, CO: Westview Press, 1989.

Bout de Papier. "Living in L.A.: an interview with the Rt. Hon. Kim Campbell Canadian Consul General in Los Angeles." *Bout de papier*.13/4 (Winter/hiver 1996): 5–8

Bowker-Saur. *Who's Who of Women in World Politics*. New York: Bowker-Saur, 1991.

Brabandt, Heike, Birgit Locher, and Elisabeth Prügl. "Normen, Gender und Politikwandel: Internationale Beziehungen aus der Geschlechterperspektive." *WeltTrends* 36(2002): S. 11–26.

Bridge Overview Reports. Accessed at: http://www.ids.ac.uk/bridge/reports_gend_CEP.html on 2 April 2006. Brill, Alida, ed. *A Rising Public Voice: Women in Politics Worldwide*. New York: Feminist Press, 1995.

British Columbia Politics & Policy. "Member of Parliament for Vancouver Centre; Kim Campbell interview." *British Columbia Politics & Policy*. 2/10 (November 1988): 12–14.

Brooke, James. "A President's Daughter Tests the Waters in South Korea." *New York Times*, 22 April 2002 (nytimes.com).

Brundtland, Gro Harlem. "Global energipolitkk. Et norsk syn." *Internasjonal Politikk*, nos. 5–6 (1987): 23–34.

——. "Global Change and Our Common Future." *Environment* 31 (June 1989): 16–43.

——. "In Tune with Nature." *World Health* (January–February 1990): 4.

——. "Empowering Women." *Environment* (December 1994).

Brundtland, Gro Harlem. *Kvinners Europa*. A-Info 30/94. Oslo, Norway: Arbeider-
bevegelsen, 1994.
——. International Conference on Population and Development, Cairo, Egypt, 1994.
——. Closing Address, Fourth World Conference on Women, Beijing, China,
1995.
——. Address to the Permanent Missions in Geneva. 10 November 1998.
——. *Mitt Liv, 1939–1986*. Oslo, Norway: Gyldendal, 1998.
Brustad, Sylvia. *Kjerringråd for kvinneliv*. A-Info 2/95. Oslo, Norway:
Arbeiderbevegelsen, 1995.
Burki, Shahid Javed. "Pakistan's Cautious Democratic Course." *Current History*
91 (March 1992): 117–22.
Burns, James MacGregor. *Leadership*. New York: Harper & Row, 1978.
Burrell, Barbara. "The Political Leadership of Women and Public Policy-making."
Policy Studies Journal 25/4 (Winter 1997): 565–569.
Butler, Francelia. *Indira Gandhi*. New York: Chelsea House, 1986. Byrne, Lesley H.
"Feminists in Power: Women Cabinet Ministers in the New Democratic
Party (NDP) Government of Ontario, 1990–1995." *Policy Studies Journal*
25/4 (Winter 1997): 601–613.
Bystydzienski, Jill M, ed. *Women Transforming Politics: Worldwide Strategies for
Empowerment*. Bloomington, IN: Indiana University Press, 1992.
——. *Women in Electoral Politics: Lessons from Norway*. Westport, CT: Praeger,
1995.
Caiazza, Amy. "Does Women's Representation in Elected Office Lead to Women-
Friendly Policy?" *Institute for Women's Policy Research: Research-in-Brief*,
May 2002.
Campbell, Kim. *Time and Chance: The Political Memoirs of Canada's First Woman
Prime Minister*. Toronto, Canada: Doubleday Canada, 1996.
Cantor, Dorothy W., Toni Bernay, and Jean Stoess. *Women in Power: The Secrets
of Leadership*. New York: Houghton Mifflin, 1992.
Carothers, Thomas. *Aiding Democracy Abroad: The Learning Curve*. Washington,
DC: Carnegie Foundation for International Peace, 1999.
Carroll, Susan, J. ed. *The Impact of Women in Public Office*. Bloomington, IN: Indiana
University Press, 2001.
CEDPA: http://www.cedpa.org/publications/pdf/promotingprowid.pdf
Centre for American Women and Politics at Rutgers University. Accessed at:
http://www.rci.rutgers.edu/~cawp/
Centre for American Women and Politics at Rutgers University. Accessed at:
http://www.rci.rutgers.edu/~cawp/
Center for American Women in Politics (CAWP): www.cawp.rutgers.edu
Center for Policy Alternatives (CFPA): www.stateaction.org
Center for Voting and Democracy: www.fairvote.org
Center for Women in Government: http://www.cwig.albany.edu/privacy.htm
Chamorro, Violeta Barrios de. "The Death of La Prensa." *Foreign Affairs* 65/2
(Winter 1986/87): 383–386.
Chodrow, Nancy Julia. "Gender, Relation, and Difference," in Hester Eisenstein
and Alice Jardine, eds., *The Future of Difference*. New Brunswick, NJ: Rutgers
University Press, 1985, 3–19.

Chowdhury, Najma. "Bangladesh: Gender Issues and Politics in a Patriarchy." in Barbary J. Nelson and Najma Chowdhury, eds. *Women and Politics Worldwide*. New Haven, CT: Yale University Press, 1994, 95–113.

Chua-Eaon, Howard G. "All in the Family." *Time* (Fall 1990): 33–34.

Clinton, H. R. (2003) *Living History*. New York: Simon & Schuster, 2003.

Collins, Patricia Hill. *Black Feminist Thought: Knowledge, Consciousness, and the Politics of Empowerment*. New York: Routledge, 1991.

Connell, R.W. *Gender & Power: Society, the Person and Sexual Politics*. Stanford, CA: Stanford University Press, 1987.

Conway, M., G. Steuernagel, and David W. Ahern. *Women and Political Participation: Cultural Change in the Political Arena*. Washington, DC: Congressional Quarterly, 1997.

Cook, Bill and Uma Kothari, eds. *Participation: The New Tyranny?* New York: St. Martins Press, 2002.

Coole, Diana H. *Women in Political Theory: From Ancient Misogyny to Contemporary Feminism*. Boulder, CO: Lynne Rienner Publishers, 1988.

Cooper, Matthew. "Call It Hillary Power: The First Lady's Focus on Females Has become American Foreign Policy." *Newsweek*, 7 April 1997: 31–33.

Corazon Aquino biography. Accessed at: http://womenshistory.about.com/cs/aquinocorazon/ and http://womenshistory.about.com/gi/dynamic/offsite.htm?site=http%3A%2F%2Fwww.wic.org%2Fbio%2Fcaquino.htm

Cott, Nancy F. *The Grounding of Modern Feminism*. New Haven, CT: Yale University Press, 1987.

Council of Women World Leaders. Transcript from 1998 Summit of the Council of Women World Leaders, John F. Kennedy School of Government, Harvard University. Accessed at: http://www.ksg.harvard.edu/ksgpress/ksg_news/transcripts/cwwl.htm

Covey, Stephen R. *Principle-Centered Leadership*. New York: Simon & Schuster, 1990.

Crapol, Edward P., ed. *Women and American Foreign Policy: Lobbyists, Critics, and Insiders*. 2nd ed. Wilmington, DE: Scholarly Resources, 1992.

Crisostomo, Isabelo T. 1986. *Cory: Profile of a President*. Yuezon City: Malaysia Pelanduk Publications, 1986.

Currimbhoy, Nayana, *Indira Gandhi*, London: Franklin Watts, 1985.

D'Amico, Francine and Peter R. D'Amico, eds. *Women in World Politics: An Introduction*. Westport, CT: Bergin & Garvey, 1995.

Davis, Angela. *Women, Culture and Politics*. New York: Random House, 1988.

DeFronzo, James. *Revolutions and Revolutionary Movements*. Boulder, CO: Westview Press, 1991.

Deutchman, Iva Ellen. "The Politics of Empowerment." *Women & Politics* 11/2 (1991): 1–18.

Dollar, D. R. Fisman and R. Gatti. "Are Women Really the 'Fairer' Sex? Corruption and Women in Government." New York. Columbia University. The World Bank—Development Research Group/Poverty Reduction and Economic Management Network. October. 1999.

Dougherty, James E. and Robert L. Pfaltzgraff Jr. *Contending Theories of International Relations*. Philadelphia, PA: Lippincott, 1971.

Dynasties and Female Leadership in Asia, Project sponsored by the German Science Foundation (DFG), April 2003–May 2005.

Eagly, Alice H., Mona G. Makhijani, and Bruce G. Klonsky. "Gender and the Evaluation of Leaders: A Meta-Analysis." *Psychological Bulletin* 111/1 (1992): 3–22.

Economic and Social Commission for Asia and the Pacific. Report of the Expert Group Meeting on the Regional Implementation of the Beijing Platform for Action. Bangkok, Thailand: Economic and Social Commission for Asia and the Pacific, 1999.

Edmisten, Patricia Taylor. *Nicaragua Divided: La Prensa and the Chamorro Legacy.* Pensacola, FL: University of West Florida Press, 1990.

Eisenstein, Hester and Alice Jardine, eds. *The Future of Difference.* New Brunswick, NJ: Rutgers University Press, 1985.

Elegant, Simon. "Mosquito Party: Can Wan Azizah lead her fledgling opposition party above marginal status?" *Far Eastern Economic Review* (5 Aug. 1999): 18–19.

Elson, Diane. *Progress of the World's Women 2000.* New York. United Nations Development Fund for Women, 2000.

Eschlee, Catherine. *Engendering Global Democracy.* Paper for the World Congress of the International Political Studies Assoc. Canada, Quebec: The New World Order; Ten Years On, Univ. of Sussex, June 2000. Accessed at: www.sussex.ac.uk/Units/IRPol/Seminars?NWO/eschle.html

Estrich, Susan. *Sex and Power.* New York: Riverhead Books, 2000.

European Commission. "Fourth Medium-Term Community Action Programme on Equal Opportunities for Women and Men (1996–2000)." *Official Journal of the European Communities* No. L 335–37, 30 December 1995.

European Women Data Base. Accessed at: http://europa.eu.int/comm/employment_social/women_men_stats/index_en.htm

European Women's Lobby. "Young Women's Guide to Equality between Women and Men in Europe." Accessed at: http://ewl.horus.be/SiteResources/data/MediaArchive/Publications/JF_EN.pdf

Evans, Sara M. *Born for Liberty: A History of Women in America.* New York: The Free Press, 1989.

Faber, Doris. *Margaret Thatcher, Britain's "Iron Lady."* New York: Viking Kestrel, 1985.

Farrel, Pam. *Woman of Influence: Ten Traits of Those Who Want to Make a Difference.* Downers Grove, IL: InterVarsity Press, 1996.

Ferguson, A. E. with Katundu, L. "Women in Politics in Zambia: What difference has democracy made?" *African Rural and Urban Studies* 1/2 (1994).

Ferraro, Geraldine A. *Changing History: Women, Power, and Politics.* Wakefield, RI: Moyer Bell, 1993.

Filene, Peter G. *Him/Her/Self.* 2nd ed. Baltimore, MD: Johns Hopkins Press, 1988.

Flax, Jane. "Postmodernism and Gender Relations in Feminist Theory." *Journal of Women in Culture and Society* 12/4 (1987): 621–643.

Forbes, Beverly A. "Profile of the Leader of the Future: Origins, Premises, Values and Characteristics of the Theory F Transformational Leadership Model." Mimeograph. Seattle, WA: University of Washington, 1991.

Forcey, Linda Rennie. "Women as Peacemakers." *Peace & Change* 16/4 (October 1991): 331–354.

Foster, A. N. "Violence Against Women; The Problems Facing South Africa." Paper presented at International Planned Parenthood Federation at the Commonwealth Heads of Government meeting 1999. http://www.ippf.org/resource/gbc/chogm99/foster.htm

Foster, Leila. *Margaret Thatcher: First Woman Prime Minister.of Great Britain.* Chicago, IL: Children's Press, 1990.

Fougner, Brit and Mona Larsen-Asp, eds. *Norden–kvinners paradis?* Copenhagen, Denmark: Nordisk Ministerråd, 1994.

Gagnon, Lysiane. "Le Canada selon Kim." *l'Actualité*.18/15 (1er octobre 1993): 23–29.

Gandhi, Indira. *My Truth.* New Delhi: Vision Books, 1981.

Gardner, Howard and Emma Laskin. *Leading Minds: An Anatomy of Leadership.* New York: Basic Books, 1995.

Gardner, Marilyn. "World Leaders' Council: Only Women Need Apply." *Christian Science Monitor*, 8 October 1997, p. 13.

Garfinkel, Bernard Max. *Margaret Thatcher.* New York: Chelsea House, 1984.

Genovese, Michael A., ed. *Women as National Leaders.* London: Sage Publications, 1993.

Gibbs, Nancy. "Norway's Radical Daughter." *Time* (25 September 1989): 43–44.

Gilligan, Carol. *In a Different Voice: Psychological Theory and Women's Development.* Cambridge, MA: Harvard University Press, 1982.

——. "In a Different Voice: Women's Conceptions of Self and of Morality," in Hester Eisenstein and Alice Jardine, eds., *The Future of Difference.* New Brunswick, NJ: Rutgers University Press, 1985, 274–317.

GNP data. Accessed at: http://www.guide2womenleaders.com/situation_in_2005.htm and http://www.worldbank.org/data/wdi2001/pdfs/tab1_1.pdf,http://www.worldbank.org/data/wdi2001/worldview.htm

Golden, Claudia. *Understanding the Gender Gap: An Economic History of American Women.* New York: Oxford University Press, 1990.

Gray, Barbara. *Collaborating: Finding Common Ground for Multiparty Problems.* San Francisco, CA: Jossey-Bass Publishers, 1989.

Gray, Charlotte. "Woman of the year: . . . Kim Campbell." *Chatelaine* 67/1 (January 1994): 28–29, 31–32, 54.

Gray, John. *Men Are from Mars, Women Are from Venus: A Practical Guide for Improving Communication and Getting What You Want in Your Relationships.* New York: HarperCollins, 1992.

Greene, Carol. *Indira Gandhi: Ruler of India.* Chicago, IL: Childrens Press, 1985.

Gupte, Pranay. "OPEC's Scandinavian Partner." *Forbes* (15 December 1986): 144–146.

Haavio-Mannila, Elina, Drude Dahlerup, Maud Eduards, Esther Gudmundsdóttir, Beatrice Halsaa, Helga Maria Hernes, Eva Hänninen-Salmelin, Bergthora Sigmundsdóttir, Sirkka Sinkkonen, and Torild Skard, eds. *Unfinished Democracy: Women in Nordic Politics.* New York: Pergamon Press, 1985.

Hakim, S. Abdul. *Begum Khaleda Zia of Bangladesh: A Political Biography.* New Delhi: South Asia Books, 1992.

Hansson, Steinar and Ingolf Håkon Teigene. *Makt og Mannefall: Historien om Gro Harlem Brundtland*. Oslo, Norway: J.W. Cappelens Forlag, 1992.

Hare-Mustin, Rachel T. and Jeanne Marecek, eds. *Making a Difference: Psychology and the Construction of Gender*. New Haven, CT: Yale University Press, 1990.

Harris, Ian M. *Peace Education*. Jefferson, NC: McFarland, 1988.

Harstock, Nancy C. M. "Prologue to a Feminist Critique of War and Politics," in Judith Hicks Stiehm, ed. *Women's Views of the Political World of Men*. Dobbs Ferry, NY: Transnational Publishers, 1984, 123–150.

Haskel, Barbara G. *The Scandinavian Option: Opportunities and Opportunity Costs in Postwar Scandinavian Foreign Policies*. Oslo, Norway: Universitetsforlaget, 1976.

Hauptfuhrer, Fred. "On Top of the World." *People* (20 April 1987): 35–39.

Hayden, Dolores. *The Grand Domestic Revolution: A History of Feminist Design for American Homes, Neighborhoods, and Cities*. Cambridge, MA: MIT Press, 1981.

Heifetz, Ronald A. and Donald L. Laurie. "The Work of Leadership." *Harvard Business Review* (January–February 1997): 124–134.

Held, Virginia. *Feminist Morality: Transforming Culture, Society, and Politics*. Chicago, IL: University of Chicago Press, 1993.

Heldman, Susan J. Carroll, and Stephanie Olson. "Gender Differences in Print Media Coverages of Presidential Candidates: Elizabeth Dole's Bid for the Republican Nomination." Accessed at: http://www.rci.rutgers.edu/~cawp/Research/Reports/dole.pdf

Helgesen, Sally. *The Female Advantage: Women's Ways of Leadership*. New York: Doubleday Currency, 1995.

Hernes, Helga M. *Welfare State and Woman Power: Essays in State Feminism*. Olso, Norway: Norwegian University Press, 1987.

Hess, Beth B. and Myra M. Ferree, eds. *Analyzing Gender: A Handbook of Social Science Research*. Newbury Park, CA: Sage Publications, 1987.

Heyzer, Noleen, ed. With Sushma Kapoor and Joanne Sandler. *A Commitment to the World's Women: Perspectives on Development for Beijing and Beyond*. New York: United Nations Development Fund for Women, 1995.

Higonnet, Margaret R., Jane Jenson, Sonya Michel, and Margaret C. Weitz, eds. *Behind the Lines: Gender and the Two World Wars*. New Haven, CT: Yale University Press, 1987.

Hill, Kevin A. "Agathe Uwilingiyimana." in Rebecca Mae Salokar and Mary L. Volcansek, ed. *Women and the Law, a Bio-Bibliographical Sourcebook*. Westport, CT: Greenwood Press, 1996, 323–328.

———. "Sylvie Kanigi." in Rebecca Mae Salokar and Mary L. Volcansek, ed. *Women and the Law, a Bio-Bibliographical Sourcebook*. Westport, CT: Greenwood Press, 1996, 118–122.

Hirsti, Reidar, ed. *Gro: Midt i Livet*. Oslo, Norway: Tiden Norsk Forlag, 1989.

History of Women's Suffrage. Accessed at: http://teacher.scholastic.com/activities/suffrage/history.htm

Hoel, Sigrun. "Moving Towards Real Rights for Women—The Legal Strategy." Mimeograph. Oslo, Norway: Norwegian Labor Party, 1994. Hollander, Jocelyn A., 2002: "Resisting Vulnerability: The Social Reconstruction of Gender in Interaction," in: *Social Problems*, 49 (4): 474–496.

Hollander, Jocelyn A., 2002. "Resisting Vulnerability: The Social Reconstruction of Gender in Interaction," in: *Social Problems*, 49 (4): 474–496.

Hookway, James. 2002. "All Things to All People." *Far Eastern Economic Review* (7 February 2002): 14–16.

http://alumni.binghamton.edu/AJ/2002/fall/feature02.htm

http://womenshistory.about.com/gi/dynamic/offsite.htm?site=http%3A%2F%2F www.unet.brandeis.edu%2F%7Edwilliam%2Fprofiles%2Fbrundtland.htm

http://womenshistory.about.com/gi/dynamic/offsite.htm?site=http%3A%2F% 2Fwww3.sympatico.ca%2Fgoweezer%2Fcanada%2Fcampbell.htm

http://womenshistory.about.com/gi/dynamic/offsite.htm?site=http%3A%2F% 2Fwww.nlc-bnc.ca%2F2%2F12%2Fh12-255-e.html

http://womenshistory.about.com/gi/dynamic/offsite.htm?site=http%3A%2F% 2Feurope.cnn.com%2Fresources%2Fnewsmakers%2Fworld%2Fnamerica% 2Fchamorro.html

Htun, Mala. "The Unfinished Revolution: New Approaches to Promoting Female Leadership." *The Inter-American Development Bank* (May 1997): 4–5.

Huddy, Leonie and Nayda Terkildsen. "The Consequences of Gender Stereotypes for Women Candidates at Different Levels and Types of Office." *Political Research Quarterly* 46 (September 1993): 503–525.

Hunt, Swanee. "Women's Vital Voices: The Costs of Exclusion in Eastern Europe." *Foreign Affairs* 76/4 (July/August 1997): 2–7.

Hurwood, Bernhardt J. "Iceland's Optimist." *Christian Science Monitor*, 16 September 1982, p. 15.

India Image. Accessed at: http://indiaimage.nic.in/

Inglehart, Ronald and Pippa Norris. "Gender Gaps in Voting Behavior in Global Perspective." 3 September 1997 paper residing on the John F. Kennedy School of Government, Harvard University, world wide Web site: http://www.ksg.harvard.edu/people/pnorris/APSA98_31_6.htm

Institute for Women's Policy Research. Accessed at: www.worldbank.org/ gender/prr

Inter-American Dialogue. Accessed at: http://www.thediealogue.org.publications/ Politicsmatter.pdf

International IDEA. Accessed at: http://www.idea.int/women/parl/toc.htm

International Woman Suffrage Timeline. Accessed at: http://womenshistory. about.com/od/suffrage/a/intl_timeline.htm

Interparliamentary Union. Accessed at: www.ipu.org

Jackson, Guida M. *Women Who Ruled.* Santa Barbara, CA: ABC-CLIO, 1990.

Jagland, Thorbjørn. *Verdier og likestilling.* A-Info 3/95. Oslo, Norway: Arbeiderbevegelsen, 1995.

Jahan, Rounaq. "Women in South Asian Politics." In: *Third World Quarterly* 3 (July 1987): 848–870.

Jalušic, Vlasta and Milica G. Antic. *Women—Politics—Equal Opportunities: Prospects for Gender Equality Politics in Central and Eastern Europe.* Ljubljana: Politike, 2001.

Jamilah Ariffin. Women and Development in Malaysia. Petaling Jaya, Selangor, 1992.

Janeway, Elizabeth. "Women and the Uses of Power," in Hester Eisenstein and Alice Jardine, eds. *The Future of Difference*. New Brunswick, NJ: Rutgers University Press, 1985, 327–344.

Jaquette, Jane S., ed. *The Women's Movement in Latin America: Participation and Democracy*. 2nd ed. Boulder, CO: Westview Press, 2000.

——, ed. *Women in Politics*. New York: Wiley, 1974.

Jeffery, Patricia and Amrita Basu. Appropriating Gender. Women's Activism and Politicized Religion in South Asia. New York: Routledge, 1998.

Johnson, Paula. "Women and Power: Toward a Theory of Effectiveness." *Journal of Social Issues* 32/3 (1976): 99–110.

Jones, Christopher B. "Women of the Future: Alternative Scenarios." *The Futurist* (May–June 1996): 34–38.

Jong, Erica. *What Do Women Want?* New York: Harper Collins, 1998.

Kahn, Kim Fridkin. "Gender Differences in Campaign Messages: The Political Advertisements of Men and Women Candidates for U.S. Senate." *Political Research Quarterly* 46 (September 1993): 481–502.

Kane, John. *The Politics of Moral Capital*. Cambridge: Cambridge University Press, 2001.

Kane, Kate. "The Harvard MBA Class of 1965 Revisited: Business School was Easy for the First Class of Women. Finding a Job after Graduation wasn't." *Women and Academia*. June 1997.

Karvonen, Lauri and Per Selle, eds. *Women in Nordic Politics: Closing the Gap*. Brookfield, VT: Dartmouth Publishing, 1995.

Keenan, Edward. "Daylight upon Magic: The Essential Truth of the Martin Coronation Metaphor" *Eye Weekly* (20 November 2003). Internet. Accessed at: http://www.eye.net/eye/issue/issue_11.20.03/city/liberals-web.html on 1 January 2006.

Kelber, Mim, ed. *Women and Government: New Ways to Political Power*. Westport, CT: Praeger, 1994.

Kerber, Linda K. "Separate Spheres, Female Worlds, Woman's Place: The Rhetoric of Women's History." *Journal of American History* 75 (June 1988): 4–39.

Khan, Stephen. "A Dynasty Revitalised: Sonia Gandhi Damns Predictions with Stunning Win," *The Independent*, 14 May 2004.

Kincaid, Diane D. "Over his Dead Body. A Positive Perspective on Widows in the U.S. Congress." *Western Political Quarterly* 31(1978): 96–104.

King, Martin Luther, Jr. *Where Do We Go from Here? Chaos or Community*. New York: Harper and Row, 1967.

Kinigi, Sylvie. "Women and Conflict Management in Africa." *Partnership*. Extracted from a presentation to the conference "Empowering Women in the 21st Century: The Challenges for Politics, Business, Development, and Leadership," Accra, January 1997.

Klenke, Karin. *Women and Leadership: A Contextual Perspective*. New York: Springer Publishing Company, Inc., 1996.

Komisar, Lucy. *Corazon Aquino: The Story of a Revolution*. New York: Lawson, 1987.

Kriesberg, Louis. "Conflict Resolution Applications to Peace Studies." *Peace & Change* 16/4 (October 1991): 400–417.

Lauria, Joe. "U.N. Confers on Protecting Women from War's Toll." United Nations Commission on the Status of Women 48th Session. Accessed at: *http://www.un.org/womenwatch/daw/csw/48sess.htm*

Leahy, Margaret E. *Development Strategies and the Status of Women*. Boulder, CO: Lynne Rienner, 1986.

Lee, Shin-wha, ed. *International Directory of Women's Political Leadership, 1991–92*. College Park, MD: Center for Political Leadership and Participation, 1992.

Lerner, Gerda. "New Approaches to the Study of Women in American History." *Journal of Social History* 3/1 (Fall 1969): 53–62.

Les Premiers Ministres du Canada, 1867–1994. The Prime Ministers of Canada, 1867–1994. Présenté par la Chambre des communes et les Archives nationales du Canada. Ottawa, Canada: les Archives nationales du Canada, 1994.

Lintner, Bertil. 2002. "The Proof of The Pudding." *Far Eastern Economic Review* (16 May 2002): 12–14.

Lipman-Blumen, Jean. *Gender Roles and Power*. Englewood Cliffs, NJ: Prentice-Hall, 1984.

——. *The Connective Edge: Leading in an Interdependent World*. San Francisco, CA: Jossey-Bass Publishers, 1996.

Lips, Hilary M. *Women, Men, & The Psychology of Power*. Englewood Cliffs, NJ: Prentice-Hall, 1981.

Lithgow, Lynette. "A Question of Relativity: The Role of the News Media in Shaping the View of Women in Asian Political Dynasties. #2000–13." The Shorenstein Center on the Press, Politics and Public Policy: Press–Politics; Public Policy. Cambridge, Mass: Harvard University, John F. Kennedy School of Government, 2000.

Longwe, S. H. (2002) NEPAD Reluctance to Address Gender Issues. Accessed at: http://www.africaaction.org/docs02/gen0211b.htm

Mac-Johnson, Rodney. "The Second Sex Comes to the Fore." *World Press News*. 2002. Accessed at: http://www.worldpress.org/Africa/538.cfm

Manor, James. "Innovative Leadership in Modern India: M. K. Gandhi, Nehru, and I. Gandhi," in Gabriel Sheffer, ed., *Innovative Leaders in International Politics*. Albany, NY: State University Press of New York, 1993, 187–215.

Marquand, Robert. "Women at Pinnacle of Power." *Christian Science Monitor*, 1 May 1998, p. 1.

Matland, Richard E. "The World's Leader in Female Representation: Norway," in Shin-wha Lee, ed. *International Directory of Women's Political Leadership, 1991–92*. College Park, MD: Center for Political Leadership and Participation, 1992, 163–167.

McCauley, Karen, *Golda Meir*. New York: Chelsea House, 1985.

McCorduck, Pamela and Nancy Ramsey. *The Futures of Women*. Reading, MA: Addison-Wesley Publishing Company, 1996.

McCoy, Jennifer L. "Nicaragua in Transition." *Current History* 90 (March 1991): 117–132.

McGlen, Nancy E. and Meredith R. Sarkees. *The Status of Women in Foreign Policy*. Foreign Policy Association. Headline Series. No. 307. Summer 1995.

McIntyre, Angus. In Search of Megawati Sukarnoputri. Working Papers, Centre of Southeast Asian Studies. Clayton, Victoria, 1997.

Millet, Richard L. "Nicaragua: A Glimmer of Hope?" *Current History* 89 (January 1990): 21–37.

Mir-Hosseini, Ziba. Islam and Gender. The Religious Debate in Contemporary Iran. Princeton, 1999.

Montagu, Ashley. *The Natural Superiority of Women.* New York: Macmillan, 1992.

Morgen, Sandra and Ann Bookman, eds. *Women and the Politics of Empowerment.* Philadephia, PA: Temple University Press, 1988.

——. "Rethinking Women and Politics: An Introductory Essay," in Sandra Morgen, and Ann Bookman, eds. *Women and the Politics of Empowerment.* Philadephia, PA: Temple University Press, 1988, 3–29.

Moser, Caroline O.N. *Gender Planning and Development: Theory, Practice and Training.* London: Routledge, 1993.

Moyers, Bill. *A World of Ideas with Bill Moyers.* "Changing Agendas with Gro Harlem Brundtland." Public Affairs Television, New York, 1990. (30 minutes).

Mrozek, Andrea, "Fighting the Native Patriarchy." *National Post.* Page A12. 11 January 2006. Source: Western Standard.

Narasimhan, Sakuntala. *Born Unfree.* Bombay: Ameet Offset, Hanuman Industrial Estate, 1989.

——. *Empowering Women: An Alternative Strategy From Rural India.* New Delhi: Sage Publications, 1999.

National Democratic Institute. Accessed at: www.ndi.org

National Organization for Women. Accessed at: www.now.org

Nazlee, Sajda. *Feminism and Muslim Women.* London: Ta Ha Publishers, 1996.

Nelson, Barabara J. and Najima Chowdhury, eds. *Women and Politics Worldwide.* New Haven, CT: Yale University Press, 1994.

New Israel Fund. Available at: http://www.nif.org/

Norris, Pippa. "Choosing Electoral Systems: Proportional, Majoritiarian and Mixed Systems." *International Political Science Review* 18/3 (July 1997): 297–312.

Norris, Pippa and Inglehart, Robert. "Cultural Barriers to Women's Leadership: A Worldwide Comparison." Quebec City, International Political Science Association World Congress. Session 16 "Social Cleavages and Elections," August 2000.

Norway's Ministry of Children and Family Affairs. "Human Development Report of 1995." Norway's Ministry of Children and Family Affairs, 1995.

Nyhamar, Jostein. *Arbeiderbevegelsens Historie i Norge.* Oslo, Norway: Arbeiderbevegelsen, 1990.

Nzomo, Maria, ed. Empowering Kenya Women; Report on a Seminar of Post-Election Women's Agenda, Forward Looking Strategies to 1991 and Beyond. Nairobi, Kenya: National Committee on Status of Women, 1993.

——. "Gender, Governance and Conflicts in Africa." *DPMF Publications: DPMF Workshop and Conference Proceedings.* Accessed at: http://www.dpmf.org/gender-maria.html

Odendahl, Teresa, and Michael O'Neill, eds. *Women & Power in the Nonprofit Sector.* San Francisco, CA: Jossey-Bass Publishers, 1994.

Ogden, Chris. *Maggie: An Intimate Portrait of a Woman in Power.* New York: Simon & Schuster, 1990.

Okin, Suan Moller. *Women in Western Political Thought*. Princeton, NJ: Princeton University Press, 1979.

Opfell, Olga S. *Women Prime Ministers and Presidents*. Jefferson, NC: McFarland, 1993.

Papandreou, Margarita. "Feminism and Political Power: Some Thoughts on a Strategy for the Future," in Ellen Boneparth and Emily Stoper, eds. *Women, Power and Policy: Toward the Year 2000*. 2nd ed. New York: Pergamon Press, 1988, xi–xix.

Parenteau, John. *Prisoner for Peace: Aung San Suu Kyi and Burma's Struggle for Democracy*. Greensboro, NC: Morgan Reynolds Publishing, 1994.

Pateman, Carole. " 'Does Sex Matter to Democracy?'—A Comment." *Scandinavian Political Studies* 13/1 (1990): 57–63.

Patricia Taylor Edmisten. *Nicaragua Divided: La Prensa and the Chamorro Legacy*. Pensacola, FL: University of West Florida Press, 1990, 72, 91; Richard L. Millet, "Nicaragua: A Glimmer of Hope?" *Current History* 89 (January 1990): 36; Opfell, 173–175; Saint-Germaine, 78–79.

Pavan-Wolfe, Lisa. "Women in the Workforce: Addressing the Challenge of Demographic Change" *European Week of Regions and Cities*. Brussels, 11 October 2005. Internet. Accessed at: http://europa.eu.int/comm/employment_social/speeches/2005/lp_111005_en.pdf

People's Daily Online. "Musharraf Greets Sonia Gandhi on Electoral Victory" 26 May 2004. Accessed at: http://english.peopledaily.com.cn/200405/26/eng20040526_144382.html

Peterson, Spike V. and Anne Sisson Runyan. *Global Gender Issues*. Boulder, Colorado, 1993.

Platform for Action and Beijing Declaration. Fourth World Conference on Women. New York. United Nations, 1996.

Political Gender Gaps in Europe. Accessed at: http://erik.kabel.utwente.nl/gg/about

Pond, Elizabeth. "Women in Leadership: A Letter from Stockholm." *The Washington Quarterly* 19/4 (Autumn 1996): 59–69.

Powers, Elizabeth. "Are Feminists Out of Touch with the Majority of Women?" *CQ Researcher* (28 February 1997).

PROLEAD. Accessed at: http://www.iadb.org/sds/doc/Prolead-MovingInto-Power-E.pdf

Pyke, Karen D. "Class Based Masculinities: The Interdependence of Gender, Class and Interpersonal Power." *Gender and Society* 10/5(October 1996): 527.

Ramphele, Mamphela. *Across Boundaries: The Journey of a South African Woman Leader*. New York: Feminist Press, 1996.

Randall, Vicky. *Women and Politics: An International Perspective*. 2nd ed. Chicago, IL: University of Chicago Press, 1987.

Rehn, Elisabeth and Ellen Sirleaf. *Women, War, Peace. The Independent Experts' Assessment On the Impact of Armed Conflict on Women and Women's Role in Peace-building*. New York: United Nations Development Fund for Women, 2002.

Reid-Merritt, Patricia. *Sister Power: How Phenomenal Black Women Are Rising to the Top*. New York: John Wiley & Sons, Inc., 1996.

Richter, Linda K. "Exploring Theories of Female Leadership in South and Southeast Asia." *Pacific Affairs*, 63(1990–1991): 524–540.

Richter, William L. "Pakistan under Benazir Bhutto." *Current History* 88 (December 1989): 433–451.

Rose, Kalima. *Where Women Are Leaders: The Sewa Movement in India*. London: Vistaar Publications, 1992.

Rosenbach, William E. and Robert L. Taylor, eds. *Contemporary Issues in Leadership*. 2nd ed. Boulder, CO: Westview Press, 1989.

Rosenberg, Emily. "Gender." *Journal of American History* 77/1 (June 1990): 116–124.

Rule, Wilma. "Women's Underrepresentation and Electoral Systems," *Political Science & Politics* 27/4 (December 1994): 689–693.

"Rwanda's Uwilingiyimana was crusader for justice." *Reuters Newswire*, 8 April 1994.

Saadawi, Nawal. *The Nawal El Saadawi Reader*. London: Zed Books, 1997.

Safir, Marilyn, Martha T. Mednick, Dafne Israell, and Jessie Bernard, eds. *Women's Worlds: From the New Scholarship*. New York: Praeger, 1985.

Saint-Germaine, Michelle A. "Women in Power in Nicaragua: Myth and Reality," in Michael A. Genovese, ed. *Women as National Leaders*. London: Sage Publications, 1993, 70–102.

Sardar, Ziauddin. "Kept in Power by Male Fantasy." *New Statesman* 127/4397 (Summer 1996): 24–26.

Sarler, Carol. 29. December 2005. "We've Gone from Being Amazons to can't cope, won't cope wusses". *Times Online*. Accessed at: *http://www.timesonline.co.uk/article/0,,1072-1961661,00.html* on 21 April 2006.

Schaef, A.E. (1981). *Women's Reality: An Emerging Female System in the White Male Society*. Minneapolis, MN: Winston Press, 1981.

Schalkwyk, J. and B.Woroniuk. Participation, Governance, Political Systems. Paper Prepared for Sida, Stockholm, Sweden,1998.

Schein, Virginia E. "Would Women Lead Differently?" in William E. Rosenbach and Robert L. Taylor, eds. *Contemporary Issues in Leadership*. 2nd ed. Boulder, CO: Westview Press, 1989, 154–160.

Schuster, Ilsa. "Political Women: The Zambian Experience" in Marilyn Safir, Martha T. Mednick, Dafne Israell, and Jessie Bernard, eds. *Women's Worlds: From the New Scholarship*. New York: Praeger, 1985, 189–198.

Schwellnus, Lesanne and Ingrid Clanchy, eds. *This is Our World: Perspectives of Young South African Women*. Joint Enrichment Project.

Schwepcke, B. *Töchter Asiens: Frauen zwischen Herrschaft und Anpassung*. Wien, 1998.

Scott, Joan. "Deconstructing Equality-Versus-Difference: Or, the Uses of Poststructuralist Theory for Feminism." *Feminist Studies* 14/1 (Spring 1988): 33–50.

Sheer, L. *Failure is Impossible: Susan B Anthony In Her Own Words*. New York: Random House, 1995.

Sheffer, Gabriel, ed. *Innovative Leaders in International Politics*. Albany, NY: State University of New York Press, 1993.

Silverstein, Josef. "The Idea of Freedom in Burma and the Political Thought of Daw Aung San Suu Kyi." *Pacific Affairs* 69(1996): 211–228.

Skjeie, Hege. "The Feminization of Power: Norway's Political Experiment (1986–)." Oslo, Norway: Institut for Samfuns-forskning Rapport, August 1988.

——. "The Rhetoric of Difference: On Women's Inclusion into Political Elites." *Politics and Society* 19/2 (June 1991): 233–263.

——. "The Uneven Advance of Norwegian Women." *New Left Review* 187 (May/June 1991): 79–102.

——. "Politisk Lederskap." *Nytt Norsk Tidsskrift* 2 (1992): 118–135.

——. "On Authority: Weberian Ideal Types and Norwegian Politics," in *Politics: A Power Base for Women?* Örebro Women's Studies, no. 3. Report from a conference in Örebro, Sweden, 12–16 May 1993.

Smyth, Frank."The Horror—Rwanda: A history lesson." *The New Republic* 210/25(1994): 19.

Solheim, Bruce O. *On Top of the World: Political Leadership in Scandinavia and Beyond*. Westport, CT: Greenwood, 2000.

——. *The Nordic Nexus: A Lesson in Peaceful Security*. Westport, CT: Praeger, 1994.

Sonia Gandhi, Accessed at: http://www.soniagandhi.org/

Sonia Gandhi Web site: http://www.soniagandhi.org/php/showContent.php?linkid=1

Spindel, Cheywa, E. Levy, and M.Connor. *With an End in Sight: Strategies from the UNIFEM Trust Fund to Eliminate Violence Against Women*. New York: United Nations Development Fund for Women, 2000.

Steinem, Gloria. "Gro Harlem Brundtland." *Ms* (January 1988): 74–75.

Stiehm, Judith Hicks, ed. *Women's Views of the Political World of Men*. Dobbs Ferry, New York: Transnational Publishers, 1984.

Stimpson, Catharine. *Where the Meanings Are*. New York: Routledge, 1990.

Swirski, Barbara and Marilyn P. Safir, eds. *Calling the Equality Bluff: Women in Israel*. New York: Teachers College Press, 1993.

Sylvester, Rachel and Alice Thomson "Cameron in Rush to Make Party Changes" *Telegraph*. 9 December 2005. Accessed at: http://www.telegraph.co.uk/news/main.jhtml?xml=/news/2005/12/09/ntory09.xml&sSheet=/portal/2005/12/09/ixportaltop.html

Takala, Annika. "Feminist Perspectives on Peace Education." *Journal of Peace Research* 28/2 (1991): 231–235.

Thatcher, Margaret. See her memoirs, *The Downing Street Years* (1993) and *The Path to Power* (1995), and her collected speeches in *The Revival of Britain*, compiled by A. Cooke (1989); studies by R. Lewis (1984), P. Jenkins (1987), and H. Young (1989).

——. *The Path to Power*. New York: HarperCollins, 1995.

The British Council. "Promoting Gender Equality Worldwide." *The British Council*. The Network Newsletter no. 23, November 2000. Accessed at: http://www.britishcouncil.org/governance/gender/netnews/pdf/network23.pdf

The Center for Legislative Development. "The Quota System: Women's Boon or Bane?" 2000. Accessed at: http://www.cld.org/waw5.htm

The Center for Legislative Development. "Women Around the World." vol. 1 No. 3, April 2000. Accessed at: http://www.cld.org/waw5.htm

The Courier (UNESCO). Accessed at: http://www.unesco.org/courier/2000_06/uk/doss22.htm

The Prime Ministers of Canada, 1867–1994=Les premiers ministres du Canada, 1867–1994. Presented by the House of Commons and the National Archives of Canada. Ottawa: National Archives of Canada, 1994.

Thomas, Sue. *How Women Legislate*. New York: Oxford University Press, 1994.

Thomas, Sue and Clyde Wilcox, eds. *Women and Elective Office: Past, Present, and Future*. New York: Oxford University Press, 1998.

Thompson, Mark R. "Frauen der Märtyrer—Töchter an der Macht." *Internationale Politik* 8(2001): S. 59–64.

——. "Damen der Dynastien: Schwierige Demokratisierung in Bangladesch, Indonesien, Pakistan und den Philippinen." In Bendel, Petra / Aurel Croissant / Friedbert W. Rüb (Hg.), *Zwischen Diktatur und Demokratie: Zur Konzeption und Empirie demokratischer Grauzonen*. Opladen, 2002, 343–358.

——. "Die philippinische Demokratie zwischen Populismus und Reform" (Philippine Democracy between Populism and Reform). *Asien* 82(January 2002): 61–78.

——. "Female Leadership of Democratic Transitions in Asia." *Pacific Affairs* 4(2002–2003): 535–555.

Tovsen, Marit. "Women in Politics in Norway." Seminar Paper for Women from Eastern Europe, Denmark, 19 August 1992, mimeograph.

Toward a New Middle East: Women and Development. Accessed at: http://www.washingtoninstitute.org/templateC07.php?CID=155

Tripp, Ailil Mari. "New Trends in Women's Political Participation in Africa." University of Wisconsin Madison. Workshop on Democracy in Africa in Comparative Perspective, 2001. Accessed at: http://www.democracy.standford.edu/Seminar/AiliTripp.pdf

Tronto, Joan C. "Beyond Gender Difference to a Theory of Care." *Journal of Women in Culture and Society* 12/4 (1987): 644–663.

Turner, Lynn H. and Helen M. Sterk, eds. *Differences That Make a Difference: Examining the Assumptions in Gender Research*. Westport, CT: Bergin & Garvey, 1994.

UNESCO. "Unfinished Democracy." 26 November 2003. Accessed at: *http://www.unesco.org/courier/2000_06/uk/doss22.htm*

United Nations. *Women: Looking Beyond 2000*. New York: United Nations, 1995.

United Nations. "Dr. Gro Harlem Brundtland." United Nations Press Release; accessed at http://www.who.org/inf-dg/biographies/gh-brundtland.html on 29 June 1999.

United Nations Development Fund For Women (UNIFEM): Strategies and Initiatives Paper; accessed at: http://www.unifem.undp.org

van Kessel, Ineke and Yvonne Jansen. "Is Democracy Good for Women: The Impact of Democratic Transitions on the Representation of Women in the National Parliaments of Southern Africa." Lecture on 14 December 1999. Accessed at: *http://www.niza.nl/uk/press/docs/women_onthe_rise/lecture_vankessel.htm* on 5 April 2006.

Vastel, Michel. "L'effet Campbell." *l'Actualité* 18/7 (ler mai 1993): 20–24.

Victor, Barbara. *The Lady. Aung San Suu Kyi. Nobel Laureate and Burma's Prisoner*. New York: Faber and Faber, 1998.

Waylen, Georgina. *Gender in Third World Politics*. Boulder, CO: Lynne Rienner Publishers, 1996.

Weigert, Kathleen Maas. "Peace Studies as Education for Nonviolent Social Change." *Annals of the American Academy of Political and Social Science* 504 (July 1989): 37–47.

Weiner, Eric. "Where Women Rule, They Leave Genderless Legacy Behind." *Christian Science Monitor*, 10 May 1995, p. 1.

Wekerle, Gerda R., Rebecca Peterson, and David Morley, ed. *New Space for Women*. Boulder, CO: Westview Press, 1981.

Wheatley, Margaret. "Goodbye, Command and Control." Reprint of *Leader to Leader*, No. 5 (Summer 1997). San Francisco, CA: Jossey-Bass Publishers, Inc., 1997.

White House Project. Accessed at: www.thewhitehouseproject.org

Williams, Christine L. "Feminist Views of the Social Sciences." *The Annals of the American Academy of Political and Social Science* 571(September 2000).

Wolf, Naomi. *Fire with Fire: The New Female Power and How It Will Change the 21st Century*. New York: Random House, 1993.

Women for Women. Accessed at: www.womenforwomen.org

Women in American History. *Britannica Online*. Accessed at: http://womenshistory.about.com/gi/dynamic/offsite.htm?zi=1/XJ&sdn=womenshistory&zu=http%3A%2F%2Fsearch.eb.com%2Fwomen%2Farticles%2Fwoman_suffrage.html

Women in Parliament: Beyond Numbers. Accessed at: http://womenshistory.about.com/gi/dynamic/offsite.htm?zi=1/XJ&sdn=womenshistory&zu=http%3A%2F%2Farchive.idea.int%2Fwomen%2Fparl%2Fch6_table8.htm

Women in the Labour Force 1900–2004. Accessed at: http://www.infoplease.com/ipa/A0104673.html

Women Leaders in Asia. Accessed at: http://womenshistory.about.com/gi/dynamic/offsite.htm?site=http%3A%2F%2Fwww.time.com%2Ftime%2Fasia%2Fasia%2Fmagazine%2F1999%2F990823%2Faquino1.html

Women's E news. http://www.womensenews.org/article.cfm/dyn/aid/2245/context/archive

Women's E-News Daily. Accessed at: www.womensenews.org on 5 April 2006.Woodward, Alison E. "Going For Gender Balance: A Guide For Balancing Decision-Making. Good Practices to Achieve Gender-Balanced Representation in Political and Social Decision-Making." Brussels, Belgium: Council of Europe, March 2002.

Women World Leaders. Accessed at: http://www.geocities.com/CapitolHill/Lobby/4642/

Young, Hugo. *One of Us: A Biography of Margaret Thatcher*. London: Macmillan, 1989.

Zakaria, Rafiq. *Women & Politics in Islam: The Trial of Benazir Bhutto*. New York: New Horizons Press, 1989.

Index

About the Authors

GUNHILD HOOGENSEN is Associate Professor of Political Science at the University of Tromso in Norway.

BRUCE O. SOLHEIM is Professor of History at Citrus College in Glendora, California.